Culture and Power

Culture and Power

A History of Cultural Studies

Mark Gibson

Oxford • New York

First published in 2007 by
Berg
Editorial offices:
1st Floor, Angel Court, 81 St Clements Street, Oxford, OX4 1AW, UK
175 Fifth Avenue, New York, NY 10010, USA

Berg is the imprint of Oxford International Publishers Ltd.

Library of Congress Cataloguing-in-Publication Data
Gibson, Mark.
  Culture and power : a history of cultural studies / Mark Gibson.
    p. cm.
  Includes bibliographical references and index.
  ISBN-13: 978-1-84520-116-6 (cloth)
  ISBN-10: 1-84520-116-7 (cloth)
  ISBN-13: 978-1-84520-117-3 (pbk.)
  ISBN-10: 1-84520-117-5 (pbk.)
  1. Culture—Study and teaching. 2. Power (Social
sciences) I. Title.

  HM623.G53 2007
  306.07—dc22

                                                    2006035441

British Library Cataloguing-in-Publication Data
A catalogue record for this book is available from the British Library.

ISBN 978 1 84520 116 6 (Cloth)

ISBN 978 1 84520 117 3 (Paper)

Typeset by JS Typesetting, Porthcawl, Mid Glamorgan
Printed in the United Kingdom by Biddles Ltd, King's Lynn

www.bergpublishers.com

Contents

Contents

Preface

Culture and Power is a book about the concept of power in cultural studies. Its approach is historical. I identify and describe some of the points at which the concept was first taken up, the reasons that motivated its adoption and the effects it has had on the shape of the field. The period in question is, roughly speaking, the fifty odd years from the 1950s to the early 2000s.

Like all histories, the book is written from the present and inflected by current concerns. Some of these are no doubt unconscious and may best be judged by you the reader, but the argument is most consciously addressed to a pervasive belief that the concept of power has become, in some fairly fundamental way, a 'problem'. The sharpest articulations of this belief have come from external critics of the field, for whom there is nothing to lose and often much to gain from pointing out its shortcomings. They crystallized particularly in the so-called 'culture wars' of the 1990s in which cultural studies was widely accused of a rampant 'political correctness' – a fanatical and unforgiving insistence on framing everything in terms of power relations. But, as I argue in Chapter 1, reservations over the use of the concept of power have not been restricted to this. They can be found both before and after the 1990s, within cultural studies itself as well as outside.

The obvious risk in writing with these concerns in mind is that the story might be depressing. There is now a veritable industry in diagnosing what is 'wrong' with cultural studies – or what has *gone* wrong. The field is often written about almost in the past tense, as something that has run its course. Some have actively wanted to call for the last rites; others have hoped to revive the field by finding a remedy. But even the latter have sometimes looked like killing the patient with their concern. In the analysis of cultural studies' flaws, we can lose any sense of why it has been an exciting and innovative field. What interest could this hold for a new generation of readers – readers whom this book certainly hopes to address?

Many have concluded that the best strategy for cultural studies now is to stop introspecting, to put the 'culture wars' firmly in the past and to turn its attention to producing good new work. There is much to be said for this strategy and there are many exciting initiatives which can be called upon to give it substance – the development of cultural studies in Asia, Africa and South America; the engagement with new technologies; alliances with 'fair trade' and 'anti-globalization' activism; a burgeoning interest in alternative sexualities; the yoking of cultural studies to the 'creative industries'; and encounters with economics, law and other disciplines not previously included in the interdisciplinary mix.

But simply 'moving on' also has its own problems. Whatever efforts are made to ignore it, unease about the concept of power continues to work away in the background, often in debilitating ways. A deliberate decision *not* to address it can actually exacerbate the unease, suggesting a dark and unresolved secret, which the field must repress. To put too strong an emphasis on bright new projects, in this context, can begin to seem hollow, robbing them of some of their shine. Looking resolutely to the future can also deny access to the *value* that can be drawn from the past. Cultural studies now has more than fifty years experience in addressing popular cultural forms, in contributing to the democratization of education, in relating culture to broader social forces, in contextual analysis and in bringing different disciplines together in productive ways. It would be a waste, to say the least, if all this experience was now simply cast aside.

For these reasons, the book suggests another strategy, not so much an alternative as a complement to 'moving on'. It is to question the assumption that there *is* a fundamental problem in the way cultural studies has approached questions of power. My intention in this is not to whitewash the field. Many shortcomings can be found with particular examples of cultural studies, just as there can with examples of history, philosophy, sociology or literary criticism. It is rather to *normalize* this state of affairs, to contest the idea that all the problems can be reduced to one big Problem that threatens to overwhelm the field. It is to suggest that where there *have* been problems in the use of the concept of power, they should be seen as problems are generally seen in other fields – as problems *in* cultural studies, not problems *with* cultural studies.

The most important piece in this argument is to reject the idea that cultural studies is *founded* on the concept of power. The most common myth of origins here is that everything begins with Marxist theories of culture – the notion, in particular, that culture needs to be understood in relation to structures of social domination. Many have tried to counter simple caricatures of cultural studies by pointing out that Marxism is a complex heritage and that, in any case, theories of power in the field have had other inputs – from feminism, postcolonialism, queer theory and the work of Michel Foucault. All of this is true, but it does not go far enough. What needs to be asked, more pointedly, is whether the assumption of Marxist origins is simply wrong. Marxist theory has been unquestionably *important* in cultural studies, but there is little justification for seeing it as *foundational*.

In establishing this point, I pay particular attention to early formations of cultural studies, which made little use of the concept of power – even, in some cases, actively resisting it. The most extended discussion here is of the British case and the work of Richard Hoggart, Raymond Williams and the early Stuart Hall, but I also draw parallels in the United States with James Carey and his associates, inspired by John Dewey and the sociology of the Chicago School. These figures were not merely vague 'precursors' to cultural studies; they gave it its first institutional form. Hoggart, for example, who was certainly not a Marxist and made no use of the concept of power, was the founder of what is still widely recognized as one of the field's most generative sites: the Centre for Contemporary Cultural Studies at Birmingham.

Against this background, I trace the *uptake* of the concept of power, its *introduction* into a field that had already established characteristic objects of study, styles of analysis and political concerns. This development involved a significant transformation of cultural studies, but never, I argue, a total one. The concept of power has remained in tension with other ways of conceiving of culture, politics and social relations. The picture which emerges from this is of cultural studies as a *respondent* to the concept of power, not, as is often implied, a zealous advocate. There may have been some instances of the latter, but taken as a whole, it would be fair to say that attitudes to the concept of power in the field, even as it has been adopted, have been marked by some degree of scepticism.

This raises an obvious question of where the concept of power *has* come from. My response to this is that we should not look, in paranoid 'Cold War' mode, for a responsible agent – the radical agitator or subversive continental theorist – but to wider cultural contexts. Agents and agitators are only truly effective when something is already in the air. More important than fixing on the former is to understand the latter. Why, at certain times and places – in recent history, for example, the 1960s and 1970s – has the concept of power had such cultural resonance? To answer this question requires something which cultural studies has *not* really attempted, except perhaps at the margins of some Foucauldian work: *a cultural history of the concept of power*. There is not space in the book to develop such a history fully, but I suggest some beginnings. A particularly fruitful starting point is to consider the relation between the concept of power and state formation. Of more immediate relevance to cultural studies are a number of developments from the mid twentieth century which allowed the concept to float free of state contexts and be applied at the level of everyday life.

Apart from a chapter on Michel Foucault, the book does not give a great deal of space to discussing major *theories* of power: the differences, for example, between Marx and Engels, Gramsci, Althusser, Nietzsche, Ernesto Laclau, Steven Lukes, Judith Butler and Anthony Giddens. The differences are significant and have been important in cultural studies, but they are extensively covered in other texts. The book is addressed to readers and teachers of cultural studies who may be interested in a subject that has become increasingly urgent, but has attracted much less attention: what Foucault once called the 'thematics' of power itself. Why the concept of power in the first place? Where has it come from? What is at stake in its use?

The argument of the book has suggested principles of selection that may need some explaining. The book is a history of cultural studies, but a history that some readers may see as incomplete. An easy answer to this would be that no book can cover everything, particularly in a field as wild, diverse and uncertain of its boundaries as cultural studies. I should also point out that the book is a history with a particular focus. There are many areas of work which, while important, have not borne centrally on the relation between cultural studies and the concept of power. Nor is there any real reason why they should. Omission, in other words, should not be taken as a sign of any judgement against them.

But there are also more particular emphases which need to be accounted for. The most surprising of these may be the decision to give as much space as I have to British cultural studies and, within British cultural studies, to the Birmingham Centre for Contemporary Cultural Studies. Where the narrative does move away from Britain, it remains largely within a rather 'Anglo' orbit, only turning in the final chapter to other contexts. Considerable efforts have been made in recent years to 'decentre' the history of cultural studies, not least by some of the authors whose work I examine. Attention has been drawn to other tributaries in Britain than Birmingham and, outside Britain, to alternative formations not just in the United States and Australia but in Asia, Africa, Latin America and elsewhere. Against this background, the book might appear a little conservative.

This requires a more substantial response. I *do* want to suggest in the book that there is a particular interest in the British case – at least for the general argument I have tried to put forward. This is argued out most fully in Chapter 3, which notes an 'ethno-historical specificity' – to borrow Paul Gilroy's term – in the way questions of power have tended to be addressed in Britain, or perhaps more precisely England. To put it simply, the English have preferred not to talk about 'power' in general terms, but more concretely about specific 'powers'. This tendency can be related, I suggest, to a distinctive pattern of modern state formation in which sovereign authority remained relatively weak and a range of other institutions relatively strong. It is a tendency that can also be found in the United States, Australia and other countries that share similar political histories. And it is a tendency that has been particularly significant for the concept of power in cultural studies.

The argument could be developed in relation to other examples than Birmingham, and indeed I sketch out in Chapter 9 how it might also be run in the American case. But Birmingham remains the most convenient, if only because the general outline of the history is relatively well known. It is precisely because orthodoxies have tended to harden around the Centre for Contemporary Cultural Studies that it makes a good test case. If the idea of a foundational commitment to the concept of power can be brought into question for the CCCS, there is good reason to think that it can be brought into question anywhere. Making this case is, again, complementary to attempts to move cultural studies elsewhere. If Birmingham does not provide a solid 'anchor' on the concept of power, then its status is normalized as a significant site, not an absolute standard or ultimate point of reference. In a final chapter, I suggest some ways in which the argument may be brought together with recent developments in international cultural studies, with a particular focus on work from Latin America.

Some may find that the book is still overhung by 'culture wars' gloom. All I can say is that I hope this is not the case! My greatest wish is that readers may come to see the history of the concept of power as I have come to see it in writing the book – not as an incubus, an awful deadweight around the neck of cultural studies, but as a living history which calls on us for continuing invention.

The ideas in the book have taken some time to mature and have benefited enormously from inspiration and feedback from others. I would particularly like to thank John Hartley, Alan McKee, Brian Shoesmith, Meaghan Morris, Tom O'Regan, Thomas Osborne and James Donald for their close reading of earlier versions and for variously providing encouragement and heading me off from egregious errors. Tristan Palmer at Berg has also been an excellent and supportive editor.

The book has been formed significantly by exchanges with colleagues, students and friends at Murdoch University and elsewhere: Lubica Ucnik, Wendy Parkins, Geoff Craig, Alec McHoul, Steve Mickler, Terence Lee, Ingrid Richardson, Felicity Newman, Kara-Jane Lombard, Pamela Martin, Collin Chua, Adam Jardine, Ned Rossiter, Jon Stratton, Terry Flew, Paul Holland, Melissa Gregg, Tom Gibson, Aurelia Armstrong, David Birch, Warwick Mules, Tara Brabazon, Tony Schirato and Susan Yell. I find it difficult to write without dialogic partners and argumentative others, real as well as textual: I thank even those with whom I have disagreed for providing a sounding board and for sustaining my belief that, if nothing else, the ideas matter. Early iterations of some of the arguments of the book have been published in *New Formations, International Journal of Cultural Studies, European Journal of Cultural Studies, Symploke, Australian Journal of Communication* and *Continuum*. I thank the editors and referees for their suggestions and for putting faith in the work. I am also grateful to Murdoch University for providing research funding and an important period of study leave.

As this is my first book, I would like to thank my mother Jenny Gibson for supporting me so fully in whatever I have done. Equal thanks are due to my father David, but unfortunately he will never get to read them. I like to think that he may have approved of some of the ideas herein. And thanks finally to Robin and Hannah for putting up with an absent-present dad through too many evenings and weekends and to Andrea Witcomb, for her endless patience, input and support.

–1–

Cultural Studies and the Concept of Power

There is no moment now, in American cultural studies, where we are *not* able, extensively and without end, to theorize power – politics, race, class, and gender, subjugation, domination, exclusion, marginality, Otherness etc. There is hardly anything in cultural studies which isn't so theorized... [T]here are ways of constituting power as an easy floating signifier which just leaves the crude exercise and connections of power and culture altogether emptied of signification.

Stuart Hall (1992), 'Cultural Studies and its Theoretical Legacies', 286

Perhaps I've insisted too much on the technology of domination and power.

Michel Foucault (1988), *Technologies of the Self*, 19

When the most basic concepts ... are suddenly seen to be not concepts but problems ... there is no sense in listening to their sonorous summons or their resounding clashes. We have only, if we can, to recover the substance from which their forms were cast.

Raymond Williams (1977), *Marxism and Literature*, 11

In the late 1950s, Raymond Williams set out to map an influential tradition of English thought, a constellation of discourse that gravitated around a single concept – 'culture'. By revealing the complicated history of the concept, he opened it to the possibility of further development, narrowing the gap between the limited range of established formal usage and new contexts emerging from a rapid democratization of British society. As Williams was the first to recognize, the project he attempted to give form to in *Culture and Society* (1958) and *The Long Revolution* (1965) was by no means his own invention. It connected not only with other important texts of the time – Richard Hoggart's *The Uses of Literacy* (1957) and E. P. Thompson's *The Making of the English Working Class* (1963); it also connected with a diverse range of initiatives in education, literary discussion groups, film societies, publishing and journalism. Nor was it entirely new. Post-war debates around culture belonged, for Williams, to a history of responses to modernity that went back at least to the eighteenth century. Even the more radical democratic initiatives had important precedents. To recognize new groups as participants to debates over culture or to broaden the reference of the term was to contribute to a process – the 'long revolution' – that was already some hundreds of years old.

But the field of which Williams is credited as a founder, cultural studies, has been organized as much around another concept – 'power'. It has often seemed, in fact, that the concept of culture has effectively been displaced. In an essay of the mid 1980s, James Carey suggested that the field might almost be renamed: 'British cultural studies could be described just as easily and perhaps more accurately as ideological studies in that it assimilates, in a variety of complex ways, culture to ideology. More accurately, it makes ideology synecdochal of culture as a whole' (Carey 1989b: 97). In the light of more recent developments, the suggestion needs to be modified. With the increasing distance from Marxism during the 1990s, the concept of ideology gave way to the concept of power (Fiske 1993). But Carey's general point still holds. As Bruce Robbins (1993: 209) has nicely summarized the transformation of the field from the 1950s to the 1990s, the emblematic figure of Matthew Arnold was replaced by that of Michel Foucault.

There has never been an equivalent for 'power' of Williams's magisterial survey of the history of 'culture'. This is not to say that power has not been theorized; it clearly has been – as Stuart Hall puts it, 'extensively and without end'. In the rejection of the English literary tradition, in the shift to Marxism and the revisions inspired by Althusser and Gramsci, in the emergence of feminism and postcolonial criticism, and in the turn to Foucault – in all these moves, power has been the single most visible theme. Nor has there been any shortage of commentary; each of the twists and turns and revisions in the theorization of power has been carefully examined and its implications discussed. There is a difference, however, between theorizing power and reflecting on the concept itself. To engage in the latter is not to ask how power operates or what forms it takes, but to ask what we *mean* by power, where the concept comes from, why we should use it, what its limitations might be. Given the importance of the concept in cultural studies, these questions have been given surprisingly little consideration.

But perhaps it is *because* of the importance of the concept. It is difficult to ask the second kind of question without a certain kind of distancing. To return to the case of culture, Williams's history of the concept required a partial disengagement from its active use. It is not an accident that most of those who took the lead in this were relative outsiders to the major traditions of use at the time. Williams himself came from a Welsh working-class background – his father a railway signalman, his grandfather a farm labourer – and many of the early figures in British cultural studies started from positions similarly removed from the English middle-class literary milieu in which the concept of culture had largely been formed. This did not mean that they necessarily rejected discourses around culture; later commentators have in fact often been surprised at the respect they showed for them. But it did mean they regarded them with some detachment – almost in the way you might respect another language, religion or worldview. The concept could not be accepted simply as given.

Cultural studies has rarely shown the same kind of detachment in relation to the concept of power. For many, indeed, the field has been *defined* by a basic commitment to the concept. In one widely cited example, Tony Bennett has suggested that cultural studies 'now functions largely as a term of convenience for a fairly dispersed array of theoretical and political positions which … share a commitment to examining cultural practices from the point of view of their intrication with, and within, relations of power' (Bennett 1992a: 23). The definition is intended to be an open one – to recognize, in Bennett's words, 'the elasticity which the term "cultural studies" has now acquired' (1992a: 23). But this openness only highlights a significant point of closure. To 'belong' to cultural studies is already to see things 'from the point of view of relations of power', to have adopted the concept as a fundamental starting point. Those who do *not* take it as their starting point, who set out instead to question it, can, by implication, be placed on the outside.

A Sonorous Summons

There are good historical reasons for this closure. There has always been more at stake in the use of the concept than purely intellectual differences. The concept of power has played a central role in arguments for greater social inclusion of women, people of colour, the working class, ethnic and sexual minorities, indigenous people and other groups who have traditionally been barred from or under-represented in the public domain. The justice of these arguments has often been felt to inhere in the concept itself. While cultural studies has often expressed reservations about some of the cruder ways they have been put, it has usually done so only in order to strengthen them. A conviction in the use of the concept of power has only been increased by the fact that the field has faced strong resistance, through much of its development, even to suggesting that culture be understood in terms of relations of power. It is natural, in this context, that the emphasis should be more on the positive use of the concept than on standing back to reflect on it. Questioning the commitment to theorizing about power has generally been seen as bringing into question the very project of cultural studies itself.

As if to confirm this, the major body of writing that has taken a critical position on the concept of power in cultural studies has done so from a position of open hostility to everything it represents. This is the conservative offensive that has emerged since the early 1990s, particularly in America, around the themes of 'political correctness' and the 'culture wars'. An emphasis on power is associated in this writing with excessive sensitivities around gender, race and ethnicity. For Dinesh D'Souza, one of the best-known proponents of this view, there has been a 'victim's revolution' on university campuses in which a fear of giving offence has come to outweigh academic values and respect for the truth:

Most American universities have diluted or displaced their 'core curriculum' in the great works of Western civilization to make room for new course requirements stressing non-Western cultures, Afro-American Studies, and Women's Studies. Since race and gender issues are so sensitive, the university leadership often discourages faculty from presenting factual material that may provoke or irritate minority students. Several professors who cross the academic parameters of what may be said in the classroom have found themselves the object of organized vilification and administrative penalties. Again, these intellectual curbs do not apply to professors who are viewed as champions of minority interests – they are permitted overtly ideological scholarship, and are immune from criticism even when they make excessive or outlandish claims. (D'Souza 1991: 5)

Among numerous other examples, D'Souza cites the case of Dante scholar Robert Hollander, who spoke against the formation of a women's studies programme at Princeton University in the 1980s on what he claimed were academic grounds: he 'remembers being subjected to a barrage of personal attacks. "I achieved instant notoriety ... colleagues I had worked with for a long time, with whom I got on extremely well, turned on me with incredible savagery"' (D'Souza 1991: 6).

At the centre of this revolution, according to the conservative analysis, has been an institutionally embedded left-liberal elite who have exploited cultural and political sensitivities to their own advantage. These 'tenured radicals', in Roger Kimball's (1990) phrase, have deliberately fostered a sense of grievance among women and minority groups as a way of furthering their own careers. To question their authority – to suggest that critical theories of power may be ill-founded or overblown – has been to risk being cast as an apologist for power, if not actually an 'oppressor'. At a deeper level, for Kimball, there has also been a more destructive motivation. The revolution has been led by those who have taken their bearings from the counter-cultural movements of the 1960s. Having found their wider political ambitions thwarted, they have sought revenge within the sheltered space of the academy: 'Their object is nothing less than the destruction of the values, methods, and goals of traditional humanistic study' (Kimball 1990: xi). The results have been nothing short of disastrous: 'Instead of reading the great works of the past, students watch movies, pronounce on the depredations of patriarchal society, or peruse second- or third-rate works dear to their ideological cohort; instead of reading widely among primary texts, they absorb abstruse commentaries on commentaries, resorting to primary texts only to furnish illustrations for their pet critical theory' (Kimball 1990: xvii).

To cite these arguments in the mid 2000s might appear to give them a longer life and wider currency than they deserve. The 'culture wars' are most closely associated with the 1990s and the debates to which they refer have often been seen as peculiarly American. In some respects, they were always a beat up, in which lurid accusations of a 'new McCarthyism' (D'Souza 1992: 13) were manufactured on the basis of a few slender anecdotes. Their credibility as analysis has been dented by revelations of corporate funding and political interests behind some of the major contributions and by detailed refutations on points of fact (Diamond 1995; Wark 1997b). It is fair to ask how relevant they are to cultural studies in the mid 2000s, or have ever been outside the United States. But it would also be a mistake to dismiss them entirely. The political dynamic they helped to crystallize cannot be entirely quarantined to the strange ideological obsessions of conservative American think tanks or the overheated climate of a few college campuses. Like the counter-cultural movements of the 1960s and 1970s – against which they have been in large part a reaction – they have reverberated widely and shown considerable capacity to endure across time. While some of their heat may have dissipated, many of the problems they raised remain.

This is certainly the way it appears as I write this in 2004 in Australia, where the terrain of cultural politics has been transformed almost beyond recognition over the past ten years. A common point of reference in tracing the shift has been an attack by Prime Minister John Howard in 1996 on what he called the 'black armband' view of Australia:

> This black armband view of our past reflects the belief that most Australian history since 1788 [the date of European settlement] has been little more than a disgraceful story of imperialism, exploitation, racism, sexism and other forms of discrimination.
>
> I take a very different view. I believe that the balance sheet of our history is one of heroic achievement and that we have achieved much more as a nation of which we can be proud than of which we should be ashamed. (Quoted in *The Australian*, 19 November 1996, p.13)

The rhetoric is less colourful than that of D'Souza, Kimball and the American culture warriors, but the commonalities are clear. Howard has exploited much the same conjuncture, in which concepts of power – 'imperialism, exploitation, racism, sexism' – have lost their positive momentum and come to be seen as a liability for those who use them. In the space of this conjuncture, he has succeeded in mobilizing considerable public support for a reversal of many of the projects closest to Australian cultural studies – multiculturalism, feminism, reconciliation with indigenous people, the attempt to define a more independent position in relation to Britain and America and to encourage a greater cultural sensitivity to Asia.

The political dynamic of the culture wars has also remained strong in the United States, even as the currency of the term itself has faded, with ongoing attempts by conservative commentators and politicians to marginalize left and left-liberal opinion. There are some paradoxes in the American case as there are also variants of conservatism which have taken ownership, themselves, of the concept of power. In *Paradise and Power*, one of the more influential books on the geopolitical situation following the terrorist attacks of September 11 2001, Robert Kagan (2003) contrasts a pragmatic recognition of the need to project military force – in his own word, 'power' – with the 'paradise' imagined by European governments and their left-leaning sympathizers in thinking that the world could function without it. Here, ironically, it is the conservative side of politics that insists on the recognition of relations of power. But Kagan's use of the concept departs from what has been the more common pattern. Like Howard's celebration of Australia's 'heroic achievements', the conservative emphasis in the United States has been on the 'positive' themes of economic growth, family, individual freedom and the 'great traditions' of the West. Those who speak too much of power, particularly in a critical mode, have continued to be represented as 'negative', dogmatic, ideologically obsessed.

The situation in Britain may appear somewhat different as the political tone has been set from the late 1990s by the progressivism of Tony Blair's 'New Labour'. But in many ways, the exception is one that proves the rule, for a condition of the renewal of left-of-centre politics in Britain has been the suppression of critical discourses on power. It is a condition which is captured in Blair's declaration to the Trades Union Council in 1996 shortly before the election which brought him to power: 'I did not join the Labour Party to protest. I joined it as a party of government.' The price of overcoming the demoralization inflicted on the left by the long years of Thatcherism has been the renunciation of the oppositional identity with which it was then associated. Indeed, this renunciation has often been more vigorous and intensive precisely because it has been pursued from 'within'. It has been more than simply a point of ritual antagonism by those who are safely distanced; it has been a project of cultural transformation by those for whom it is fundamental to their political identity. A major casualty in this has been critical discourses on power.

In none of these cases, then, has the climate been an easy one in which to ask questions about the concept of power. It should be recognized that many in cultural studies have resisted the temptation simply to strike back against their critics, demonstrating in their response that the field is more open and tolerant than the picture of zealous ideological obsession that the latter have drawn. Some have even admitted a truth to certain allegations. As Stuart Hall conceded in the debate around political correctness, there *are* elements on the left who have adopted a narrow and prescriptive 'politics of truth' – 'a substitution of false racist or sexist or homophobic consciousness by "true consciousness"' (Hall 1994: 181; see also Epstein 1995; Carey 1997b; Morris 1997b). But it has also been necessary to set limits. There is never any question for Hall that racism, sexism and homophobia are real phenomena which have demanded not just attention but action. A continued commitment to the concept of power is the major way in which this position has been affirmed. As Sarah Dunant summarizes it, in her introduction to the volume in which Hall's essay appears, the debate around political correctness has been about more than equality or tolerance: 'It is about power, who has it and what they do with it' (Dunant 1994: ix). This, for most, has been a bottom line.

The major aim of this book, beyond providing an overview of the use of the concept of power in cultural studies, is to suggest that it may now be time for this point of closure also to be reviewed. This is emphatically not to side with D'Souza,

Kimball and the conservative culture warriors in seeking to discredit or reject the 'point of view of relations of power'. My position is that this point of view has been, in general, an honourable one. It is rather to argue that it is nevertheless *only* a point of view – one that has a particular historical formation, particular material conditions and social locations. Its achievements should not be attributed to having told 'the truth' about society – the truth, that is, of power – but to having responded constructively to an identifiable set of needs, desires and aspirations. It is to these we should now return. It is time to recognize, in Williams's terms, that power has become no longer a 'concept' but a 'problem'. It is time we ceased listening to its 'sonorous summons' and 'resounding clashes' and attempted to recover 'the substance from which its forms were cast'.

Of Epicycles and Orreries

While taking this course could appear to be a capitulation, removing the most important bulwark which cultural studies has maintained against the erosion of past achievements, I believe it has the potential, paradoxically, to strengthen its position. However much the field may have sought to demonstrate openness within the scope of a commitment to the concept of power, the critics have sensed that there *is* an inflexibility in the commitment itself. They have been remarkably successful in representing this as a form of left-political fundamentalism and there is every sign that they will continue to press their advantage so long as it holds. To think in terms of bulwarks or barricades, to attempt merely to hold ground that was won in the past, is to accept a defensive position. Standing back from the concept of power may shift the terms of debate and open the possibility of regaining the initiative. As I will point out in later chapters, cultural studies has not *always* been defined by a commitment to the concept of power; there have been other ways in which it has projected itself. If this is so, there is no reason to think that it *has* to be so defined in future.

But there are other reasons for reviewing the commitment to the concept of power than attempting to win ground against opponents. It may be important for cultural studies quite independently. One of the reasons the field has found it difficult to respond to criticisms about its orientation to questions of power is that there is deep ambivalence about the concept *internally*. It is true, as Bennett's definition of cultural studies suggests, that it has had a central place through most of its history, but it is equally true that there have always been those who have regarded it with some misgivings. The contradictions here have now become acute.

While it is often implied that there was once a time when cultural studies' commitment to the concept was straightforward, it is difficult in fact to find any such moment. The most obvious candidate might be the high point of Marxist cultural studies at the Birmingham Centre for Contemporary Cultural Studies in the mid 1970s, but it is questionable whether even this would qualify. As Stuart Hall set out to correct the record some twenty years after the event, the embrace of Marxism was not as unqualified as it has often been made to appear: 'for five or six years, long after the resistance to theory in cultural studies had been overcome ... we walked right around the entire circumference of European thought, in order not to be, in any simple capitulation to the *zeitgeist*, Marxists' (Hall 1992: 280). At the centre of this hesitation was a set of reservations about the simplifying effect of reducing social relations to structures of dominance and subordination. The relation of cultural studies to Marxism, for Hall, was always one of 'wrestling with angels': while the field may have embraced the general proposition of class domination, it was uneasy from the very beginning about many of the implications of doing so.

This ambivalence is not restricted to the case of Marxism or the early writing on class. It can also be found in the development of critical theories around gender and race. There are close parallels with Hall's 'wrestling with angels', for example, in Meaghan Morris's early feminist contribution to the field in the essays collected in *The Pirate's Fiancée* (1988). The sceptical relation of Hall and his colleagues to orthodox Marxism finds an analogue in Morris in a critical distance from the radical feminism of figures such as Mary Daly. The same general stance can be found in black cultural studies in writers like Paul Gilroy, whose work has developed as a critical counterpoint to the 'ethnic absolutism' (Gilroy 1992) of more trenchant oppositional critiques of white power originating particularly from the United States. In each case, cultural studies has set itself off against more straightforward and unreserved applications of the concept of power. In contrast, in many ways, to the reputation it has gained, it has sought not so much to *promote* the use of the concept as to *moderate* a use that has been promoted by others.

Until the 1990s, tensions around the concept of power in cultural studies were managed largely through relations with these others: The field aligned itself with propositions about power put forward by Marxism, but rejected the dogmatic excesses of 'orthodox' Marxism; it aligned itself with feminism, but rejected authoritarian tendencies in certain kinds of 'radical' feminism; it aligned itself with movements against continuing white dominance over political life and public culture, but rejected their 'ethnic absolutist' forms. In recent years, however, this positioning has become increasingly difficult to sustain. Three related developments can be identified here. The first is simply that the 'others' have largely disappeared from view. This is most obvious in the case of Marxism: with the fall of the Berlin Wall and the continuing drive in China towards a fully-fledged market economy, it has become difficult to find an 'orthodox' Marxist anywhere. But it can also be observed in the other cases: the political energies which drove the more revolutionary forms of feminism and black radicalism in the 1970s and 1980s have faded, giving way to more moderate and institutionally embedded forms.

A second development, more difficult to locate precisely, has been a creeping recognition that problems associated with the use of the concept of power may be more fundamental than they were earlier thought to be. If, in the past, there was already an awareness of the *potential* for these problems to emerge, this was balanced by the belief that greater theoretical sophistication could prevent them from actually doing so. The early adoption of Marxism was facilitated, for example, by the argument, taken from Louis Althusser, that economic forces – the basis for class power – were determining only 'in the last instance'. This caveat allowed some scope for admitting processes and phenomena that were not immediately reducible to a simple model of class domination. As was increasingly conceded, however, these processes and phenomena could never be granted more than a secondary status (Hall 1996b: 45). E. P. Thompson made the point early and, in retrospect, brilliantly in *The Poverty of Theory* (1978), comparing the Althusserian model to an orrery – the complicated model of the solar system developed before Copernicus in an attempt to account for the movement of the planets. However ingenious Althusser's innovations on the orthodox Marxist model, they appear as futile, in this picture, as the epicycles that were hypothesized by the Ptolemaists to preserve the assumption of celestial orbit around the earth. The tendency to fundamentalism was not so much rejected as disguised in order that its life might be prolonged.

Theoretical work in cultural studies could be seen in many ways as a restless search for a more satisfactory solution than the Althusserian formula – a way of restraining the simplifying thrust of the concept of power in such a way as to make it acceptable. But with each stage in this search, as earlier solutions have been discarded, a suspicion has grown that the search itself may need to be reviewed. As Chris Rojek has put it of the theoretical oeuvre of Stuart Hall:

> One has the feeling that Hall himself is no longer able to give shape to his labours. In reviewing Hall's work at length, I am struck by the image of a master builder who has added so many rooms, doors and passages to his house that he is no longer able to find his way around the premises (Rojek 1998: 61).

Hall's guiding commitment has always been to resist the hardening of cultural studies into orthodoxy, to maintain what he has called 'the *process of theorizing*, of the development and refinement of new concepts and explanations which, alone, is the sign of a living body of thought' (Hall 1996b: 45). We should not forget how important this contribution has been (cf. Fiske 1996). The very vigilance of Hall's campaign raises questions, however, about why it should be necessary. There is a point at which one is tempted to ask whether the propensity to closure should not be recognized and addressed at some more basic level.

The third development, already mentioned, has been the emergence of critics outside cultural studies who are determined precisely to punish this propensity. It might be objected that the field has always had its opponents. As Dunant pointed out in relation to the political correctness debates, there are some obvious continuities: 'Take almost any recent tabloid headline, substitute the words "loony left" for "PC" and I guarantee you'll not be able to tell whether the story came from 1994 or '84'

(Dunant 1994: x). But there are also important differences. The character of the criticisms has been altered since the 1990s by a sharper awareness, in a sense, of the problems that moderate elements on the left, including cultural studies, have always known were there. The difference from the way these problems have been addressed within cultural studies itself, of course, is that they have not been coupled with any sense of obligation to the field or the movements with which it has been associated. The motivation, on the contrary, has been to drive a stake through the heart.

Taken together, these three developments have placed cultural studies in what can only be described as an uncomfortable position. With the retreat of the more radical 'others' – those who once set a direction in the use of the concept of power but in a way that was seen as dogmatic or extreme – its position in relation to the concept has had to be redefined. Where the field could appear earlier as moderating the concept, it has more recently had to assume more of the burden of promoting it. This shift, in which cultural studies has widely come to be seen as a *primary* advocate for the concept, has coincided with increasing suspicions internally that the problems associated with it may be intractable. Finally, and to exacerbate the situation, much of the analysis of the liabilities of the concept of power has been appropriated by external critics intent on using them as a bludgeon to damage the credibility of the field.

What to do with the Corpse?

The effect of all this could be seen in a palpable frustration during the 1990s with the whole direction of cultural studies, even – or perhaps especially – by those most involved in its development. In a particularly striking metaphor, Hall described a feeling that debates in the field had become a 'struggle over the remains, over the corpse': 'I don't really want to write about cultural studies, as such, any more ... I want to do some new work, to use cultural studies to open up new questions about globalization, new questions about ethnicity. I want to move it on. I don't want to wrangle with it' (Hall 1996c: 398). In a similar mode, Meaghan Morris urged Australian cultural studies also to move on: 'I believe that it is high time for more Australian practitioners to put their heads down, ignore the flak, and start producing the substantive accounts of cultural life, past and present, that we claim our field can generate and that would clarify our project' (Morris 1997a: 37). Many statements of similar kind can be found from other leading practitioners.

Surveying the field in the mid 2000s, it would be fair to say that it has succeeded in 'moving on'. But it has done so in large part by abandoning, or at least toning down, its earlier emphasis on the critical analysis of power. There have been many examples of this tendency, including the so-called 'turn to ethics' (Garber, Hanssen and Walkowitz 2000), the rediscovery of aesthetics and phenomenology, suggestions that cultural studies engage in government policy formation (Bennett 1992a;

Cunningham 1992) or that it contribute to the development of 'creative industries' (Hartley 2005). A number of these will be discussed in following chapters. There has been, in addition, a widespread move towards more 'empirical' approaches, which avoid the problems that have developed around theoretical work on power by focusing more closely on actual cultural sites and processes. It is striking, in browsing current issues of cultural studies journals or in attending conferences in the field, how little of recent work is, in fact, still explicitly engaged in theorizing power.

I do not want to suggest that there is any problem with this in itself. There is no reason why cultural studies must always be fully engaged with these questions. The new initiatives that have emerged over the last ten years have succeeded in many cases in overcoming the malaise that was felt at the height of the culture wars, producing some excellent work and demonstrating a capacity for renewal. But a string of questions is left unanswered. Does the turn from the concept of power imply that it is no longer important? How should we now regard the theoretical work of the 1970s and 1980s? Is cultural studies engaged in the same project as it was then, or has it, in effect, been reinvented? Can we still define the field in terms of 'the point of view of relations of power'? If not, then what *does* now define it? There are few clear answers to these questions. The 'departure' from the concept of power can only be described as messy and unresolved.

It is often ambiguous, in fact, whether it has been a departure *within* cultural studies or a departure *from* cultural studies. A good example here is the 'policy' initiative that I discuss further in Chapter 11. As presented at various times by its chief proponent Tony Bennett, this was an attempt to renovate cultural studies – a reform by which the field 'may be deflected from those forms of banality which, in some quarters, have already claimed it while also resisting the lure of those debates whose contrived appearance of ineffable complexity makes them a death trap for practical thinking' (Bennett 1992a: 33). But the rejection of existing practice – as caught between 'banality' and 'contrived complexity' – was often so general and so damning that it raised questions whether the turn to policy was not rather a decision simply to abandon cultural studies and set up elsewhere. This rejection was even sharper in the case of other 'policy' proponents. For Stuart Cunningham, for example, writing in 1992: 'Cultural studies remains fixated on theoretical and textual orientations which provide little purchase in seeking to equip students with knowledge and skills for citizenship and employment in the 1990s' (1992: 177).

Departing from cultural studies is much more an option than it would be in other disciplines, because 'belonging' to the field has usually been overlaid on other affiliations – to media studies, film studies, sociology, literary studies, anthropology or education. 'Defecting' in this context means little more than retreating to one of these other bases of intellectual identity. Indeed, defection does not even need to be declared. Bennett and Cunningham have both maintained some relation to cultural studies. Bennett has taken the chair previously occupied by Stuart Hall, no less, at the Open University. But like many senior figures who were active in the 1970s and 1980s, the relation has also become somewhat enigmatic. It is clear that their opinion of the 'mainstream' of the field is less than flattering and that their continued affiliation has become a qualified one.

There is often an implication in these contexts that the 'real' cultural studies, the one most centrally located, is that which engages in the critical analysis of power. There are a number of factors contributing to this impression. The majority of undergraduate teaching materials and introductions to the field are still located here. There are reasons for this beyond the lag found in any discipline between new developments and their translation to the level of pedagogy. Whatever else may be said of them, critical theories of power have proved to be eminently teachable. They have been condensed in relatively formal propositions which can often be applied in 'problem-solving' ways: 'Apply Barthes' concept of ex-nomination to explain how the authority of dominant social groups is made invisible in the media'; 'Use Foucault's model of panoptic surveillance to discuss the political implications of security monitors and identity cards': there is something in such exercises which many students can grasp intuitively, but they also involve a clear element of challenge – a valuable combination in any attempt to develop analytical skills.

A second major factor has been the nature of the uptake of cultural studies in the United States. It is not an accident, I think, that the alarm expressed by Hall in the opening quotation to this chapter is an alarm most specifically about *American* cultural studies. It has been there, above all, that the inflation of the concept of power has occurred. There is, as Hall says, something of a surprise in this, as the American academy has often been seen as *allergic* to the concept, most notably in its historical resistance to Marxism. His earlier fear had been that the translation of cultural studies to America might 'formalize out of existence the critical questions of power, history and politics' (Hall 1992: 286). Instead, paradoxically, power became during the 1990s the central focus around which the field was received. At the same time, the size and relative wealth of the American academy has meant that the centre of gravity of cultural studies is now seen to reside there. The result has been that the field has come to be defined, for many, by a highly professionalized, American-centred theoretical discourse on power.

Thirdly, and more controversially, it could be argued that many of the departures from the critical analysis of power in cultural studies have needed the image of a 'bad other' to set themselves against. However real the problems associated with the concept, there has also been a certain amount of polemical exaggeration of their extent. There has been a tendency, as Hall observes, to advance by repudiating what went before, 'a sort of desire to advance only by way of wreaking an Oedipal revenge' (Hall 1996c: 398). One of the effects of this is that cultural studies has often been projected by internal critics almost as the conservative culture warriors have sought to represent it, as a field in the grip of a fanatical and destructive obsession with power.

Finally, and perhaps most decisively, there are few obvious *alternatives* to the definition of cultural studies in terms of its commitment to the concept of power. The departures from the concept have developed along a number of quite different lines and none have succeeded in consolidating themselves to the same degree. They are held together tenuously by the fact that they occupy a similar space – addressing 'culture' in some form, but outside the traditional disciplinary frameworks of anthropology, literary criticism or fine art – and that cultural studies now has an institutional form in teaching programmes, journals and conference circuits. But there is also a sense in which they still need the idea of a central core of debates around power to *be there* in order to define themselves. There are few who have much enthusiasm any more for wading into these debates: recent memories of the culture wars and disciplinary necrophilia are a continuing deterrent! But there are numerous ways – in the vocabulary that is used, in the starting point against which positions are marked out, in assumptions about the concerns of others – that they continue nonetheless to be invoked. The problem of power in cultural studies has not been resolved, in other words, so much as suppressed. The corpse of past controversies has not been given decent burial and continues to haunt the present.

Live the Legend, Collect the Power!

A major belief in writing this book has been that this situation should not be allowed to stand. Cultural studies deserves a clearer affirmation. This is not to suggest, by any means, that it is flawless; many of the problems that its critics have pointed out are real. But it is important to look beyond these to the *space* that the field has attempted to hold – a space that opened up in the second half of the twentieth century with the expansion of higher education, mass media and the governmental administration of everyday life. The key insight of the early figures in the field was that this terrain required quite a different style of intellectual exchange from those inherited from the closer, more bounded intellectual cultures of the past. There is little to suggest that this insight is less relevant today than it was in the 1950s and 1960s, when cultural studies first emerged in the encounter between middle-class dominated educational institutions and students from working-class backgrounds. The reality of life in the twenty-first century is that we are required to engage constantly with others who have had very different experiences from our own, who do not share our assumptions or frames of reference. Whatever its flaws, cultural studies has been right in seeking to embrace this reality.

The field has also been right, in my view, to recognize the importance of the concept of power. The conservative attack on cultural studies of the last fifteen years has been surprisingly successful in associating the concept with intellectual 'elites' – in representing it as a peculiar obsession of Kimball's 'tenured radicals'. But any open review of the evidence reveals it to be a far more general concern. As I write this in a space cleared from the debris of domestic life, I notice a *Bionicle Collector's Sticker Book* left on the floor by my five-year-old son: 'Live the Legend, Collect the Power!'. The bionicle universe is an elaborate fiction created to trade off and give life to a phenomenally successful line of Lego models of humanoid creatures – bionicles. Set on a volcanic island, Mata Nui, it has something of the feel of Polynesian legend, but a central element is a drama played out around power. Like many others who spend time around children, I have had to learn the attributes of the 'kanohi masks of power', used by the heroes, the Toa, in resisting the evil designs of Makuta: 'These masks supply the Toa with their great powers. Each Toa has to collect six masks – each mask provides the Toa with a different power'. Kanohi Akaku: power: X-ray vision. Kanohi Kakama: power: speed. Kanohi Hau: power: shielding… (Farshtey 2003)

This is but one small instance of a sprawling cultural phenomenon. In fact, the terrain on which questions of power is engaged is vast. As children's media specialist Marsha Kinder (1991) has argued, 'playing with power' is a central element of mainstream commercial children's media culture – from *Teenage Mutant Ninja Turtles* and *Power Rangers* to the *Powerpuff Girls*. And it is equally evident in more adult domains. For all its stylistic sophistication and philosophical provocations, a film like the Wachowski brothers' *The Matrix* has a similar imaginative structure to the bionicle legend: a faceless and malevolent agent seeks to concentrate power in itself, destroying or narcotizing all possible sites of resistance; a motley crew of outsiders must learn to trust each other and pool their resources in order to defeat it. The only major difference is the use of everyday points of reference to establish a more realist mode – the displacement of human interaction by new technologies, the modern corporation, the unsettling tension between the tranquil surface of everyday life as it is often experienced in the West and knowledge of unprecedented destructive potential. Further along this continuum, one might place the gritty street references of Public Enemy's 'Fight the Power' or a newspaper story about the visits to Australia of American and Chinese presidents George W. Bush and Hu Jintao – 'Power at Stake', with an accompanying image of Bush's hand outstretched over a map of Australia and South East Asia (*The Australian*, 25–6 October, 2003).

It may seem frivolous to mix these examples in the context of a discussion of the concept of power in cultural studies. The concept has generally been reserved for theorizing serious social and political issues – sexism, racism, military domination, institutional discrimination and exploitation. Certainly, the relative seriousness of different contexts needs to be respected: what is at stake in a children's sticker book cannot be compared with that, say, of a bloody military conflict in Iraq. But there is a way of articulating the difference that, nonetheless, I do want to resist. This is to say that some discourses of power identify fundamental social realities while others do not, that 'real' power can be distinguished from mere 'playing with power' and that those who have the expertise to recognize its forms and mechanisms should be granted an authority to speak over others.

If cultural studies has stood for anything in responding to the pluralism of the contemporary public sphere, it has been a suspicion of unthinking tendencies to privilege certain perspectives over others. It was a central motivation of the early efforts of British cultural studies to refuse suggestions in the 1950s and 1960s that 'culture', with all its positive connotations, was an exclusive preserve of the middle class: if the concept was to continue to serve as a major rubric for public discussion and debate, it had to be extended from canonical art and literature to include popular music, film and television, even trade unions and other working-class political organizations. It has also been the motivation of feminism in pointing out the masculine assumptions of established definitions of politics and history, of postcolonial studies in seeking to relativize a Western frame of reference and of queer theory in refusing assumptions of a single model of sexuality. In each case, cultural studies has rejected lazy claims for the authority of certain positions as 'normal', 'natural' or engaged with the 'real'.

The argument I wish to make is that a similar scepticism should be extended to the concept of power. There is little reason to think that claiming knowledge of 'real' power is any less problematic than claiming knowledge of 'real' culture, 'real' history or 'real' literature. To be consistent, cultural studies must accept that concepts of power may be as local, specific and historically formed as any other concept; that to insist on one's own concept as the only 'true' one may be as overbearing and dogmatic as a claim that true culture resides only in the art gallery or literary journal. It is here that the charges of a left-liberal 'elitism' do begin to bite and, however questionable the motivations behind them, it may not be a bad thing, in some cases, that they do. The issue is not a commitment to the concept of power as such; it is the modesty – or even, more simply, the 'good manners' – with which it is articulated in the public domain.

It should be recognized that modesty in these matters is not easily achieved. Williams's observations on the parallel case of the concept of culture provide, again, a useful guide: 'The hesitation, before what seems the richness of developed theory and the fullness of achieved practice, has the awkwardness, even the gaucherie, of any radical doubt. It is literally a moment of crisis, a jolt of experience' (Williams 1977: 11). For cultural studies to hesitate in its use of the concept of power, to forgo the 'fluency' which Hall identified in 1992, may appear a needless regression, if not a betrayal of all that the field has achieved. It should be remembered, however, that much the same doubts were expressed in the 1950s and 1960s over a hesitation in the use of the concept of culture. The benefits of the latter are now clear in the breadth of connections which cultural studies has been able to make with an extraordinary diversity of 'cultural' experiences. Similar benefits should be possible in the case of the concept of power today.

–2–

With Respect to Foucault
Towards a Critique of the Thematics of Power

It would be difficult to reflect on the concept of power – not just in cultural studies, but in the humanities and social sciences more generally – without paying respect to Michel Foucault. His work over a lifetime left an enormously rich and influential body of writing on the concept, not only at a theoretical level, but in close empirical studies of medical practices, sexuality, systems of knowledge, 'arts of government', prisons, schools, hospitals and other modern institutions. Some readers of the last chapter may wonder why it has not already been invoked. Am I perhaps trying to claim as new an approach to power that is already quite familiar? Has not Foucault already taught cultural studies precisely to 'hesitate' in its use of the concept? Has he not already provided the resources through which we can free our thinking about power from misplaced certainties? What more needs to be done than to continue to develop and extend the Foucauldian project?

One response to this would be to point out that Foucault consistently refused the role of 'master theorist', the authority on a subject to whom all must defer. He often presented his work as exploratory, even experimental:

> I like to open up a space of research, try it out, and then if it doesn't work, try again somewhere else. On many points ... I am still working and don't yet know whether I am going to get anywhere. What I say ought to be taken as 'propositions', 'game openings' where those who may be interested are invited to join in. (Foucault 2000a: 223)

It would be quite contrary to the politics of intellectual work professed by Foucault himself to suggest that the horizon of thought on power must always be 'Foucauldian': 'Under no circumstances should one pay attention to those who tell one: "Don't criticize, since you're not capable of carrying out a reform." That's ministerial cabinet talk' (Foucault 2000a: 236).

But in view of the problems set out in Chapter 1, there is another reason for wariness about appealing too easily to Foucault. Whether he can himself be held responsible, Foucauldian propositions, concepts and formulations have become central to the 'fluency' – precisely the *lack* of hesitation – with which power has sometimes been spoken of in cultural studies. 'Power-knowledge', 'discursive regimes' of power, 'modalities' of power, 'juridico-discursive' power, 'disciplinary' power, 'pastoral' power, 'technologies' of power, 'panopticism', 'governmentality'.

If one looks at the contexts in which Foucault first introduced these concepts, it is often clear that he intended them to unsettle or displace earlier – and, as he saw it, more dogmatically held – positions on power. But taken together, they also hold a seductive promise of a kind of theoretical mastery. Certain ideas, such as that of a 'micro-physics' of power, suggest almost a *science* of power, a meticulous and objective account of how it 'actually works'.

The tendency was acutely observed by Jean Baudrillard in *Forget Foucault*. For all the scepticism expressed by Foucault, there is, for Baudrillard, a suggestion in his work of a 'definitive understanding about power, sexuality, the body, and discipline, even down to their most delicate metamorphoses' (1987: 11). Foucault speaks to us about power 'in *real* objective terms which cover manifold diffractions but nonetheless do not question the objective point of view one has about them' (1987: 11). The point has been confused, unfortunately, with Baudrillard's own insistence that 'power is dead', that it no longer exists. If this is the conclusion to be drawn from questioning an 'objective point of view' about power, most in cultural studies have been less than inclined to follow the argument. Power is too important a term, too crucial in identifying problems that matter, to simply dismiss; to contemplate doing so is to risk being caught in pointless philosophical mind-games. The spectre of Baudrillard has become the major obstacle, in this context, to his own suggestion that we 'forget Foucault'.

Eventalizing Foucault

But there is another direction than Baudrillard's which might follow on from questioning too confident an objectivism in relation to power. This is one which is more in tune with Foucault's own method as applied to other concepts: 'man', 'the author', 'madness', 'the prison', 'knowledge'. The point, for Foucault, in questioning these concepts was never to suggest that the phenomena they point to 'do not exist'. It was rather to urge a recognition of the contingency and historical specificity in the way they are marked out and comprehended. In an interview on 'Questions of Method', already cited above, he describes his approach as 'eventalization': 'What do I mean by this term? First of all, a breach of self-evidence. It means making visible a *singularity* at places where there is a temptation to invoke a historical constant, an immediate anthropological trait, or an obviousness that imposes itself uniformly on all' (Foucault 2000a: 226). To 'eventalize' is to draw attention to the specificity of contexts in which concepts operate. The concept of 'man', for example, has only come to appear 'obvious', 'natural' as a result of complex historical developments – involving public institutions, systems of knowledge and economies – gathering momentum since the eighteenth century.

There are moments in Foucault where this approach does appear to be brought to the concept of power. In 'The Subject and Power', an essay widely regarded as definitive (Gordon 2000: xii), he distances himself from the assumption that 'power is something that exists with its own distinct origin, basic nature, and manifestations' (Foucault 2000d: 336). Rather than enquiring into the causes or nature of power, he suggests, we might start at a more descriptive level, tracing simply 'what happens'. To proceed in this way is:

> to introduce the suspicion that power as such does not exist. It is, in any case, to ask oneself what contents one has in mind when using this grand, all-embracing, and reifying term; it is to suspect that an extremely complex configuration of realities is allowed to escape while one endlessly marks time before the double question: what is power, and where does power come from? The flat empirical little question, 'What happens?' is not designed to introduce by stealth a metaphysics or an ontology of power but, rather, to undertake a critical investigation of the thematics of power. (Foucault 2000d: 336–7)

The statement comes surprisingly close to a Baudrillardian scepticism about the very 'existence' of power. It suggests that Foucault did at times contemplate withdrawing from the positive use of the concept to reflect upon it at more distance.

A 'critical investigation of the thematics of power': if this is placed centrally, the approach to questions of power I have suggested in Chapter 1 might indeed be described as 'Foucauldian'. But, as with many major figures, it has become necessary to indicate *which* Foucault one might be claiming as an inspiration or ally. The Foucault I wish to align myself with in this book is Foucault the advocate of a certain tact and humility in intellectual work (cf. Osborne 1998). His positions here are strikingly reminiscent, in places, of those developed by early British cultural studies. What is important for Foucault, as it was for Raymond Williams, Richard Hoggart and Stuart Hall, is to find a way of speaking which recognizes the plurality of the public domain, which does not impose established or dominant ways of knowing upon others:

> I take care not to dictate how things should be. I try instead to pose problems, to make them active, to display them in such a complexity that they can silence the prophets and lawgivers, all those who speak for others or to others. In this way, it will be possible for the complexity of the problem to appear in its connection with people's lives; and consequently, through concrete questions, difficult cases, movements of rebellion, reflections, and testimonies, the legitimacy of a common creative action can also appear. (Foucault 2000b: 288)

It may be relevant to draw attention to some biographical details here – not so much Foucault's often-cited homosexuality, but the fact that he was never entirely comfortable in the metropolitan intellectual milieu on which he nevertheless had such an influence. He came from a provincial background and after his studies in Paris spent considerable time outside France – in Sweden, Poland and Tunis (see Eribon 1992). His most formative political experiences were, by his own account, not in Paris, but Tunisia: 'I was compelled to join the political debate. It wasn't May '68 but March '68, in a country in the third world' (Foucault 2000b: 280). Much of his work can be seen as insisting, as Williams did at Cambridge, that the perspective of metropolitan intellectual culture not be simply presumed.

My main argument in this chapter is that it is important now to distinguish this Foucault from Foucault the theorist of power, even to the point of playing them against each other. It is time, as Peter C. Herman (2004) and his collaborators have suggested, to 'historicise theory'. If we are to avoid turning Foucault himself into a 'prophet and lawgiver', it is time to 'eventalize' his own writing, to make it visible as a 'singularity' so that the 'legitimacy of a common creative action' in relation to power can be brought into view. There is little in the voluminous commentary on Foucault's writing on power that situates it historically – the tendency has been very much to consider his positions for their general applicability. But much can be gleaned from his own writings and interviews, which did not seek to hide their immediate formation.

There are two contexts, it seems, which first motivated Foucault's engagement with the concept of power. The first was a desire to unsettle the authority of the intellectual culture dominant in France in the 1950s. As he describes this himself in a preface to Gilles Deleuze and Félix Guattari's *Anti-Oedipus*:

> During the years 1945–1965 (I am referring to Europe), there was a certain way of thinking correctly, a certain style of political discourse, a certain ethics of the intellectual. One had to be on familiar terms with Marx, not let one's dreams stray too far from Freud. And one had to treat sign-systems – the signifier – with the greatest respect. These were the three requirements that made the strange occupation of writing and speaking a measure of truth about oneself and one's time acceptable. (Foucault 1983: xi)

Marx, Freud, semiotics: the elements of this intellectual culture were not entirely monolithic – the most obvious common element is a certain abstraction and subordination to philosophical concerns. Elsewhere, Foucault adds Hegelian philosophy, phenomenology and existentialism (Foucault 2000b: 246–8). But it is clear that it was experienced in its totality as complacent and even oppressive.

A major concern for Foucault was the dominant view of the human subject, particularly the assumption that it constituted a coherent centre of experience and meaning. Along with a number of contemporaries, he felt 'a certain pressing desire to raise the question of the subject in a different way, to free ourselves of the fundamental postulate that French philosophy had never abandoned since Descartes, that was reinforced, even, by phenomenology' (Foucault 2000b: 251). Another significant object of criticism was an understanding of history, derived from Hegel, as an unbroken and intelligible totality, offering a rational and detached perspective even on such tragic events as the Second World War. In combination with the theory of the subject, this provided an all too coherent interpretive frame from which to think and act.

The determination by Foucault and his contemporaries to find alternatives was strongly conditioned by the geopolitical context of the Cold War in which political options appeared to be reduced to a choice between 'the America of Truman and the USSR of Stalin':

> The experience of the war had shown us the urgent need of a society radically different from one in which we were living, this society that had permitted Nazism, that had lain down in front of it, and that had gone over *en masse* to de Gaulle. A large sector of French youth had a reaction of total disgust towards all that. We wanted a world and a society that were not only different but that would be an alternative version of ourselves. (Foucault 2000b: 247)

In contrast to this, everything that was offered by the French academy, and even outside it by Sartre's existentialism, seemed to confirm, depressingly, the already known.

The Meanness of Small Beginnings

Three names stood out as inspirations for Foucault in developing a different way of seeing: Friedrich Nietzsche, Maurice Blanchot and Georges Bataille. For each of these, 'experience has the function of wrenching the subject from itself, of seeing to it that the subject is no longer itself, or that it is brought to its annihilation or its dissolution' (Foucault 2000b: 241). Bataille's idea of a 'limit-experience' – one that displaces the subject from itself – is an important one for Foucault, providing a way of conceptualizing his own work. But the most important influence in explicitly articulating the shift was Nietzsche, and it is through this influence that the concept of power is brought into play.

In Nietzsche's work itself, the concept appears in the context of an iconoclastic attempt to smash the idols of metaphysics – those comforting illusions, as he saw it, through which man persuaded himself of his central place in the world. It was associated with an attempt to reveal beneath the claims of truth and beauty a seething mass of conflicts and passions. Much of this structure of argument carries over directly into the work of Foucault. He picks up particularly on an argument in Nietzsche that there is no affinity between knowledge and the world to be known:

> Knowledge must struggle against a world without order, without connectedness, without form, without beauty, without wisdom, without harmony, and without law. That is the world that knowledge deals with… [T]here can be no relation of natural continuity between knowledge and the things that knowledge must know. There can only be a relation of violence, domination, power and force, a relation of violation. (Foucault 2000c: 9)

What is important about power, in this context, is that it is ignoble, 'mean'. In appreciating the pervasiveness of power, 'We see the meanness of … small beginnings as compared with the solemnity of their origin as conceived by philosophers' (2000c: 7). The function of the concept is iconoclastic; it brings into question the authority of established ways of seeing.

The second major context for Foucault's engagement with the concept of power is the subterranean currency that it had gained during the 1950s and 1960s. It invoked a widespread political unrest outside formal public debate and the academy, despite a relative peace and prosperity:

> What was it that was everywhere being called in question? The way in which power was exercised – not just state power but the power exercised by other institutions and forms of constraint, a sort of abiding oppression in everyday life… From all these experiences, mine included, there emerged one word, similar to those written with invisible ink, ready to appear on paper when the right reagent is applied – the word 'power'. (Foucault 2000b: 283–4)

The reference to 'everyday life' confirms Foucault's desire to recognize areas outside formal political processes and discourses, not only in France but also in the societies he witnessed in his time abroad. To speak of power was to connect with experiences shared even by those under very different political regimes – of French students dissatisfied with the intellectual culture in which they found themselves, of ordinary Swedes in an efficient but over-administered society, of Poles confronting a curtailment of political freedoms and of young Tunisians opposed to continuing colonial rule.

The double function of the concept of power – both loosening the authority of the dominant intellectual culture he was working against and articulating the experiences of those outside it – led Foucault to give it quite a novel emphasis. Power is 'central' to social relations, a 'ground' on which everything else takes place: 'Between every point of the social body, between a man and a woman, between the members of a family, between a master and his pupil, between every one who knows and every one who does not, there exists relations of power' (Foucault 1980: 187). He sometimes projects this emphasis onto Nietzsche, drawing a comparison with the emphasis in Marx on economic relations of production: 'It was Nietzsche who specified the power relation as the general focus, shall we say, of philosophical discourse – whereas for Marx it was the production relation' (Foucault 1980: 53). But the centring of the concept of power might equally be attributed to Foucault himself.

The danger with this centring is that similar certainties may come to attach to the concept of power as have attached to those it is designed to displace. The comparison with Marxism should be a warning here, as the history is well known. In centring economic relations of production, Marx succeeded in displacing the idealist assumption of autonomous individuals freely entering into contracts with others, bringing sharply into question the authority of bourgeois political economy. The cost, however, was a tendency to another kind of economic fundamentalism, in which relations of production are elevated as an absolute truth. Whether this tendency can be found in Marx himself has been a matter of long dispute. There is no doubt, however, that it has been a major feature of historically significant Marx*isms*.

Power is often introduced by Foucault as a substitutive concept: its function is to assume the explanatory burden of other concepts, thereby weakening them or exposing them as redundant. Accounts of the world in terms of the human subject are replaced by an account in terms of power; accounts of knowledge as a relation of perception or cognitive apprehension are replaced by an account of knowledge as a relation of power. In a discussion of the concept of power in Nietzsche, Foucault draws attention, himself, to the way it substitutes for God: 'If there is no relation between knowledge and the things to be known, if the relation between knowledge and known is arbitrary, if it is a relation of power and violence, the existence of God at the center of the system of knowledge is no longer indispensable' (Foucault 2000c: 10). The risk here is that the metaphysical weight of the displaced concept is simply transferred to the concept of power. God's withdrawal from the scene does not in fact mean that there is 'no relation between knowledge and the things to be known'; the relation is accounted for in positive terms by power.

Five Foucaults

Foucault was more than aware of the general problem; it is explicitly identified in the passage already cited above, in which he disavows an intention to 'introduce by stealth a metaphysics or an ontology of power' (Foucault 2000d: 337). It is also a central concern in his criticisms of the use of the concept by others. His major target here was an idea of power as a general prohibition or 'Thou shalt not', an idea through which 'one single and identical "formula" of power (the interdict) comes to be applied to all forms of society and all levels of subjection' (Foucault 1980: 140). The universalism implicit in reducing power to an abstract principle of negation is related to a tendency to 'subjectivize' it: 'In the aspect of its exercise, power is conceived as a great universal Subject which pronounces the interdict... In the aspect of subjection to power, there is an equal tendency to "subjectivise" it by specifying the point at which the interdict is accepted, the point where one says yes or no to power' (Foucault 1980: 140). Rather than initiating a departure from a universalist metaphysics, the use of the concept of power comes, in this case, only to reinforce it.

A further danger in the idea of power as a negation or prohibition is the moral force it carries with it. By denouncing power, one comes to be seen as pure, untainted, authorized to pronounce on others but beyond criticism oneself. There was a very immediate historical context, for Foucault, in addressing this problem: the shadow of Stalin. As he saw first-hand in Poland, a revolution against one form of oppression does not mean that the revolutionaries themselves will not install another. In many of his more political interventions, he challenged the French left for their failure fully to absorb this lesson. In an interview with Maoists, for example, he questions the idea that 'people's courts' would necessarily be an improvement on the 'bourgeois' legal system they wished to overthrow: 'Can we not see the embryonic, albeit fragile form of a state apparatus reappearing here? The possibility of class oppression? ... I am wondering whether the court is not a form of popular justice but rather its first deformation' (Foucault 1980: 2). Again, the concept of power carries its own certainties, providing an opening for new forms of absolutism and a potential for tyranny.

Much of Foucault's writing on power can be read as an attempt to find ways to resist these tendencies, to inject doubt into the way the concept is used. Consistent with his reluctance to project himself as 'the authority', no single solution is offered. Five approaches, at least, are experimented with. The first is to suggest that power be regarded not as a substantive entity but as a *relation*. In the passage cited earlier, where he expresses scepticism about the existence of 'power as such', he goes on to qualify the approach he is recommending: 'It is to give oneself as the object of analysis *power relationships* rather than power itself ... there is no such entity as power... Power exists only as exercised by some on others, only when it is put into action...' (Foucault 2000d: 339–40). The significance of this suggestion is that it brings into question any attempt to *locate* power, to say who 'has' it and who does not: 'Power is not something that is acquired, seized, or shared, something that one holds on to or allows to slip away' (Foucault 1981: 94). Despite its pervasiveness, it is an elusive phenomenon, one that shifts continually as new relations take form.

A second and related approach is to see power as a matter of 'mechanisms' or 'techniques'. A major discovery here was Jeremy Bentham's eighteenth-century programme for maintaining prison discipline through the 'panopticon'. The discussion of the panopticon is central to the argument of *Discipline and Punish* (Foucault 1979: 195–228) and the positions developed there continue to inform much of Foucault's later writing. What is significant about Bentham's texts was their suggestion that the analysis of power might be transferred entirely from the speculative level of subjective intentions or motivations to the level of practical arrangements or 'technologies'. In the case of the panopticon itself, these were architectural: the situation of an observation tower in a central position surrounded by multiple prison cells created a potential for a single observer to see many others without themselves being seen. The implication, more generally, is that power is best described at a specific, technical level; general philosophical discourses of power are correspondingly invalidated.

A third approach is what might be called a 'miniaturization' of power – its conceptual relocation to the 'molecular' level (cf. Baudrillard 1987: 33–4). This emerges from a critique of a widespread tendency to equate power and sovereignty. In *Discipline and Punish*, Foucault argues that in contemporary societies power has been separated from the will of the sovereign, becoming independent, in fact, of any central organ of the state. It is now to be found at the microscopic level of timetables, surveillance regimes, minute corrections to bodily dispositions. Relations of power 'go right down into the depths of society, ... they are not localized in relations between the state and its citizens or on the frontier between classes and ... do not merely reproduce, at the level of individuals, bodies, gestures and behaviour, the general form of the law or government' (Foucault 1979: 27). It becomes impossible, if we accept this, to give any broad characterization of power at the general or 'molar' level.

A fourth approach is to suggest that there is no single *form* of power. Much of the originality of *Discipline and Punish* is in offering a '*history* of power relations' (Foucault 1979: 24, emphasis added). This is not a history of the transfer of power between different individuals or groups; it is a history of the very 'modalities' of power itself. Through a study of systems of discipline, punishment and surveillance since the eighteenth century, Foucault identifies three 'mechanisms' or 'technologies' of power: one based on the old monarchical law, in which the vengeance of the sovereign was marked on the body of the condemned; a second, developed by reforming jurists, in which punishment was seen as 'a procedure for requalifying individuals as subjects'; and a third, emerging in the prison system, in which punishment become a 'technique for the coercion of individuals' (Foucault 1979: 130–1). The implication, once again, is that caution is required in speaking of power; there is little that can be said about it in general.

Finally, Foucault resists the tendency to place power in opposition to other phenomena: 'Relations of power are not in a position of exteriority with respect to other types of relationships (economic processes, knowledge relationships, sexual relations) but are immanent in the latter' (Foucault 1981: 94). A significant inspiration here appears to have been the philosophy of Spinoza, with its refusal of the Cartesian distinction between mind and body. As an immanent principle formally equivalent to Spinoza's God (the plane in which mental and material attributes both inhere), power can be thought of not as negative but as positive. It does not act 'against' the purposive actions of groups or individuals but 'in and through' them:

> The individual is not to be conceived as a sort of elementary nucleus ... on which power comes to fasten or against which it happens to strike... In fact, it is already one of the prime effects of power that certain bodies, certain gestures, certain discourses, certain desires, come to be identified and constituted as individuals. The individual, that is, is not the *vis-à-vis* of power; it is, I believe, one of its prime effects. (Foucault 1980: 98)

A similar argument informs the concept of 'power-knowledge'. If power is the basic substrate of human activity, knowledge cannot stand 'against' power because it is an attribute or *effect* of power. Despite the 'mental' associations of knowledge and the 'material' associations of power, they are substantially identical, differing only as aspects of the same phenomenon. The significance of this is to blunt the moral authority of those who speak against power; if there is no 'outside' to power, we must all accept our implication in power relations.

An Awful Vortex

In practice, Foucault combines these approaches in highly original ways, fusing them into a distinctive vision and bringing them to bear in compelling ways on actual discourses and practices. It is worth noting, however, that they are conceptually distinct: power could be a matter of 'technique' without being 'molecular'; there could be multiple 'modalities' of power without their being 'immanent' within sexual or epistemological relations. Furthermore, some approaches do not appear to be entirely consistent with others. According to the 'Spinozist' conception, power is clearly substantial. The ontology involved, like Spinoza's own, is an unorthodox one, collapsing everything under a single category; but it is, nevertheless, an ontology. Foucault sometimes describes power as a fundamental substratum, a 'concrete changing *soil*' in which sovereignty and other social institutions are '*grounded*' (Foucault 1980: 187, emphasis added). It is never explained how this can be made to fit with the strictly relational understanding which he insists upon elsewhere.

More importantly, however, for the general problem I outlined in Chapter 1, none of Foucault's innovations go any way towards a critique of the *thematics* of power. In fact, they do the opposite, directing our attention to the positive analysis of power itself. As we consider whether power is substantial or relational, microscopic or macroscopic, even as we contemplate a history of power relations, we are led further and further from reflecting on why we have chosen, in the first place, to use 'this grand, all-embracing, and reifying term'. Even in his scepticism, Foucault often succeeds only in *deepening* our investment in the concept. This is particularly the case with the multiplication of forms of power. As we are led to doubt whether any single characterization of power can be applied to all times and places, we are invited to believe that *some* characterization can always be found. The implication is sometimes confirmed explicitly: 'In a society such as ours, *but basically in any society*, there are manifold relations of power which permeate, characterise and constitute the social body' (Foucault 1980: 93, emphasis added). In emptying the concept of any specific historical content, Foucault increases the temptation to apply it universally.

A similar paradoxical fate has befallen attempts by others to renovate the concept of power from within. Perhaps the most noteworthy, within the orbit of reference of cultural studies, is Ernesto Laclau and Chantal Mouffe's attempt to identify a discursive aspect to power. In *Hegemony and Socialist Strategy* (1985), Laclau and

Mouffe draw a distinction between 'subordination' and 'oppression'. A relation of 'subordination' is one in which 'an agent is subjected to the decisions of another – an employee with respect to an employer, for example, or in certain forms of family organization the woman with respect to the man, and so on' (Laclau and Mouffe 1985: 153). A relation of 'oppression', by contrast, is one in which relations of subordination have 'transformed themselves into sites of antagonism' (1985: 154). The important point is that 'oppression' is not conceived as a universal phenomenon, but as discursively produced in particular historical circumstances. The understanding of social relations as 'oppressive' is, for Laclau and Mouffe, a specific achievement only made possible by the emergence in modernity of the 'democratic discourse': 'Our thesis is that it is only from the moment when the democratic discourse becomes available to articulate the different forms of resistance to subordination that the conditions will exist to make possible the struggle against different kinds of inequality.' (1985: 154)

Like Foucault's multiplication of forms of power, the argument works, at one level, to limit universalizing claims and allow greater sensitivity to different historical contexts. Oppression can no longer be pointed out simply as fact but must be presented more persuasively, openly setting out to win over constituencies to what is only a particular way of seeing. The distinction between 'subordination' and 'oppression' is part of an attempt by Laclau and Mouffe to insist on the democratic responsibilities of left political projects. But as with Foucault, there is a cost in the way their theoretical leverage is achieved. As with any distinction between a 'discursive' and a 'real' aspect of a phenomenon, the aspect which is marked as 'real' – in this case 'subordination' – is further universalized, becoming rigorously set apart from historical considerations. Subordination comes to be conceived by Laclau and Mouffe as a bedrock of power, entirely independent of its various instances or the way it might be framed. There is always a risk, in fact, that the democratic thrust of their argument might collapse. Given the continued assumption of a fundamental underlying phenomenon (subordination), the question must arise whether the independence of the discursive aspect (oppression) can be sustained. Discourses of power remain grounded, ultimately, in a simple universal truth.

Another revisionist approach to theories of power has been to turn them on themselves. A good example of this strategy is an attempt by Bruce Robbins to deflate the authority of Pierre Bourdieu in debates around popular culture. Where, for Bourdieu, we must always enquire into the interests of those who speak of popular culture, Robbins suggests that we might equally enquire into the interests of those who speak of *power* – not least, the interests of Bourdieu himself:

It is hard not to notice ... that Bourdieu's interest in defending the notion of a single 'dominant form' [of culture] coincides with an interest in defending the 'symbolic profits' he himself has drawn from analyzing that dominant form, that is, from the discovery or the invention of 'cultural capital'. The threat to cultural capital posed by cultural studies is clear. For Bourdieu, culture is necessarily empty of any popular or democratic input. Its contents are arbitrary, fixed in advance by the state, and ruled only by the goal of allowing the dominant class to win at the 'main social games'... If culture's contents were *not* arbitrary..., if 'the people' had some special access, competence, or authority where culture is concerned, then the system would not work as he describes... [T]he metaphor of cultural capital would collapse. (Robbins 1993: 208)

A slightly different variant of the argument has been developed by John Hartley in criticism of the classical cultural studies paradigm of the Birmingham Centre for Contemporary Cultural Studies. Hartley (1992: 25) speculates whether the oppositional intellectuals of the 1970s were interested in the 'manipulation of the masses' because they themselves wished they were able to do so. Similar arguments have also become common in debates within feminism in criticism of fundamentalist tendencies in claims about patriarchal domination (Roiphe 1993; Denfeld 1995; Lumby 1997).

Once again, these arguments are effective in unsettling an aura of moral certainty often associated with the use of the concept of power. But they also follow other revisionist approaches in further entrenching the universalism of the concept. The use of theories of power *against* theories of power sets up a vicious cycle in which the attribution of positions to strategies of power becomes a self-fulfilling prophecy. What are the interests of Robbins or Hartley in drawing our attention to the interests of those who theorize power? What are my interests here in drawing attention to their interests? The only conclusion that can be drawn from this game is a confirmation and extension of Bourdieu's reduction of positions to power games played out around the accumulation of cultural capital. While the motivation for criticizing this reduction may be discomfort with its relentless zero-sum negativity, the criticisms only further eliminate any space for the recognition of other possibilities.

The difficulty of escaping the vortex of the concept of power may help to explain the often hysterical quality of the 'culture war' debates discussed in Chapter 1. Even the conservative critics of cultural studies – those most damning of the concept – have sounded at times like the theorists they set out to criticize. If it were not for their targets, D'Souza and Kimball's analysis of a class conspiracy by left-liberal 'elites' could almost be mistaken for a Marxist critique of ideology or a Foucauldian study of power-knowledge. The inflation of their rhetoric could be read, perhaps, as a symptom of a certain despair, a sign of just how close they are to those they oppose. The uncanny grip of the concept of power may also explain why many of those who have sought new directions in cultural studies have opted, rather abruptly, to draw a line against it. To attempt to 'settle accounts' with debates around power may seem only to risk being drawn back into the quicksand, to be claimed by an increasingly ugly and destructive debate. As already noted, there is often a tendency simply to repress or disown this debate rather than to deal with it in a more substantial way.

Powers Originall and Instrumentall

Is there an alternative? It should be clear by now that I believe there is. I will finish this chapter by further clarifying the possibility I began to develop in Chapter 1. It might now be described as an opposite approach from the major one pursued by Foucault. Rather than purging the concept of power of specific historical associations – with sovereignty, for example – it is to consider how the concept of power itself has been historically formed. It would be better, in fact, if we take this line, to speak in the plural of *concepts* of power. Foucault demonstrates brilliantly that the concept that is founded on the model of sovereignty is not well suited to analysing the disciplinary regimes of prisons and hospitals. It may be a mistake, however, to respond to this as he does, by distinguishing between different 'forms' of power. To do so is to fuel the dream of a master concept, which can be adapted to any and every circumstance. It would be better, according to Foucault's own principles, to see each concept of power as a 'singularity' with no necessary relation to the next. Only in this way, as he argues so well for other concepts, can the concept be shorn of a spurious authority.

A useful lead in this direction is provided by Barry Hindess in his book *Discourses of Power* (1996). It is not immediately obvious, as the book is presented as a historical study of theories of power culminating in, and clearly aligned with, Foucault. Foucault represents, for Hindess, a 'radical alternative to conventional understandings of power' (1996: 151–2) in which various inadequacies of earlier theories are largely superseded. But there are moments in his argument that go well beyond a comparison of different 'understandings', bringing into question the whole thematics of power. These begin to open up quite different lines of analysis from those that would normally be thought of as 'Foucauldian'.

As presented, Hindess's argument is that there have been two main conceptions of power in Western political thought in the modern period:

> One, which has been especially prominent in recent academic discussion, is the idea of power as a simple quantitative phenomenon. Power, in this sense, is nothing more than a kind of generalized capacity to act. The second, more complex, understanding is that of power as involving not only a capacity but also a *right* to act, with both capacity and right being seen to rest on the consent of those over whom power is exercised. (Hindess 1996: 1)

The argument is an interesting one in itself and Hindess develops it with exemplary clarity. In doing so, however, he introduces another distinction which is perhaps more significant in its implications. This is a distinction between the idea of power in general (whether as capacity or right) and the idea of distinct and specific *powers*.

The distinction appears most clearly in a discussion of the concept of power in Thomas Hobbes's great seventeenth-century political treatise *Leviathan*. Chapter

X of *Leviathan* opens with a simple definition: 'The power of a man is his present means to obtain some future apparent Good'. Hobbes amplifies by distinguishing between 'Originall' and 'Instrumentall' powers. The first refers to faculties of body or mind such as 'extraordinary Strength, Forms, Prudence, Arts, Eloquence, Liberality, Nobility'; the second to 'those powers, which acquired by these, or by fortune, are means and instruments to acquire more: as Riches, Reputation, Friends, and the secret working of God, which men call Good Luck'. As Hindess points out, 'power in this view ... refers to any one, or any combination, of a remarkably heterogeneous set of attributes which appear to have in common the fact that they may be useful to their possessor in pursuit of at least some of his or her purposes' (1996: 23). On the basis of this definition, he goes on,

> there would be little that could usefully be said about power in general... Rather than investigate the properties of power as such, any serious enquiry would have to concern itself separately with the discrete powers associated with extraordinary Strength or Eloquence, or with Riches, the secret working of God and other such attributes, as well as with the diverse uses to which those powers can be put. (1996: 24)

The question that is pressed here is why we should talk of 'power' in the singular at all. If powers are heterogeneous and diverse, why not restrict ourselves instead to talking of 'strength', 'eloquence' or 'riches'? Foucault, as we have seen, does occasionally recognize this question, but only in passing before returning to his positive 'anatomy' of power. Hindess centres it more fully, pursuing it in a much more structured way.

Further than this, he indicates a context in which we might begin to explain the formation of at least one concept of power 'in general' – the development of the modern state. The process can be observed in Hobbes. As Hindess points out, Hobbes does not in fact limit himself to talking of particular powers; there is another understanding of power in play:

> one in which power refers not to extraordinary Strength, Eloquence, Riches or whatever, but rather to something that these various attributes are thought to have in common ... some common stuff, some shared underlying capacity or essence of effectiveness, which each of these attributes possesses in some quantity, and which accounts for their utility in obtaining 'future apparent goods'. (1996: 24–5)

The appearance of this concept is intimately connected with the attempt to provide an account of the political function of the sovereign – at a time, it should be remembered, in which this function was still emerging. It is in developing such an account that Hobbes is drawn to write of power as a single, homogeneous phenomenon. He suggests, specifically, that the discrete powers of many individuals might be 'united by consent' to form a power greater than all. It is in the disposal of this power that sovereignty is held to consist.

As Hindess points out, the suggestion introduces three important propositions which exceed the simple definition of powers as capacities: first, that power is a 'quantitative and cumulative phenomenon'; second, that it is 'capable of aggregation'; and third, that it is generally determining of events, those who possess a greater 'quantity' prevailing in a global sense over those who possess lesser quantities (Hindess 1996: 25–6). Whether or not it can be attributed entirely to Hobbes, they are propositions that have since developed into basic assumptions. The implication of an 'essence of effectiveness' has become fundamental to most modern conceptions of power.

A Common Creative Action

The only problem with Hindess, if we are attempting to particularize concepts of power, is that he continues to assess them according to whether they are, in some universal sense, 'correct'. In a test of Hobbes's supplementary propositions, he asks us to imagine a contest between heterogeneous powers: 'the power of extraordinary Strength on the one side and the power of Riches on the other, or an international dispute in which tanks are pitted against submarines' (1996: 29):

> There is little point in considering these cases in terms of the sheer quantities of power involved on the two sides. What matters rather is the presence or absence of conditions under which the means of action available to the contending parties can in fact be deployed... Means of action of different kinds will be effective under different conditions, and in this respect the idea of an underlying common substance or essence of power is clearly unsatisfactory. (1996: 29)

On these grounds, for Hindess, the whole tradition of Western political thinking since Hobbes must be seen as flawed. There can be no 'essence of effectiveness'; to assume one is to continue to perpetrate a fundamental conceptual error.

The point is very sharply made and does tell us something about concepts of power: that they cannot be justified simply on the grounds of a supposed veridical reference. But it also reveals a continuing tendency in much 'Foucauldian' commentary towards an abstract universalism. There is still something in Hindess's writing of the Althusserian Marxist of the 1970s, ever in search of the 'epistemological break' between an ideological past and a scientific future (see Hindess and Hirst 1975; 1977). Foucault himself does indeed begin to figure here as a 'master theorist', one who has led us out of confusion, if not towards a simple 'truth', then to a complex and sophisticated understanding which we can hope might serve for all time.

To indicate, more directly, the problem with the argument, a comparison might be made between the concepts of power and wealth. If the case can be made against a generalized use of the former, why not also the latter? What authorizes us to speak of two individuals or organizations as 'wealthy'? Will we not find in every case that their possessions are different – a large house and expensive art collection in one case, a fat share portfolio or successful business in another? To translate Hindess's argument in relation to power, we would have to say that any equation between the two must imply an 'essence of wealth', a notion which can be questioned on just the same grounds as the idea of an 'essence of power'. Where beneath the particular possessions – the house, the artwork, the share portfolio, the business – are we to find this essence? The answer, of course, is nowhere; there is nothing to be found but the possessions themselves. Are we then to conclude that any analysis of 'wealth in general' is in error, that virtually the whole of modern economic thought is to be dismissed as simply mistaken?

What restrains us from drawing this conclusion is the knowledge that concepts function in more practical and situated ways than that which is being implied. Whatever we might think of the philosophical justification for doing so, equivalences of wealth are routinely drawn between different sets of possessions. There is a medium of exchange – money – and a whole complex of institutions – banks, treasuries, governmental agencies – which institutionalize these equivalences, making it virtually impossible to live in contemporary societies without giving them some recognition. Whether, if we stood back from all this, we might judge them to be illegitimate is, in the bad sense, academic. To attempt to do so would be to imagine a world in which concepts are developed in some pure theoretical realm before being handed down to circulate among actual historical contingencies. All the evidence suggests the reverse: that it is among the contingencies that they first take form.

One might ask, of course, whether the social institutions for drawing equivalences between different powers are quite as developed as the mechanisms for drawing equivalences between possessions. They almost certainly are not. While it is common to imply an 'economy' of power – speaking of some individuals, organizations or nations as having 'more' or 'less' power than others – such comparisons cannot be quantified in the same way as citing an 'estimated net worth' or 'gross domestic product'. But this does not mean that practical mechanisms for equating powers do not exist. To return to the case of Hobbes, it should be remembered that he was not just a political theorist but also a political *architect*. His works were read not only as an account of how things are, but as a set of arguments as to how they *should be*. The idea that political subjects might 'combine' their powers to underwrite the function of the sovereign might be read in this context not so much as a philosophical proposition as a practical political invention. If we *think* of power as quantitative and cumulative, what political forms can then be contemplated?

If we accept this possibility, a window is opened to retrieve Foucault to the role of the 'specific intellectual'. His significance was not in making a 'radical departure' in which the concept of power was purified of past confusions and errors. It was in developing a constructive response, from his position as a European intellectual, to some of the major political problems of the mid twentieth century. His importance for the concept of power was not in handing down a theoretical approach that we can now simply apply; it was in contributing to a 'common creative action' in which we are all continually involved.

–3–

Power and the State
The Peculiarities of the English Revisited

The development of the modern state is not the only context in which we might locate the formation of concepts of power. There are clearly others. In his fascinating book *Crowds and Power*, Elias Canetti explores a number of more basic experiential contexts, particularly the concentration of bodies and a resulting sense of oneness in 'the crowd' – another characteristic phenomenon of modern societies. Canetti distinguishes between power and force, illustrating with the relation between cat and mouse:

> The cat uses force to catch the mouse, to seize it, hold it in its claws and ultimately kill it. But while it is *playing* with it another factor is present. It lets it go, allows it to run about a little and even turns its back; and, during this time, the mouse is no longer subjected to force. But it is still within the power of the cat and can be caught again... The space which the cat dominates, the moments of hope it allows the mouse, while continuing however to watch it ... – all this together, space, hope, watchfulness and destructive intent, can be called the actual body of power, or, more simply, power itself. (Canetti 1992: 327)

This suggests a concept of power independent from, and probably much older, than the state. It has something in common with Hobbes's account of sovereignty in that it is associated with a generalization away from the particular: what distinguishes power is 'a certain extension in space and in time' (Canetti 1992: 327). But if cats and mice can be used as examples, modern political arrangements are not the only way this generalization can suggest itself. Canetti's use of the concept has no obvious relation to the state.

The same may be true of the concept of power as an 'abiding oppression in everyday life' which was identified by Foucault as so widespread in the 1950s and 1960s. This is important to remember, as it has probably been the most significant concept for the development of cultural studies. I will return to it later, particularly in relation to the influence of feminism, discussed in Chapter 8.

The political form of the state must nevertheless be recognized as a major point of reference for concepts of power. It is still dominant in many everyday usages, as in discussions of who is 'in power'. What this usually means is the party who occupies government within a given territory and thereby controls the agencies of the state. It is probable, furthermore, that concepts of power developed with reference to the state have some influence on concepts developed elsewhere. Even for Foucault, they are a significant point of departure. Notwithstanding his determination to displace the state from its privileged place in political theory, he spends considerable time reflecting on it. One of his most illuminating and enduring contributions may indeed have been in bringing critical attention to the relation between the concepts of power and sovereignty.

This chapter continues, therefore, the discussion opened up at the end of the last, considering the extent to which state formations may be relevant to understanding concepts of power in cultural studies. But it is also focuses, more specifically, on the particular *kind* of state formation in which the field has largely taken form. Cultural studies has been a development most notably of the Anglophone academy, with major bases in countries which share not only a language – English – but also overlapping political histories. The term 'cultural studies' was, itself, an English coinage, first institutionalized by Richard Hoggart in establishing the Birmingham Centre for Contemporary Cultural Studies in the 1960s, and despite some criticism of the fact (Chen 1992; Turner 1992; Frow and Morris 1993), its British version has been particularly influential. Much of its theory has been borrowed from continental Europe and it has now established significant bases in locations with little historical association with Britain or America. But the state formations in which cultural studies has emerged have been overwhelmingly Anglo-derived: Britain, the United States, Canada, Australia and New Zealand.

An Ethno-Historical Specificity

There are good reasons for thinking this may be relevant to the concept of power in cultural studies. The controversies surrounding the concept in the 'culture war' debates of the 1990s were quite specific to 'Anglo' societies. Originating for the most part in the United States, they resonated in Britain and Australia but not, for example, in France (see Appignanesi 1994). A particular 'Anglo' sensitivity to the concept of power can also be seen, at an earlier moment, in the reception of Marxism. As Meaghan Morris pointed out of the Australian case in the late 1970s, 'marxism ... has a local subversive potential unthinkable to most European intellectuals, when deployed in a culture where the most elementary affirmation of the existence of class struggles past or present is capable of triggering explosions right and left' (Morris 1988: 52). The point might equally have been made of Britain, the United States or – with some qualifications, perhaps – other Anglophone locations. There is a certain distinctiveness in the way these societies have responded to questions of power.

To foreground this point may appear to suggest some Anglo essence, persisting in all cases despite historical divergences. Any such idea would need to be challenged. Cultural studies, above all, has sought to demonstrate that American, British, Australian, Canadian and New Zealand cultures are *not* simply 'Anglo', that they are equally composed of contributions from other immigrant groups, not to mention from indigenous peoples. But there is a significant point, which has often been missed in these arguments. As Jon Stratton has argued, again for the Australian case, they have paid little attention to legal and governmental institutions. If Australian cultural expression is, in a broad sense, 'multicultural', the same cannot be said of the institutional matrix in which it is embedded: 'The political and legal spheres remain, in unalloyed fashion, dominated by British, and not even continental European, premises and institutional forms. Indeed, it is remarkable how little the fundamental assumptions of government have changed since the advent of the policy of multiculturalism...' (Stratton 1998: 11). Along with Britain and the United States, Australia is a common law society and longstanding democracy, whose political structures are largely Anglo-derived. It is these institutional forms – not a supposed essence of 'Englishness' – that I am wishing here to bring into focus.

It is worth noting that patterns of state formation have been widely recognized as important for the concept of *culture*. In its modern use, the latter is a particular product of Germany (Berlin 1976; Elias 1994; Sahlins 1995: 10–13). It developed in the eighteenth century as part of a reaction to the political ascendancy of France and England, whose pre-eminence was expressed in the universalizing concept of 'civilization'. The situation of the Germans, as Norbert Elias points out, was

> a situation of a people which, by Western standards, arrived at political unification and consolidation only very late, and from whose boundaries, for centuries and even down to the present, territories have again and again crumbled away or threatened to crumble away. Whereas the concept of civilization has the function of giving expression to the continuously expansionist tendency of colonizing groups, the concept of *Kultur* [culture] mirrors the self-consciousness of a nation which had constantly to seek out and constitute its boundaries anew ... and again and again to ask itself: 'What really is our identity?' (Elias 1994: 7)

To draw these connections is not to imply an essence of 'Germanness'. It is simply to recognize, as Elias puts it, that concepts are primarily used 'by and for people who share a particular tradition and a particular situation' (1994: 8). Historically at least, these situations have been significantly defined by the state formations in which they have found themselves.

The 'particular situation' of England itself was highlighted, in fact, in the early formation of British cultural studies in a famous debate over the 'peculiarities of the English'. On one side, represented by Perry Anderson, Tom Nairn and the editorial team of *New Left Review*, it was seen in unrelentingly negative terms. Britain, it was argued, was politically malformed. Having failed to make an unambiguous transition to modernity, it had retained a '"feudal" hierarchy of orders and ranks, distinguished by a multiplicity of trivial but ceremonial insignia – accent, vocabulary, diet, dress, recreation etc.' (Anderson 1964: 39). The consequences of this were disastrous:

> Traditionalism and empiricism ... fuse as a single legitimating system: traditionalism sanctions the present by deriving it from the past, empiricism shackles the future by riveting it to the present. A comprehensive, coagulated conservatism is the result, covering the whole of society with a thick pall of simultaneous philistinism (towards ideas) and mystagogy (towards institutions) for which England has justly won an international reputation. (Anderson 1964: 40)

'Englishness' was defended, on the other side of the debate, by E. P. Thompson (1965), but there was little doubt on either side that the issues at stake were substantial. Notwithstanding Thompson's mockery of Anderson's idealization of 'Other Nations', both agreed that the political formation of England was distinctive, with significant implications for its intellectual culture – including its receptiveness to 'theory', its tolerance of political radicalism and the place it accorded to the concept of power.

In the subsequent development of cultural studies, questions of 'Englishness' have been more submerged. From the 1970s, in line with Anderson's criticisms, 'Anglo' associations became deeply unfashionable, even in England itself. As Dick Hebdige admitted of his own work at the end of the 1980s:

> My reluctance to acknowledge my own 'englishness' is inscribed in the sources I cite. Many of the theoretical and critical reference points which provide the primary orientations in this book are French. Some are American. A few are Italian and German. Very few are identifiably British. Like so many arts and social science graduates educated in the late 1960s and 1970s, I tried to escape the English tradition, to find my own 'elsewhere', to stage-manage my own symbolic defection. (Hebdige 1988: 11)

As Hebdige suggests, the defection has been more than his alone. Those outside Britain have used their distance to disown any association with an English intellectual inheritance (Gibson 2001), while those within have found other ways to disavow it. With few exceptions (Gikandi 1996; Brabazon 2000), 'Englishness' has been seen as no longer needing to be recognized or worked through in cultural studies so much as simply consigned to history.

My argument in what follows is that it is important now to question this tendency if we are properly to contextualize the concept of power. As Hebdige recognizes, the suppression of 'Englishness' may have had certain costs in self-understanding. Despite his own efforts at denial, 'the legacy of an English education (however poorly assimilated, however badly understood) shows through' (Hebdige 1988: 11). Nor is this reflection necessarily parochial. In Hebdige's sense, 'Englishness' is not a simple matter of identity. It is characterized by a 'sense of awe engendered by the incandescence of the particular, the reverence for the irreducibility of the thing-in-itself and on the other, a faith in correspondence, a faith in the endurance, the relative stability through time of that which *is*' (1998: 11–12). The outlook corresponds to a scepticism towards 'reasoning from universal premises taken on trust from authority': '[W]e are left after Occam, after Bacon, Hume, Locke and Berkeley, to generalise from what we know and see' (1998: 12). If we keep our eye on political arrangements rather than national characters, an understanding of this style of thought may be relevant not only for the English, but also for those whose history and institutions they share.

Assimilating America to this perspective may appear questionable. The United States was founded, after all, on a revolution *against* Britain and is now so dominant on the world stage as to be widely accepted as a case apart. The question of American cultural studies will be returned to in Chapter 9. Suffice it to say here that, despite its differences, the United States has some obvious similarities with Britain at the level I am considering. As David Simpson has argued, in an excavation of the background to polemics against 'theory' in both countries, there is a shared history at least in the political systems to which they have been opposed: 'federalist America worked almost as hard as conservative Britain to keep out the contamination of French ideas in the 1790s and 1800s. There is enough common history to make the substance of the present study important to an understanding of the contemporary educational polemics in both cultures' (Simpson 1993: 5). Paul Gilroy has asked, along similar lines, whether evidence might not also be found in cultural studies itself: 'It is impossible not to wonder how much American enthusiasm for cultural studies is generated by its association with England and Englishness. This question can be used as a threshold into consideration of the ethno-historical specificity of cultural studies itself' (Gilroy 1992: 187).

A Hobbesian Disappointment

Although there is some risk, in returning to it, of losing a wider focus, the 1960s' debate over the peculiarities of the English is still a useful starting point in reflecting on this ethno-historical specificity. While certain assumptions might now be questioned, it remains instructive in tracing connections between political forms, 'Anglo' institutions and the concept of power.

The debate arose from a frustration of a younger generation on the left with the relatively subdued response in Britain to the revolutionary temper of the times. While activist student movements had developed in Germany, Italy and France, students in Britain remained, in Anderson's words, 'muzzled and quiescent', bound by a culture which was 'mediocre and inert' (Anderson 1968: 4). A similar malaise was found in British intellectual life. The ascendant discipline which elsewhere provided the basis for a critical social awareness – sociology – had developed only a weak and ineffective presence: 'despite the recent belated growth of sociology as a formal discipline in England, the record of listless mediocrity and wizened provincialism is unrelieved' (Anderson 1968: 8). Under the influence of Ludwig Wittgenstein, English philosophy had come to 'consecrate the banalities of everyday language' (1968: 21). Under Karl Popper and Isaiah Berlin, political theory was reduced either to a 'manichean morality tale' or a prophylactic against revolutionary ideas (1968: 26). While F. R. Leavis's literary criticism had some ambition to comprehend social totalities, it offered no general theoretical position. The only achievement of international significance, Keynesian economics, refused to question a cyclical view of time in which all that can be expected are periodic fluctuations of capitalism within a social order which remains unchanged.

The analysis of these shortcomings was conducted in Marxist terms and focused historically on the Enlightenment. The problem with Britain, for Anderson, was that it had bypassed a classical modern revolution in which class antagonisms were fully exposed. The Civil War of 1640–9 shattered the old feudal institutions, clearing the way for the development of a modern capitalist society, but it failed to clarify any structural social contradiction. It was a 'clash between two segments of a landowning class, neither of which were *direct* crystallisations of opposed economic interests' (Anderson 1964: 28). As a consequence, 'the ideological legacy of the revolution was almost nil... Because of its "primitive" pre-Enlightenment character, the ideology of the Revolution founded no significant tradition and left no major after-effects' (1964: 30). Never having to stage an open revolution against the aristocracy, the English bourgeoisie was not spurred, as elsewhere, to articulate a comprehensive vision of society: 'It handed on no impulse of liberation, no revolutionary values, no universal language' (1964: 43).

As Thompson pointed out in his response to Anderson, the implicit ideal against which England was being measured was France. It is the French Revolution, above all, which provided the paradigm of all that England had missed out on. As Thompson himself characterized the difference:

> The French experience was marked by a clarity of confrontation, a *levée en masse* of the intelligentsia, a disposition towards systematizing and towards intellectual hierarchy – the staff officers, attachés, and so on, who grouped around the great radical *chef de bataille*. The English experience ... did not encourage sustained efforts at synthesis; since few intellectuals were thrown into prominence in a conflict with authority, few felt the need to develop a systematic critique. They thought of themselves, rather, as exchanging specialized products in a market which was tolerably free, and the sum of whose commodities made up the sum of 'knowledge'. (Thompson 1978: 59)

It was the French pattern – a clarity of confrontation, systematic critique, organized and intellectually directed forms of political action – which Anderson and his collaborators wished to introduce to Britain.

The irony in this admiration for the grand totalizing moves of French intellectual culture is that at almost the same time French intellectuals themselves were becoming acutely aware of their *costs*. It was these costs, as we have seen, which came particularly to concern Foucault. As he put it in 1976:

> [W]hat has emerged in the course of the last ten or fifteen years is a sense of the increasing vulnerability to criticism of things, institutions, practices, discourses. A certain fragility has been discovered in the very bedrock of existence... But together with this sense of instability and this amazing efficacy of discontinuous, particular and local criticism, one in fact also discovers something that perhaps was not initially foreseen, something one might describe as precisely the inhibiting effect of global, *totalitarian theories*. (Foucault 1980: 80)

The problems perceived by Foucault and Anderson in their respective societies could hardly have been more different. What appears as the relative *in*vulnerability to criticism of things, institutions, practices and discourses in Britain is directly related by Anderson to an *absence* of totalizing theory. The relative *in*efficacy of criticism within British intellectual culture was a consequence of the fact that the bourgeoisie 'refused ever to put society as a whole in question. A deep, instinctive aversion to the very category of totality marks its entire trajectory' (Anderson 1968: 13).

This suggests, in itself, that the context for the concept of power in British cultural studies may be quite different from the one we considered in Chapter 2 for Foucault. The concept is developed in the course of different debates and performs different functions. For Foucault, as we have seen, it is deployed as part of an attempt to bring into question universalizing philosophical concepts such as 'the human subject'. For Anderson, by contrast, it is associated with the *importation* of such concepts to make up for a local absence. The naming of social relations as relations of power is part of the same project as the introduction to Britain of 'fundamental concepts of man and society' (Anderson 1968: 5). The concept of power could perhaps be seen as a point of *convergence*, a zone in which French debates have become less philosophically oriented and English debates more so. But it would be a mistake to ignore the different points from which they began. The mere existence of common terms should not distract us from the distinct, even contradictory, motivations behind them.

But the differences between England and other European states can be taken deeper. As a Marxist, Anderson tends to assume that fundamental social contradictions can be found in any society; the only question is the extent to which they are recognized. The central 'peculiarity of the English', from this perspective, is that they have been blind to a reality that others have seen. At certain points, however, another interpretation comes into view: that the moment or axis of social contradiction in England is actually more difficult to locate. In 'Origins of the Present Crisis' (originally published 1964), Anderson presents this, in terms also derived Marx, as a problem of the 'supremacy of civil society over the state': 'Schematically, three main idiosyncrasies of [the modern British] structure of power stand out: the relative insignificance of bureaucratic or military forms, the unusually immediate striking capacity of economic forms, and the ultimately crucial importance of ideological and cultural forms' (Anderson 1992b: 40). In sum, Britain is less organized than other societies around the state. State-related functions – the bureaucracy and the military – are relatively weak; functions more independent from the state – the economy, ideology and culture – are relatively strong.

The significance of this is that there is no clear focus or centre of power. At a purely formal level, it might look the other way. England is unusual in the absolute sovereignty vested in parliament: 'no other modern capitalist state has ever taken the risk of dispensing with a written constitution' (Anderson 1992b: 41). In theory, this should provide an opportunity for radical governments, allowing them untrammelled freedom in remaking society. In practice, however, the opening is illusory as the power of the state is itself so limited. The gap between sovereignty and an actual capacity to bring change is illustrated by the repeated frustration of governments with radical ambitions: 'When a Labour government holds office, it is an isolated, spotlight enclave, surrounded on almost every side by hostile territory, unceasingly shelled by industry, press and orchestrated "public opinion". Each time it has in the end been overrun' (Anderson 1992b: 42). Like Foucault, but for reasons more related to the specific case he is considering, Anderson dismisses an equation between power and sovereignty. The sovereign authority, in the English case, can only ever be seen as *a* power; it is difficult to mistake it for power as such.

To recall the discussion at the end of last chapter, one might say that England has been a Hobbesian disappointment. Hobbes's prescription for a stable and prosperous Commonwealth was the formation of Leviathan, the 'Greatest of humane powers ... which is compounded of the Powers of most men, united by consent, in one person, Naturall, or Civil, that has the use of all their Powers depending on his will' (Hobbes 1914: 43). In Hobbes's own country, this supreme sovereign power has been only weakly established: the powers of most men have *not* been united in one person; the sovereign authority has *not* had the use of all their powers depending on its will. In a further irony, the result has not been, as Hobbes would have predicted, a perpetual state of war, but quite the opposite – a peculiarly stable society, tending to smugness in its insulation against revolution or political extremes. As Anderson resonantly described them in reference to the 1950s, England's faults have been the opposite of hot-headed or sanguinary – a society which is 'glutinously chauvinist – reverent worship of Westminster, ubiquitous culture of constitutional moderation and common sense, ritualised exaltation of tradition and precedent' (Anderson 1980: 144).

Singular or Plural?

It may be helpful, in drawing further connections between concepts of power and the English pattern of state formation, to examine more closely what actually happens with the formation of a sovereign authority. Before doing so, however, I want to sharpen a distinction which has already emerged in the discussion so far, between an idea of distinct and specific *powers* and the idea of a general phenomenon *power*. In linguistic terms, the word 'power' in the former case is used as a count noun. As with apples or oranges, one can have one power, two powers, three or more powers, but it makes no sense to talk of power 'as such'. In the latter case, by contrast, power is used as a mass noun. It is assumed to identify a general phenomenon, more like water, which may be 'distributed' or 'concentrated' in various ways, which may take different 'forms', but which remains at some fundamental level the same. Powers as distinct and specific must be identified in the plural or with an article or deictic – 'a power', 'the power', 'this power', 'that power'. Power as a general phenomenon is identified in the singular and without an article – simply 'power'.

This is very close to the distinction that Hindess draws in his discussion of Hobbes. As he points out, the idea of power in general appears to have a metaphysical implication. It suggests 'some common stuff, some shared underlying capacity or essence of effectiveness' to be found in every instance in which the word 'power' is applied (Hindess 1996: 25). The idea of powers as distinct and specific does not carry this implication. The possibility is allowed that the different phenomena that we choose to name as powers may have nothing *essentially* in common. The focus of attention is directed as much to the differences as the similarities. If we were forced to give an account of why the same word is used in each case, the answer would have to be at the level of how we use words.

Once this distinction is recognized, a movement backwards and forwards between different uses of the word 'power' can be found everywhere in cultural studies. A particularly striking example is John Fiske's *Power Plays, Power Works*, which is unconsciously structured around it. Fiske's overall argument, almost the trademark for which he has become known, is that 'the people' – those excluded from access to dominant social institutions – have more resources at their disposal than an exclusive focus on their marginalization or subordination would lead us to believe:

> The people do not have easy access to the system of power and cannot, in general, turn it to their own advantage. They do, however, have access to their own forms of power which, though socially weaker, are far from ineffective... The 'weak' powers available to the people are so different from the power to which the power-bloc enjoys privileged access as to require different names. I propose to call strong, top-down power 'imperializing' and weak, bottom-up power 'localizing'. (Fiske 1993: 11–12)

'Imperializing power' carries the burden, here, of negative associations of power – its aim, Fiske says, is to dominate, 'to extend its reach as far as possible'. 'Localizing power' is, by contrast, represented positively – it is 'not concerned to dominate other social formations, not concerned with constantly expanding its terrain but interested in strengthening its control over the immediate conditions of everyday life' (1993: 12).

Fiske has often been criticized for the naïvety of his oppositions between 'bad' and 'good', 'domination' and popular 'resistance', but there is a dimension to his arguments which, to my knowledge, has never been remarked and which suggests a greater complexity. At the level of overview, it appears that he is comparing different 'forms' of power. In actual practice, however, he compares the tendency or not to *totalize* power, to see it as a general phenomenon. As indicated in the slippage from the singular in the passage quoted above ('forms of power' to 'powers'), 'weak' or 'localizing' powers are most often identified as *plural*. The play between singular and plural becomes particularly significant when Fiske puts forward his vision for a positive political transformation. This is

> one in which imperializing power will diminish, and localizing powers will increase, or, to put it another way, weak powers will gain strength and strong power will weaken... We may characterize such a change as one between a homogeneous system of strong power and a more diverse system of weaker powers... [S]ome of the weak powers will strengthen and move inwards while the strong power will weaken and allow others access to its centrality. (Fiske 1993: 52)

The difference between singular and plural is here strictly observed. What is proposed, given this, is not a simple populism in which 'the people' struggle for power against a dominator or oppressor. It might be described as a counter-Hobbesian politics in which we unlearn *Leviathan* – refusing to think *in terms* of power in order to acquire again an appreciation of particular *powers*.

The movement between 'power' and 'powers', while clearly important in Fiske, is never explicitly recognized and is elsewhere made rather casually. But the same can be said of thinkers like Foucault who, in other ways, have brought to the concept a certain theoretical rigour. The movement in Foucault is often the opposite of that in Fiske: particular powers are translated to the general level of 'power'. In the essay 'Truth and Juridical Forms', for example, he meditates at length on questions of power through a discussion of Sophocles' tragedy *Oedipus the King*. At one point, he quotes a line given to Oedipus in his dispute with Creon: 'You have brought an oracle from Delphi, but you have falsified that oracle, because, son of Laius, you claim a power that was given to me'. Foucault comments on this as follows: 'Oedipus feels threatened by Creon at the level of power... What's at issue in all these confrontations of the play's beginning is power' (Foucault 2000c: 25). Strictly speaking, the comment is not supported by the quoted line from Sophocles: what is at issue for Oedipus is not power but *a* power – the power specifically of the oracle.[1]

The point is more than a linguistic quibble because the choice of the singular or plural ('power' or 'powers') gives expression – or at least *can* give expression – to different institutional arrangements. The singular, 'power', is associated in particular with the institution of sovereignty. The sovereign authority within a given territory is generally spoken of not just as *a* power to be considered alongside others, but as representing power 'as such'. If Hobbes is a reliable indicator, as probably the greatest early theorist and observer of the modern state, the impulse towards speaking of power in general is closely bound up with the establishment of a supreme political authority, the sovereign. In a first step, the individual powers existing within a territory are brought conceptually within a space of quantitative comparison – one in which it is possible to equate powers or compare them as 'more' or 'less' than each other. In a second step, it is imagined that all these powers might be 'combined' and put at the disposal of the sovereign. It is at this point that we can talk not of individual powers, but simply of 'power'.

A Symbolic Currency

At the end of Chapter 2, I suggested a comparison between the generalizing impulse in the concept of power and the generalization of economic assets through money. A theoretical elaboration of this can be found, in an unlikely quarter for cultural studies, in the sociological theory of power developed in the 1960s by Talcott Parsons. The theory was designed in large part to counter the influence of concepts of power in the work of critical sociologists such as C. Wright Mills, whose classic *The Power Elite* (1956) represented power in strongly negative terms similar to those which later gained currency in cultural studies. Much of the point of the comparison between power and money, for Parsons, was to demonstrate that power can be seen as a 'positive' phenomenon enabling constructive social action. Consistent with the general cast of structural functionalism, there is a certain idealization both of capitalist economies and of political structures as simply facilitating the achievement of worthy social ends. For this reason, the theory has been widely dismissed as 'conservative'. But the analysis can, to some extent, be extracted from this context and is illuminating in the attempt to understand generalized concepts of power.

1. It may be worth pointing out that the distinctions here are not just an artefact of the English translation. The quoted line from Sophocles refers, in the original French, to '*un pouvoir*' (a power). Foucault's comment on this is '*Ce qui est en question … c'est le pouvoir*' (Foucault 1994: 563). If he had meant to refer specifically to the power of the oracle, he would have used '*ce pouvoir*'. The distinction between individual powers and power in general is marked in the French not through the presence or absence of an article ('a power'/'power'), but by use of the demonstrative adjective ('*ce pouvoir*'/'*le pouvoir*').

The central insight to be distilled from the comparison between power and money is that power, in the generalized sense, is *symbolic*. It would make little sense, for Parsons, to attempt, as Foucault did, to locate the actual 'mechanisms' or 'connections' of power: 'Power ... is the *means* of acquiring control of the factors in effectiveness; it is not itself one of these factors, any more than in the economic case money is a factor of production' (Parsons 1994: 19). Admittedly, there are points in the political system where symbolic values appear to be anchored in material realities. As in the economic case, where worthless paper money has been accepted historically on the promise that it may be redeemed for gold, power is often thought to rest ultimately on physical compulsion – the ability of those 'in power' to call out the army or police. But in both cases, the system as a whole far exceeds these apparent guarantees. 'If the security of monetary commitments rested only on their convertibility into metal, then the overwhelming majority of them would be worthless, for the simple reason that the total quantity of metal is far too small to redeem more than a few' (1994: 23). So it is too with political commitments: even the largest army or police force could never enforce them all.

The question which occurs here is why, if power is symbolic, it 'works' so effectively? Why, if political commitments can be only marginally enforced, are they, on the whole, adhered to? Parsons's answer is functionalist and utilitarian. Polities are organized, in his view, to permit 'effective collective action in the attainment of the goals of collectivities' (Parsons 1994: 18). Like the function of money in facilitating economic relations, the symbolic order of power increases the effectiveness of collective action. We are led to suppose that the majority of people understand this and, recognizing the benefits of collective action, give their support to the system. But the general analysis of power does not commit us to such an anodyne and rationalist social psychology; there is room for other answers to the question. A useful point of contrast is provided by Jean-Joseph Goux in *Symbolic Economies*. Despite its roots in Marxist political economy, a starting point which could hardly be more distant from Parsons', Goux's account of political structures is strikingly similar, working the same homology with the monetary system. The difference is in the explanations he offers of how symbolic orders are established and maintained.

Goux's enquiry is actually wider than a comparison between the economic and political, extending ambitiously to all processes by which symbolic equivalences and hierarchies of value are established. These also include the linguistic and libidinal 'registers' – the symbolism of words and of eroticized objects in an 'economy' of desire. But the paradigm case is, again, the economy proper. Unlike Parsons, Goux does not assume as a model a fully developed capitalist system in which cash transactions, banks and credit have been established as second nature. Drawing on Marx's analysis in *Capital* of the origins of monetary exchange, he insists that we examine the *genesis* of the value form on which the system now rests (Goux 1990: 11). This genesis can be traced in four stages, starting with the principle of barter, in which one commodity is declared identical to another commodity, and culminating with the establishment of a 'general equivalent', money, which 'confers a value – a fixed worth, or price – on each commodity' (1990: 16). As in Marx, the whole purpose of the analysis is to strip away the obviousness of current modes of economic thinking, thereby opening them to criticism.

The same approach is carried over by Goux into the political domain. The political counterpart of barter, he suggests, is the recognition of an equivalence of status between local rulers within decentralized feudal systems (Goux 1990: 40). The counterpart of a fully developed monetary system is the ascension of a sovereign authority who becomes the general equivalent in the political register – the universal measure of power. As with Parsons, power is understood here as symbolic; it is not to be confused with the actual mechanisms by which things are achieved. But the political system, for Goux, is far from a rational arrangement simply designed to realize collective goals. The elevation of the sovereign has, in a Marxist sense, a fetishistic aspect. It involves the overvaluation of the general equivalent and the systematic erasure of its genesis. Like the general equivalent in other registers, the sovereign authority comes to appear a universal necessity rather than the artifice that it is. It has, in this, a certain tyrannical quality: 'Supplanting the diversity of relationships among elements is [a] univocal, exclusive relationship to the general equivalent which *magnetizes* or *funnels* towards its ideal center all value relationships, making them its tributary rays' (1990: 44–5).

There are, then, at least two opposing answers to the question of what is invested in concepts of power formed around the establishment of centralized political authorities. According to the first (Parsons's), it expresses a rational desire for a generalized medium of political calculation in order that collective goals can be more effectively achieved. According to the second (Goux's), it betrays a fetishization of the sovereign and an impulse towards systematizing and ordering, tending, in its advanced forms, towards a kind of tyranny. But I would like to finish the chapter by suggesting a third, represented in an approach developed in the 1930s by the English political philosopher Michael Oakeshott. Oakeshott's perspective allows some room for both Parsons and Goux. It is also particularly helpful, to return to the main theme, in understanding the 'peculiarities of the English' and therefore the context of the concept of power in cultural studies.

A Multiplicity of Semi-Independencies

In contrast to Anderson, Oakeshott is drawn to early modern or 'pre-Enlightenment' political history, seeing it as having continuing relevance to the understanding of contemporary politics. This brings the English case into focus in more positive terms. The English Civil War, in particular, appears as much more than a premature and malformed rehearsal for the French Revolution; it was played out, in Oakeshott's view, around stakes that are still recognizable today. The French Revolution occurred at a time when a sovereign authority had been established without question; indeed the absolute monarchy in France was the paradigm of political centralization. Attention, in this context, was focused largely on the *disposal* of sovereignty – its transfer from the monarch to 'the people', the balance to be found between the different classes or estates. The high points of English political history were organized, for Oakeshott, around a different question: the *status and desirability* of a sovereign authority in the first place. We might agree with Anderson that lines over the *constitution* of modern government in England were confused, but the important differences, in Oakeshott's perspective, were not over this but the *purpose* of government as such.

On this latter question, Oakeshott distinguishes two basic political dispositions – 'the politics of faith' and 'the politics of scepticism'. In the former, 'the activity of governing is understood to be in the service of the perfection of mankind' (Oakeshott 1996: 23). What distinguishes it is not simply optimism; it has been opposed, in fact, to older religious forms of optimism. It is an optimism specifically about the capacities of government: 'Human perfection is to be achieved by human effort, and confidence in the evanescence of imperfection springs here from faith in human power and not from trust in divine providence' (1996: 23). The 'perfection' envisaged may take many forms, including utopian visions that now appear archaic: 'it may range from a condition of moral virtue or religious salvation to a condition of "prosperity", "abundance" or "welfare". In short, there are versions of this style of politics appropriate not merely to the circumstances of the eighteenth and nineteenth centuries, but even to those of the sixteenth' (1996: 24). The politics of faith is nevertheless, for Oakeshott, a specifically *modern* phenomenon. The prime condition for its emergence has been 'a remarkable and intoxicating increase of human power' (1996: 24).

In the 'politics of scepticism', by contrast, 'governing is understood to be a specific activity, and in particular it is understood to be detached from the pursuit of human perfection' (Oakeshott 1996: 31). Oakeshott is careful to distinguish this from simple anarchy, the rejection of government as such. The desire is not that there be *no* government, only that government be *limited*:

> Human imperfection (so the argument runs) may be evanescent, and, moreover, it may be a single and simple condition of human circumstances…, but, even on these assumptions, to pursue perfection in one direction only (and particularly to pursue it as the crow flies, regardless of what there may be to do in the interval before we embrace it) is to invite disappointment and (what is worse than the mortification of non-arrival) misery on the way. (Oakeshott 1996: 31)

Like the politics of faith, the politics of scepticism has emerged from a recognition of the *potential* in modernity for an extraordinary coordination of social actions in pursuit of collective goals. Its response, however, has been to find ways of *preventing* this potential from being fully realized – to restrict government to maintaining a certain basic order.

Unfortunately, Oakeshott does not distinguish much more clearly than Fiske or Foucault between 'powers' in the plural and the singular 'power'. But it is clear that there is some relation between these different usages and the two styles of politics he outlines. He does point out that a major historical project of the politics of scepticism has been the 'separation of powers', the development of arrangements to ensure the independence first of church and state and then, within government, of the major branches and agencies – classically the executive, legislature and judiciary. The reason he does not place more weight on this is that he thinks the separation of powers has hardened into an 'over-formal doctrine' (Oakeshott 1996: 85). There is a common temptation in the politics of scepticism, he argues, simply to oppose the abstract ideals of the politics of faith with counter-ideals, at which point it loses its distinctiveness. The general point, however, remains clear: the politics of scepticism is associated with the idea of a 'multiplicity of semi-independencies' (1996: 87) – what we might naturally call 'powers'; the politics of faith is associated with a totalizing political vision expressed in the singular 'power'.

These connections are confirmed if we bring Oakeshott together with Parsons and Goux. It is clear, in Parsons, that the symbolic extension of the concept of power is associated with a certain enthusiasm for coordinated social action. To participate in this extension is, like participation in the monetary system, to support the conditions for 'the attainment of the goals of collectivities'. Parsons's unreserved investment in the concept of power is an index, in Oakeshott's terms, of a tendency towards the politics of faith. The converse holds of Goux's *resistance* to the symbolic extension of the concept of power – his resistance, that is, to a simple acceptance of the general equivalent that allows us to talk of power 'as such'. This resistance can be seen as an index of a tendency towards the politics of scepticism. In drawing attention to a historical past in which powers have *not* been subordinated to a common measure, in alerting us to the ongoing suppression of difference which this subordination necessarily involves, he urges a continuing regard for a 'multiplicity of semi-independencies'.

The Nemesis of Scepticism

We might expect, given the strong opposition between faith and scepticism, that Oakeshott would recommend one or other side. Which of the two styles of politics should we regard as preferable? But one of his most useful insights is that the answer may depend on the *context* in which it is asked. Each style of politics has its limitations and, if left entirely to itself, provokes a characteristic 'nemesis':

> when either of these styles of politics claims for itself independence and completeness, it reveals a self-defeating character. Each is not less the partner than the opponent of

the other; each stands in need of the other to rescue it from self-destruction, and if either succeeded in destroying the other, it would discover that, in the same act, it had destroyed itself. (Oakeshott 1996: 91–2)

Oakeshott's analysis of the limitations of the politics of faith has striking similarities with Goux's analysis of highly centralized regimes of value and, even more so, with Foucault's analysis of disciplinary regimes of power. Government in the style of the politics of faith is, he argues, 'minute, inquisitive, and unindulgent: society will become a *panopticon* and its rulers *panoverseers*' (Oakeshott 1996: 29, original emphasis). An intimate relation forms between knowledge and power, a relation which was recognized as early as the sixteenth century by Francis Bacon: 'Knowledge, he perceived, could provide power, and the organized pursuit of knowledge could provide power in great quantity: it was power he was interested in, and he imagined it as the mastery of the world for the benefit of mankind' (1996: 55). It is not enough, in the politics of faith, that citizens or subjects conform to the law; claims are made over what Foucault would call 'the soul': 'mere obedience is not enough; it must be accompanied by fervour... [W]henever our politics have turned decisively in the direction of the horizon of faith government has always demanded not acquiescence but love and devotion' (1996: 97).

The nemesis of the politics of faith is found, paradoxically, in a tendency towards the abolition of politics. It appears at first quite the opposite – a problem of political *excess*. Governing in the style of the faith is conceived as a 'total' activity:

> [T]his means that every permitted action is itself an activity of governing..., and that every subject legitimately employed is *eo ipso* an agent of government... There is, then, in such a community only one work being carried on; and the various manners in which it may be pursued (sleeping, agriculture, painting pictures, nurturing children etc.) are not distinct and independent activities, they are the indistinct components of a single pattern... And the threefold division of activities possible elsewhere – governing, going about one's lawful business, and behaving unlawfully – is reduced to two by the coalescence of the first and the second. (Oakeshott 1996: 93)

At the limit, however, governing loses any capacity to distinguish itself: 'When [it] is understood as an activity of limitless control, it finds itself with nothing to control: a *factotum* has no subjects who are not opponents' (1996: 94). Specifically political processes are replaced with a simple exercise of force.

The general object of these criticisms – essentially an inherent totalitarian tendency in modern politics – is one that is familiar in cultural studies, particularly through the influence of French writers (including Goux and Foucault). What is not often noted, however, is that of any societies the analysis probably applies *least* to those in which the field has actually taken form. The point was recognized, in fact, by Foucault: 'If there is one country that was not totalitarian in the history of

Europe, it is undoubtedly Britain' (Foucault 2000b: 293). A more general resistance to systematic political organization has been largely inherited by the major Anglo political offshoots outside Europe – the United States, Canada, Australia and New Zealand – in which cultural studies has also emerged. In this context, the criticisms that need more to be heard are those of the *opposite* tendency – criticisms, that is, of the politics of scepticism. It is here that Oakeshott provides a perspective that is not easily found elsewhere.

The limitations of scepticism, for Oakeshott, spring from 'the severe self-limitation which belongs to its character' (1996: 106). In restricting itself merely to maintaining a 'relevant public order', governing in the style of scepticism is prone to overlook even the wider conditions of that order: 'It abdicates exactly at the point where the activist expects an assertion of authority, it withdraws where he expects it to proceed; it insists on technicalities; it is narrow, severe and unenthusiastic; it is without courage or conviction' (1996: 109). Under modern conditions of rapid social change, where crises are frequent and calls for urgent action widespread, the intellectual distinctions of scepticism come to appear irrelevant: 'in a world where all other activities are serious, where diligence is a virtue and energy excellence, they fix upon government the character of frivolity' (1996: 110). At the limit, government itself becomes compromised. Unable any longer to command respect, it is unable even to maintain a public order. The final nemesis of scepticism is a 'disposition to reduce politics to play' (1996: 110).

It would be difficult to think of anything that resonated more clearly with the analysis of intellectual entrepreneurs like Anderson at the early formation of cultural studies. The problem they confronted was not a panoptic society in which behaviour was minutely governed within a single encompassing 'regime'. The weak coordination of political functions would have made such a regime impossible, even if it had been wished. The issue, on the contrary, was an 'entropy', a 'lassitude', an appalling 'amateurism', a lack of any organized response to the 'crisis' which could be seen at every turn: 'stagnant industries, starved schools, run-down cities, demoralized rulers, parochial outlooks' (Anderson 1964: 50). It is equally clear that the only remedy, for Anderson, was, in Oakeshott's terms, an injection of the politics of faith. Britain needed to learn from societies that had developed more coordinated forms of collective action – Germany, France, Italy, Japan – not only in political theory but also in practical arts of governing: 'The indicative planning typical of … neo-capitalism demands technocratic skills and a powerful administrative apparatus. In England, the traditions of the governing class have not provided for this' (Oakeshott 1996: 51).

If all of this remains at the level of broad overview, it provides *something* of a context for the concept of power in cultural studies. It helps to explain, for example, why, as often noted, it has always had a certain aura of 'foreignness' about it. To invoke the concept from an 'Anglo' location is immediately to gesture towards an intellectual space more associated with continental Europe – above all France.

The background offered here also provides us with a starting point from which to investigate the actual development of the concept in the field. It warns us particularly against taking the formal theoretical positions of cultural studies as too clearly indicative of actual motivations. The latter, for the most part, have not been derived from local intellectual resources and have been conditioned by quite different political contexts.

Revisiting the Andersonian moment in debates around power may be particularly useful now as a reminder of the complexity of motivations surrounding the concept. There has been a tendency since the 1960s to reduce these motivations to those projected by continental European theories. Consistent with Anderson's recommendations – and to no small extent through the influence of the journal he edited, *New Left Review* – the British New Left moved decisively in the 1970s and 1980s to embrace the latter. In many cases, British theorists so thoroughly adopted continental European frames of reference as to internalize continental problems as their own. As Donald Sassoon pointed out in a perceptive early assessment, the project of *New Left Review* quickly enclosed itself in an 'international ghetto': 'We were better informed and more interested in those small groups with which the British New Left bore some resemblance than with wider social forces' (Sassoon 1981: 238). One of the more lasting effects of this, it could be argued, has been a tendency to forget the different functions the concept of power can serve. A desire to identify a tyrannical coordination of political functions is only one context; the concept can also express a desire that there be *more* coordination than there is.

–4–

Cultural Studies 'before power'
The First Generation

In an interview with Raymond Williams in the late 1970s, the editorial committee of *New Left Review* summarizes a series of responses to questions about his childhood and adolescence:

> One might say, then, that in your boyhood there was an absence of the typical town-country relation, absence of direct confrontation between privileged exploiters and working people, an absence of antagonism between manual and mental labour. Your early experience appears to have been exempt from a whole series of typical conflicts and tensions which most people of your generation from working-class families would have felt at some point. Your own history seems to have escaped nearly all of them. (*New Left Review* in Williams 1979: 35)

The repetitive emphasis of this resumé – if not by Perry Anderson, then by close collaborators Anthony Barnett or Francis Mulhern – reflects a certain frustration at an inability to place Williams in relation to structural contradictions in British society. After a failure of various attempts to draw him on the issue, his biography begins to appear as lacking any positive political points of reference, as nothing more than a series of 'absences'. Even the accumulated evidence of these absences leaves Williams unmoved; he does not attempt to deny them: 'I think it is true' (Williams 1979: 36).

Yet his response cannot have been surprising. Williams's view of his own formation remained quite consistent throughout his life. It can be traced back twenty years to 'Culture is Ordinary' (first published 1958), where he denied a sense of contradiction between his Welsh working-class background and studying at Cambridge:

> I was not … oppressed by Cambridge. I was not cast down by old buildings, for I had come from a country with twenty centuries of history written visibly into the earth: I liked walking through the Tudor court, but it did not make me feel raw… Nor was learning, in my family, some strange eccentricity; I was not, on a scholarship to Cambridge, a new kind of animal up a brand-new ladder. Learning was ordinary; we learned where we could. (Williams 1989b: 5)

At this point, furthermore, his self-understanding was clearly consistent with his political vision. Responding to an argument, particularly common among Marxists at the time, that working people were 'excluded from English culture', he dismisses it simply as 'nonsense':

> They have their own growing institutions, and much of the strictly bourgeois culture they would in any case not want. A great part of the English way of life, and of its art and learning, is not bourgeois in any discoverable sense... The leisure which the bourgeoisie attained has given us much of cultural value. But this is not to say that contemporary culture is bourgeois culture... There is a distinct working-class way of life. (Williams 1989b: 7–8)

It was not only that Williams himself did not feel 'excluded'; he doubted whether any systematic exclusion existed.

The frustration, then, is not one of thwarted expectations but of a more substantial incomprehension: How could Britain's leading socialist writer of the post-war period *not* have been inspired by a stronger sense of social injustice? It is a question that had been raised more aggressively by Anderson in 'Origins of the Present Crisis' where he traced it to the 'proletarian positivity' of the English working class (Anderson 1964: 44). The criticism was extended not only to Williams but also to Richard Hoggart:

> The whole dense, object-infested universe described by Hoggart in *The Uses of Literacy* testifies to the monumental positivity of the oldest working-class in the world. Too much so... The very density and specificity of English working-class culture has limited its political range and checked the emergence of socialism in England. Williams's attempt to solve the difficulty by attributing an indefinite extendability to working-class ... institutions, besides its factual weakness, rests on an evacuation of conflict concepts from his whole idiom. (Anderson 1964: 45)

The later interview with Williams, along with others collected in *Politics and Letters*, was conducted in a spirit of reconciliation, occasioned particularly by Williams's much-celebrated turn to 'rejoin a wider international Marxist debate' (*New Left Review* in Williams 1979: 9). Yet it is clear that differences in political assumptions and motivations remain. They are differences that run as continuing tension through the history of the British New Left.

The British Matrix

The relation of *cultural studies* to this history is paradoxical. While Williams and Hoggart are generally recognized, together with E. P. Thompson, as the key 'founders' of the field in Britain, it is the position represented by Anderson that is usually taken to *define* it. The consensus here is succinctly stated by Graeme Turner in his introduction to British cultural studies: 'Work in cultural studies has consistently addressed itself to society's structures of domination' (Turner 1996: 5). The view is one for which the early work of Williams and Hoggart can only appear ambiguously – present, as Williams appeared to *New Left Review*, only as an absence. The pair are sometimes referred to, with post-feminist irony, as the 'founding fathers', but if we are to invoke metaphors of patriarchal gender relations they might better be described as 'mothers'. By most accounts, they provided little more than fertile ground on which the seeds of others were laid. As Turner puts it of Williams's *The Long Revolution*, 'it lacks a theory of cultural structure and an appropriate method of textual analysis... It is difficult to read the book's focus on the constitutive "patterns" of cultural relationships ... without regretting the absence of structuralist methodologies' (Turner 1996: 55, 57). The achievement of the book, for Turner, was to offer a receptive matrix for cultural studies, 'ready for the influence of European Marxism and structuralism to provide the methodologies for its future development' (1996: 58).

My aim in this chapter is to offer a more positive account of the early initiatives in British cultural studies. My motivation in doing so is not so much to right a historical wrong as to open the way for a different understanding of cultural studies in the present. As I will argue in Chapter 6, the introduction of Marxism and structuralism which occurred during the 1970s was less revolutionary than it has often been seen. The shift was certainly significant, but the new theoretical imports did not enter an empty vessel; they were overlaid on well-formed intellectual and political positions which transformed them as much as those positions themselves were transformed. To represent European 'theory' as providing the only positive terms for the development of cultural studies is, therefore, systematically to distort our understanding of it. Most significantly, it limits the resources on which the field is now able to draw. The situation has a certain perversity: precisely the qualities which have made cultural studies distinctive in relation to comparable intellectual traditions – its *differences* from 'European Marxism and structuralism'– are ruled out of consideration as it seeks to reinvent itself after the Cold War.

At the centre of these issues is the concept of power. The concept is, in many ways, the defining 'absence' attributed to the first generation of British cultural studies, an absence set off against a later 'presence'. It is this opposition that determines the peculiar relation of the field to its own past. If, as Turner suggests, it was only with the introduction of European theoretical perspectives that questions of power could be adequately addressed, then it can only have been then that cultural studies came properly to 'exist'. The ambiguous status of Williams and Hoggart follows directly from this logic. Their absence of address to power locates them outside the field whose birth they can only appear as vaguely 'facilitating'. If the relation, then, between the first and later generations of cultural studies is to be reviewed, it is the use and significance of the concept of power that, above all, must be examined.

My suggestion in what follows is that the point of difference between early cultural studies and later theoretical perspectives needs to be recast. It is, in fact, misleading to say that the former neglected questions of power. It is true that the *term* was relatively absent, but this cannot be equated to an absence of address to the *phenomena* it identifies. These phenomena – including violence, exploitation and other social abuses – were clearly recognized; they were just not conceived, as they were later, under a single rubric. To draw on the discussion of the last two chapters, the relevant distinction is between an assumption of a plurality of powers and an assumption of a single, global phenomenon 'power'. Any 'absence' from the work of Williams and Hoggart is therefore only a relative one. It is more important in understanding the history of cultural studies to recognize the *presence* of quite a different approach to questions of power (or powers). This approach may have become relatively invisible, but it has continued to exercise a significant influence.

None of this is to judge, in absolute terms, the relative merits of thinking in terms of powers, in the plural, or the singular 'power'. My position is that it there is little sense in doing so. The two intellectual styles respond to different historical circumstances and can only be assessed in terms of the quality of responses *to* those circumstances. The weaknesses of early cultural studies in the context of Britain in the 1970s and 1980s have been more than adequately rehearsed and were partly conceded, at least by Williams. My proposal is only that recognition also be given to its possible *strengths*. These have sometimes been seen most clearly by observers who are somewhat removed. A striking example is Jean-Claude Passeron's contrast between 'French' and 'English' approaches to the study of class in his introduction to the French edition of Hoggart's *The Uses of Literacy*:

> The discussion of the realities of class is certainly to the credit of numerous fractions of the French intellectual milieu, but it is not altogether wrong to suppose that its theoretical and abstract tone serves also to keep at bay a whole set of realities at once simple and scandalous – or worse than scandalous, vulgar. The whole empirical force of these realities is evident when a description at once ethnographic and autobiographical such as Richard Hoggart's brings them into focus directly, above literary artifice and scholarly exercises. (Passeron 1971: 130)

Passeron, best-known as a co-author with Pierre Bourdieu (Bourdieu and Passeron 1979; Bourdieu and Passeron 1990; Bourdieu, Chamboredon and Passeron 1991; Bourdieu, Passeron and de Saint Martin 1994), was engaged in precisely the theoretical projects which cultural studies came, after Hoggart, to admire. It is instructive, then, at the point where Hoggart himself has almost been forgotten, to see that a certain admiration has also flowed the other way.

It has often been suggested that one of the revolutionary moments of post-war cultural criticism was Roland Barthes' analysis in 1959 of a cover of the magazine *Paris Match* picturing an African soldier saluting the French flag. As Stephen

Muecke writes, it was, for many, a moment of revelation: 'Being at the time of the Algerian war, this image was that of a European power sending a clear ideological message about its relationship to its colonies. But what was new and surprising about Barthes' analysis was that previously nobody expected to find ideology while flicking through popular magazines in the hairdresser's' (Muecke 1997: 168).

But exactly contemporary with Barthes' essay was a less-remembered 'English' revolution, which needs to be understood in different terms – the moment when Richard Hoggart's grandmother's ironing appeared as an object of serious contemplation before an educated reading public (Gibson 1998). Unlike Barthes' ideological analysis of popular culture, Hoggart did not seek to connect ordinary experience with issues of world-historical importance, to capture the weighty political significance of ideology or myth. He showed simply that it could be considered in its cultural specificity, for no more than what it is.

Two paradigms?

Before the case can be made more fully, some work is required to disentangle Williams and Hoggart from received accounts of their significance. The major point of reference here is Stuart Hall's essay 'Cultural Studies: two paradigms', which set much of the framework for representing the relation between the early initiatives in cultural studies and later theoretical perspectives. The essay is perhaps unique in the sympathy and depth of understanding it shows for both sides. As I will argue in Chapter 5, much of the significance of Hall within British cultural studies has been in maintaining a productive tension between the 'first' and 'second' generations in the field. While he is often read simply as a 'theorist', he has always retained a connection with what he called the 'indigenous' or 'native' tradition (Hall 1996a: 33), a connection that goes well beyond mere sentimental attachment or personal loyalty. But his major public statement on the specificity of this tradition was made at a high point in the ascendancy of European theoretical imports. It is deeply marked by the 'structuralist moment' and has never seriously been revised.

The 'structuralist' bias of Hall's account is evident in its very title. The term 'paradigm' has perhaps softened now to the point where it sometimes means little more than 'approach'. But in the 1970s and early 1980s it had a more precise meaning, derived particularly from Thomas Kuhn's (1970) *The Structure of Scientific Revolutions*. In drawing his points of contrast, Hall assumes, as Kuhn had argued, that intellectual positions are informed by general governing principles which structure thought and perception. The provenance of the assumption is explicitly anti-empiricist. What is important in examining a position is not – so the argument goes – its relation to 'experience' or 'evidence', but the categories it employs in *organizing* experience. The classical exposition of the general perspective is in Kantian and post-Kantian philosophy, in which 'forms' of thought and experience are considered in abstract from their specific 'contents'.

Such a mode of analysis is thoroughly at odds with early British cultural studies. As Hall himself recognizes, one of the most distinctive characteristics of the latter was its *resistance* to abstraction (Hall 1996a: 39). This was a resistance, most notably, to the separation out of different instances of the social – 'culture', 'the economy', 'social institutions' – as if these had a merely external or mechanical relation with each other. But it was also a resistance to the separation out of forms or structures of thought and perception from their contents. The style of thought represented by Williams and Hoggart is strongly historical. Ideas, like other cultural phenomena, are related to the particular times and places in which they take form and are not seen as transcending them. Hence there is no question of distinguishing general structures from the various instances in which they are merely 'applied'.

What occurs in Hall's essay is not, therefore, a neutral representation of early cultural studies, but an active *translation* of its concerns into a different intellectual idiom. There is an obvious context for this in his efforts to mediate between different generations and intellectual commitments whose relations had become fraught, if not openly antagonistic. The essay can be read as an attempt to address what he describes at one point as 'the sectarian and self-righteous climate of critical intellectual work in England' in which 'arguments and debates have most frequently been over-polarized into their extremes' (Hall 1996a: 42). The desire to establish a more productive dialogue leads Hall to seek terms in which different positions can be represented to each other. Given the ascendancy of 'structuralism', it is from the structuralist lexicon that these terms are drawn. Hence, early British cultural studies, cast as 'culturalism', is tailored for diplomatic purposes as a fully respectable 'paradigm'.

It may be that no better solution could have been found at the time and it succeeded, at least, in ensuring that dialogue at some level remained open. This does not mean, however, that the strategy remains good for all time. In fact, it has increasingly come to have an opposite function from that which Hall initially intended it. Its long-term effect has been to place the early work of Williams and Hoggart in an inherently weak position in which it can be represented only in terms which are not its own. The result has been to burden it with criticisms that appear insurmountable, consigning it effectively to the dustbin of history.

The most damaging of these criticisms have been charges of 'expressivism', 'humanism' and 'essentialism', all of which claim to identify uncritical or dogmatic ontological assumptions. The terms derive from Althusserian Marxism, but have survived well beyond the point where Althusser himself has faded from view. Their sense was originally developed out of quite a specific engagement with 'Hegelian' versions of Marxism, which gained influence in France in the post-war period (Althusser 1971). In the wake of the Liberation, the French Communist Party and other Marxist-inspired left political movements attempted to claim some of the aura of nationalist mythology by emphasizing collective human agency in effecting historical change. Support was found at the doctrinal level in the rediscovery of the 'early Marx', which still showed the clear influence of Hegelian conceptions of the realization of the human subject in History. Althusser's theoretical project can be read as an attempt to head off what he saw as fundamentalist tendencies in this development (Benton 1984: 14ff). While 'humanist' Marxism congratulated itself on its distance from Stalinism, it was, in his view, no less prone to dogma. The root of this dogma lay in an absolute faith in a human 'essence' which, while it was held to exist independently of specific historical contexts, was believed nevertheless to 'express' itself in historical processes.

The translation of Althusserianism to the British context was assisted by two factors. The first was an identification by Althusser between 'essentialism' and 'empiricism'. In the French context, 'empiricism' had already become established in left political debates as little more than a term of abuse, being closely associated with the authoritarianism of Stalinist claims to possession of the 'facts' of history. Althusser's provocation was to suggest that humanist Marxism, which saw itself as *rejecting* empiricism in this sense, was in fact little different from the positions it claimed to oppose: If 'empiricism' presupposed an essence in objective reality, then 'humanism' presupposed an essence in human subjectivity; one could be seen as merely the mirror of the other. In the British context, the significance of Althusserianism was quite different. Given that versions of empiricism were openly professed, it did not trap its interlocutors in the contradictions of their own logic, but appeared instead as an assault on the very style of intellectual debate. The term 'empiricism' functioned, however, as an important point of translation.

The second factor in easing this translation was, ironically, attempts by some to oppose it. The most significant of these for cultural studies was E. P. Thompson's *The Poverty of Theory* (1978). While Thompson was virulent in his opposition to Althusserian 'theoretical practice', his engagement with Althusser succeeded in casting empiricism as, precisely, a 'theoretical' position. The paradox is one that Anderson had recognized as afflicting any attempt to provide empiricism with a general theoretical defence. The most common of these was an appeal to the criterion of 'verifiability'. As Anderson noted, 'Empiricism pushed to this extreme was subversive of the very experience it should have underwritten: the criterion of verifiability was itself notoriously unverifiable' (Anderson 1968: 21). But the significance of Thompson's anti-theoretical theorizing goes further than this. In rejecting Althusser's emphasis on 'structure', he appealed to the category of human 'agency', appearing in doing so to confirm his vulnerability to Althusserian criticisms. The emphasis on agency appears not only in overt polemic, but also thematizes Thompson's monumental *The Making of the English Working Class* (1963) which, in its framing rhetoric, might perhaps be described as 'expressivist'.

Much of the confusion over the significance of early British cultural studies has resulted from a tendency to make Thompson the representative figure. The precedent here was set, again, by Hall. He is clearly aware in 'Cultural Studies: two paradigms' of substantial differences between Thompson and Williams – differences, as he points out, which were sharply articulated by Thompson himself in a review of Williams's *The Long Revolution*. Yet when he comes to summarize the general principles of 'culturalism', it is Thompson's positions, not Williams', which are abstracted. Hoggart, who showed little interest in general theoretical debates, disappears from view entirely. The result is that Williams and Hoggart are assimilated first to Thompsonism and then, more bizarrely, to Althusser's 'Hegelianism'. However much Hall resists the polemical tendencies of British Althusserianism, he is compelled in conclusion to indicate general 'weaknesses' in early cultural studies. These are almost exactly the weaknesses which Althusser had identified in 'humanism': a tendency to voluntarism and populism, theoretical inadequacy, a naïve 'expressivist' view of social totalities and a fundamentalism of subjective 'experience'. It is at this point that Hall's continued attachment to early cultural studies comes to *appear*, despite protestations, as little more than sentimental.

The full extent of the damage here becomes evident in Paul Gilroy's *There Ain't No Black in the Union Jack* (1987), where the claimed essentialism of Williams and Hoggart becomes further associated with a fundamentalism of race and nation. Gilroy takes the point so far as to associate Williams with the racial exclusionism of Enoch Powell and Peregrine Worsthorne: 'The distinction which Powell and Worsthorne make between authentic and inauthentic types of national belonging, appears in an almost identical form in the work of Raymond Williams. It provides a striking example of the way in which the cultural dimensions of the new racism confound the left/right distinction' (Gilroy 1987: 49). It is unlikely that Hall would have pressed quite the same charge, but he contributed to the context in which it could be made. A clear suggestion of his characterization of Williams was that he claimed experience as 'authenticating' in some absolute sense (see Hall 1996a: 45). This is a characterization not so much of empiricism as of *positivism*. It is in the confusion between these two that the left/right distinction in British politics was 'confounded'. Significant differences in political and intellectual orientation were erased as the entire terrain to which they belong became identified simply with 'conservatism'.

Reasoning and Experience

It should now be possible to ask, however, whether this tendency might be reversed. When viewed outside the context of the debates above, the association between early British cultural studies and 'Hegelianism' appears as highly idiosyncratic. There is little direct evidence in Williams or Hoggart of any significant influence from the German metaphysical tradition. Where the latter is recognized – as an influence, for example, on some of the writers reviewed by Williams in *Culture and Society* – it often appears in a negative light (see, particularly, his comments on Carlyle in Williams 1958: 76–7). Williams was much criticized, in fact, for his reluctance to engage with continental philosophy. Hoggart was so remote from doing so that the point has not even been considered worth making. Nor were either involved in the kinds of liberationist politics which Althusser set out to criticize in France. The logic of translation from French to English debates belonged to a particular historical conjuncture and has no more substantial justification.

It is questionable whether an alternative philosophical genealogy should be sought for the early work of Williams and Hoggart; it may be better to say simply that it did not owe much to philosophy. It is useful, however, in freeing it from the terms through which it has been read, to consider a *point of intersection* with philosophical concerns. This is in a similarity in key terms and characteristic arguments with the more local tradition of British empiricism. Here there is at least some evidence, a useful point of reference being an essay on David Hume in Williams's *Writing and Society*.

The essay is significant not only in revealing clear connections between Hume's style of thought and Williams's own, but also in indicating how Williams regarded philosophy. He finds a precedent on this question in Hume himself, for whom philosophy was a variety of *letters*: 'We can quote his most recent and best biographer, Ernest Mossner, for the opinion that from the beginning Hume "regarded philosophy as part-and-parcel of literature. To be a philosopher is to be a man of letters: the proposition was received by Hume and the eighteenth century as axiomatic"' (Williams 1983: 121). Williams cites this view in order to revive it; the remainder of his essay is an attempt to show that Hume's philosophy can *still* be read as a certain kind of writing. The important point in the argument is that the specialization of philosophy in abstract 'reason' does not distinguish it categorically from writing that is immersed in the particularities of 'experience'. It is a point, again, on which Williams follows Hume. As he understands Hume's empiricism, it is not a doctrine that reason gains *authority* from experience, but a view of the two as *inseparable*.

It is significant that Williams does not attempt to justify this view in general terms; consistent with the style of thought to which it belongs, he traces the circumstances in which it arose. As he points out, Hume's historical position was perhaps unique: it was possible, in eighteenth-century Scotland, to recognize the transformative power of a developing capitalist economy, to sense the tempo and texture of modernity, but not yet to have obvious cause to regard it as cataclysmic or revolutionary. The space of his thought was one that was sensitized to the kind of change that has since come to be accepted as an inescapable dimension of modern life, but where it could be considered in a way that was even and contemplative.

It is in this context, for Williams, that the major themes of Hume's philosophy are best understood. The most familiar of these is his empiricist scepticism, his distrust of reasoning from abstract or universalist premises:

I found that the moral Philosophy transmitted to us by Antiquity, labor'd under the same Inconvenience that has been found in their natural Philosophy, of being entirely

Hypothetical, and depending more upon Invention than Experience. Every one consulted his Fancy in erecting Schemes of Virtue and Happiness, without regarding Human Nature, upon which every moral Conclusion must depend. (Hume quoted in Williams 1983: 123)

Where Williams's interpretation of this differs from most is that he does not take it to be pitched exclusively at the level of formal argument; nor does he see it as preparing the way for an alternative ontology or conceptual system. Its impulse arises, he suggests, from a troubled relation between the formal discipline of writing and the elusive qualities of enthusiasm, passion and warmth of social engagement. It is on this point that Hume considers the weaknesses of other positions: 'I have notic'd in the Writings of the French Mysticks, and in those of our Fanatics here, that, when they give a History of the Situation of their Souls, they mention a Coldness and Desertion of the Spirit, which frequently returns, and some of them … have been tormented by it many Years' (Hume quoted in Williams 1983: 123). And it is on the same point that he is troubled by tendencies in himself: 'I dine, I play a game of back-gammon, I converse, and am merry with my friends; and when after three or four hours' amusement, I wou'd return to these speculations, they appear so cold, and strain'd and ridiculous, that I cannot find in my heart to enter into them any farther' (Hume quoted in Williams 1983: 127). For Williams, the whole of Hume's moral philosophy might be read as an attempt to develop a response to this problem – to define a new relation between reasoning and experience, writing and social engagement, the time of the study and a wider world whose pace was visibly increasing.

The Present View of the Object

The distinctiveness of Hume's approach to this problem lies, for Williams, in a complex relation to *convention*. On the one hand, he directs an insistent scepticism against formalism and dogma, whether in social and political institutions or in thought and writing. As in the case of 'the moral Philosophy transmitted to us by Antiquity', these qualities are taken more generally to imply a fixity and irrelevance. But on the other hand, he openly *appeals* to convention in defining a relation between reason and experience. This is evident in stylistic devices used to engage the assent of the reader, particularly small affirmative judgements on questions where a basis for common agreement is assumed – ''tis evident, 'tis certain, 'tis undeniable'. Hume admits that the use of such expressions might be seen to contradict his scepticism, but defends himself against the charge of authoritarian intent: '[They] were extorted from me by the present view of the object, and imply no dogmatical spirit, nor conceited idea of my own judgement, which are sentiments that I am sensible can become no body, and a sceptic still less than any other' (Hume quoted in Williams

1983: 128). While 'the present view of the object' may be conventional, it is also *negotiable*, being always qualified by the particular circumstances – 'according to the light' (1983: 128) – in which it arises. The approach is one that does not judge tradition and convention in themselves, but only for the kinds of communicative relation they do or do not allow.

Williams's commentary on this is as revealing of himself as it is of Hume. While he notes certain limitations in Hume's thinking, and criticizes some of the positions which have been abstracted from it, his exposition overall is clearly sympathetic. Most telling, perhaps, is a defence of Hume's position on religion: '[H]ere (we have still to observe, in twentieth-century England as well as in eighteenth-century Scotland) an obstinate kind of questioning, a scepticism, can lead, suddenly, to a cry of fire. Angry prejudices are released, only to turn suddenly and assume the name and body of love' (Williams 1983: 130). There is no question, for Williams, that this concern must be taken seriously; but it is not, he argues, an objection that can be made against Hume. It is true that he questioned the consequences of religion as he saw it practised and expounded, but this questioning never ignited a desire that the institution of religion itself be destroyed. Hume's temper here is clearly regarded by Williams as a virtue, illustrating precisely the attractions of his style of thought: its ability, particularly, to combine an open tolerance – which does not wish people to be fundamentally other than they are – with a force of critical intellect brought to bear on petty dogmas, tyrannies and complacencies.

There are unmistakable parallels between themes in Williams's own work and those he identifies in Hume. His classic formulation 'structures of feeling', is Humean in exactly the sense that he himself outlines, resisting an opposition between the formal aspects of phenomena and those qualities which give rise to affirmation. The same might be said of the idea of the 'long revolution'. Williams's vision of the process of democratic social transformation is not of one carried forward by 'an obstinate kind of questioning'; nor is it one in which tradition is simply rejected in favour of 'the new'. It is a process in which there is a gradual synchronization of reasoning and experience, in which traditional institutions and conventions are gradually adjusted to respond to modernity. Perhaps most importantly, there are similarities in the principles employed in judging social or political arrangements. Like Hume, Williams insists on the qualification of judgements by the 'light' in which they are made: '[M]y general position [is] to seek the maximum disclosure of the circumstances of judgment, which would allow someone else to dissociate himself from it; but then openly and not by a presumptive category' (Williams 1979: 347).

It is here, then, that we might clarify some of the bearings of early British cultural studies. If Hume represents for Williams 'a whole movement of thought – in effect the movement of empiricism' (1983: 126), the 'empiricism' in question has a very different sense from that assumed by Althusser. When Althusser used the term it was an abstract metaphysics which he clearly had in mind – the positing of substances or 'essences' understood as independent not only from theoretical discourse but also from evidence. This is almost the opposite of Humean empiricism, which is distinguished precisely by a *rejection* of the metaphysical category of substance. The category, Hume argued, was a 'fiction of the antient philosophy'. The belief in substances was merely a habit of mind which reconciled the contradictory appearance in phenomena of similarities and variations through time: 'In order to reconcile which contradictions the imagination is apt to feign something unknown and invisible, which it supposes to continue the same under all these variations; and this unintelligible something it calls a *substance, or original and first matter*' (Hume 1978: 220).

Similar caution is required in relation to 'humanism'. If Williams might be described as a 'humanist', it is in the same sense, again, as the term might be applied to Hume. As Williams summarizes the basic assumptions, they are of 'the shared conventions of humane feeling; the certainty that these are embodied in the common language of approval and disapproval; the conviction that moral activity is the use of this language, and that reasoning is necessary mainly to confirm this use and to expose the inadequacy of other definitions of morals' (Williams 1983: 134). These convictions might be criticized for many things, but the assumption of an ontological essence in 'man' or 'Spirit' is not one of them. Hume was no less sceptical of such assumptions than he was of a metaphysics of 'substances'. The point of this scepticism, for Williams at least, was precisely to deny to reason any absolute court of appeal. There is no alternative, in the Humean tradition, than to engage communicatively in 'the common language of approval and disapproval'; it is only from this that 'humane feeling' gains its point of reference.[2]

An Unclarified Affair

One of the most immediately illuminating points to begin in considering the relevance of all this to questions of power is Williams's ambiguous 'conversion' to Marxism. Perhaps the most decisive passage appears in a discussion of the concept of hegemony in *Marxism and Literature*. Having given an outline of the concept, Williams considers, then rejects, an objection to its use:

> There is of course the difficulty that domination and subordination, as effective descriptions of cultural formation, will, by many, be refused; that the alternative language of co-operative shaping, of common contribution, which the traditional concept of 'culture' so notably expressed, will be found preferable. In this fundamental choice there

2. McKenzie Wark (1997a: 194–6) has made a useful suggestion in coining the term 'Humean nature'. The term introduces a similar distinction to the one I am drawing between Humean empiricism and metaphysical humanism.

is no alternative, from any socialist position, to recognition and emphasis of the massive historical and immediate experience of class domination and subordination, in all their various forms. (Williams 1977: 112)

This is undoubtedly an important turning point in Williams's writing. His reference to the 'alternative language of co-operative shaping' is very close to a description of his own earlier work and the decision to reject it is clearly arrived at with difficulty. But the significance of the turn should not be overstated. The terms of Williams's engagement with Marxism remain very much his own.

The point here was not lost on Terry Eagleton, one of the keenest observers at the time. As both a one-time student of Williams and a rising exponent of Marxist cultural criticism in Britain, Eagleton had an intense interest in the question. Like many others of a younger generation, he clearly sought the vindication of Williams's recognition of Marxist theory, but he could not help but find his turn to Marxism disappointing. The key term in contention is, significantly, 'experience':

> It is symptomatic of Williams's whole method that he should point to the *experiential* force of hegemony, as an index of its structural primacy. Hegemony is deeply, pervasively lived... It goes logically with this confusion that his concept of hegemony is a structurally undifferentiated one: 'a central system of practices, meanings and values' which is not distributed into its constitutive economic, political and ideological formations. Williams's rapprochement with Marxism is still, evidently, a fraught, dissentient, intellectually unclarified affair. (Eagleton 1976: 23, original emphasis)

Even in what appears to be Williams's clearest announcement of a commitment to Marxism, there is a crucial reservation. At no point are 'domination' and 'subordination' recognized unequivocally as fundamental social realities; the terms are granted no further validity than that they correspond to a 'historical and immediate experience'. The decision to adopt them avoids any question of final correctness, appearing instead as a choice, given particular political commitments ('socialism'), of an appropriate 'language'. Williams does not so much reject an earlier position as find ways of adapting a Marxist vocabulary to what remains a highly sceptical view of general theoretical principles.

The example is a striking illustration of my overall argument in this chapter: that the approach to discourses of power in early British cultural studies is, in the Humean sense, an empiricist one, reluctant to allow a separation between 'reason' and 'experience'. Where for Eagleton, 'domination' and 'subordination' are properly theoretical concepts, with a validity independent of experience, their status for Williams is quite different. They are concepts which have developed within particular historical contexts and whose meaning is rooted *in* those contexts. Any role for theory is limited to a clarification of the ways in which they are used and a demonstration of the inadequacy of attempts to ground them at some more fundamental level.

But to consider the issues only as they are clarified by an engagement with Marxism is also, in some ways, misleading. It suggests, firstly, that an attention to questions of power is confined to those who use the concept or related concepts in their most generalized forms – to those, that is, who speak of 'power' or 'domination' in the abstract. Secondly, and perhaps more importantly, it suggests an equation between generalized concepts of power and a recognition of social *conflict*. This equation is explicit in the way Williams frames his 'fundamental choice': on the one hand, the 'language of co-operative shaping', on the other, the language of 'domination and subordination'. There is no place in this presentation of options for a consideration of social relations that are *neither* cooperative *nor* subsumed under a generalized rubric of power.

The point is important because it has haunted attempts to resist generalizing theoretical tendencies in cultural studies. The problem was already present in Williams, whose work was always highly sensitized to Marxism even when not clearly 'Marxist'. It can be stated as a simple dilemma: whether to emphasize conflict or whether to emphasize local differences and historical particularities.[3] The 'unclarified' character of Williams's Marxism can largely be attributed to a continuing discomfort with settling for either of these options over the other. References to conflict evoke, for Williams, a universal form of human relations – 'domination' – an implication that he must then strain to circumvent. But to avoid such references is to suppress an obvious dimension of social experience. The problem has proved remarkably persistent in cultural studies. As we will see in Chapters 10 and 11, it has reappeared in recent attempts to disengage from general theories of domination. These attempts have been shadowed by much the same criticism that Thompson made of the early Williams: that he had 'evacuated conflict concepts from his whole idiom'. As Meaghan Morris has put it, borrowing terms from Michel de Certeau, the move away from general theories of domination has been accompanied by a loss in cultural studies of a 'polemological edge' (Morris 1990: 31).

Policemen don't shit Roses

For an indication of why the dilemma may be misleading, it is necessary to look to the figure in the development of British cultural studies who was least sensitized to Marxism: Richard Hoggart. There is a paradox here: while Hoggart is further than Williams from Anderson or Eagleton, he is not so open to their criticisms. There is a directness about social conflict in his writing which is not hedged by

---

3. It was a dilemma which was personified, for Williams, by the figures of Marx ('conflict') and F. R. Leavis ('culture'). As is clear from 'Culture is Ordinary', Williams's thought, from his days as a student at Cambridge, was always located somewhere in the tension between these two (see Williams 1989b).

elaborate qualifications. A dislike of an artificial smoothing of human relations is, in fact, one of his most persistent themes. As he put it in *The Uses of Literacy*: '"Everyone's entitled to his own opinion" may indicate strength or weakness; but when, as today, it is constantly surrounded by appeals for the "open mind" and for "broadmindedness" – open for its own sake and broad enough not to cause any unpleasantness by requiring disagreement from anyone – one knows where the emphasis lies' (Hoggart 1957: 177). Yet Hoggart is the figure, more than any other, who resisted both a generalized concept of power and universalizing theoretical tendencies. His blindness to Marxism undoubtedly had its costs – in an inability, particularly, to engage with the concerns of a younger generation. But it is a blindness that may now have a certain virtue. Hoggart's writing preserves the memory of different understanding of conflict – not as an index of structural contradictions but as a contingent quality of social encounters.

A good example here is his comments on the relation between working-class communities and the police – an issue more famously addressed from a 'Marxist' perspective by Stuart Hall and others in *Policing the Crisis* (1978). There is no question, for Hoggart, that the relation has always involved a major element of conflict and he is critical of those who fail to recognize it. In an essay of 1960 on television, for example, he calls attention to the absence of representations of conflict in the popular police drama *Dixon of Dock Green*:

> Traditional working-class attitudes to the 'cops' were a compound of suspicion, scorn, laughter, and respect. Compare that with the clean, simplified, kindly figure of the 'cop' in *Dixon*. Where is the world in which the police beat you up at the station if you've made it difficult for them to get you there? in which you suspect they always stick together and will lie to the magistrates to do so? in which you believe they are lenient with the local nobs? (Hoggart 1970: 158)

The observation is not an isolated one; similar criticisms are made of 'concerned' social documentaries: 'on the "colour" problem, nuclear warfare, "the problem of youth", and so on' (Hoggart 1970: 154). These are, for Hoggart, 'informed with intelligent good intentions' but 'almost always off-key, irrelevant to the lived pressure and depth and grotesqueness of "problems"' (1970: 154):

> Most of them give as nearly as they can a 'balanced', an 'objective' picture, one which represents a 'fair cross-section' of the 'typical people' involved in the 'problem'. I wonder what effect they have at the level at which we say 'bloody niggers' or 'those damn teenagers ought to be horsewhipped'. (1970: 154)

Yet the analysis is quite distinct from a critique of ideology, attempting to expose an 'underlying' structure of relations which there is an interest somewhere in concealing. As Hoggart goes on to clarify his remarks on police violence: 'I am not saying these qualities exist all the time and are unrelieved. But one knew and knows that they do exist, within a whole texture of attitudes to the police, a texture that has been formed in the stress of experience, a texture that is not simply mean and suspicious but is subtle and qualified' (Hoggart 1970: 158).

As part of a 'whole texture', conflict does not reveal a more fundamental level of reality than other qualities of social relations. It is to be noted in a documentary mode rather than seized upon as a key for analytic penetration. Hoggart's lead in this is not so much from any intellectual authority as from vernacular working-class traditions. As he relates it in later autobiographical reflections: 'The standard working-class phrase before all discreditable behaviour in the police was the dour: "Policemen don't shit roses"' (Hoggart 1988: 128).

Here, then, is a 'purer' empiricism with respect to power than can be found in Williams. Society, for Hoggart, is composed of a multiplicity of powers – the powers of the police, the magistrates, the bosses, as well as those available to working-class communities. The exercise of these powers is often dominative and sometimes violent, but such qualities do not represent a fundamental social 'truth'. Powers have relations with other powers – the magistrates with certain middle-class institutions, the police with the 'local nobs' – but these relations are contingent. They are not reducible to a basic structuring principle that would allow power to be considered as one.

Hoggart is *aware* of a more totalizing view of power as well as its tendency to fasten on evidence of conflict. He recognizes it most explicitly in his essays on student politics and changes in universities during the late 1960s:

> The extreme student radicals argue that society is thoroughly corrupted and at bottom authoritarian; that the amiable part-yielding that it (like the universities) seems capable of is worse than frank opposition because, in the end, it gets you nowhere but meanwhile blunts your cutting edge... The much talked-about patience of the police is only a façade. If anyone really tries to push things to the point at which they challenge the structure, then the mask is dropped and the police become ruthless, exposed as the agents of naked power. (Hoggart 1982: 27)

But Hoggart is more secure than Williams in holding to an alternative view. It is not necessary, as he sees it, to minimize conflict, merely to recognize it as part of a 'mongrel mixture of attitudes': 'There are a great many rigidities and snobberies... But there are also a great many decencies' (Hoggart 1982: 26).

–5–

'A Whole Way of Conflict'
The Turn to Power

If my argument so far is generally accepted, the interesting question which emerges is why an empiricism with respect to power has been eclipsed in more recent cultural studies. It becomes no longer possible to offer the common progressivist account according to which later theoretical positions replaced earlier positions because of a failure of the latter to recognize power. Nor can it be suggested that later positions have been superior in their recognition of social conflict. Attention must be directed to quite a different set of questions: Why has there been a tendency to *totalize* power? Why has power come to be considered in the abstract? Why has social conflict been so widely accepted as an index of structural contradictions?

The answers to these questions can only be sought in the contexts in which the developments have taken place. For the British case, this requires us to look more closely at the history of the New Left, particularly its response to a rapid expansion of what John Hartley has called the 'G-E-M' complex, the interlinked agencies of government, education and the media (Hartley 1999: 5–7). The initial catalyst for this expansion was the Second World War, which displaced unprecedented numbers of people from what had been their expected activities and locations, involving them in more rationalized, centralized organizations. But the tendency was confirmed in the post-war period. Industrial restructuring, increasing prosperity and a removal of obstacles to social mobility all raised the prospect of a break-up of established class cultures. At the same time, previous limits to cross-demographic communication were breached as business and media organizations moved to establish mass markets and audiences. Further contributing to the tendency was the development of the welfare state, which required greater penetration by government agencies into 'ordinary lives'.

The relevance of this to the above discussion is touched upon obliquely in Williams's essay on Hume. The greatest *limitation* of Hume's moral philosophy, for Williams, is that it is not immediately suited to contexts of social diversity. The problem is evident in an ambiguity in Hume's use of the word 'society' itself. At some points, it carries an old sense of 'the company of one's fellows'. Where this is the usage, appeals to shared conventions appear a plausible way of achieving consistency between individual reason and wider 'social' experience. But at other points, Hume refers to 'society' in the more abstract modern sense of a 'system of common life' (involving not only one's 'fellows' but also those with quite different experiences). As Williams identifies the problem:

> Hume, unconsciously assimilating 'society', at many points, to a sense not far from the class-based 'company of his fellows', misses what seems to me the central difficulty in his whole argument... [He] is trying to generalize and even universalize, in the matter of virtue and society, while retaining within this crucial term not only an unconscious particularity but also, largely unanalysed, the essential complexities of the operative and connecting word. (Williams 1983: 140)

In Hume's time, the problem may not have been acute: the intellectual exchanges he was engaged in were still, effectively, internal to a particular class, gender and geopolitical location. But where this condition no longer holds, the whole approach is brought into question.

If there is any origin of the 'crisis' in English intellectual life identified by Anderson in 1964, it appears to have been here, in the difficulty of adapting an empiricist style to increasingly pluralistic contexts of public discussion and debate. As Anderson himself pointed out in 'Components of the National Culture', English cultural criticism up to F. R. Leavis employed a characteristic mode of address. The reader was engaged with a rhetorical question which was implied, if not actually explicit: 'This is so, is it not?' (Anderson 1968: 52) So long as there are sufficient similarities of experience between addresser and addressee for the answer, in general, to be 'yes', then the strategy can work effectively; common ground can be negotiated for more developed arguments. But where, instead, the answer becomes uncertain, the very conditions for public discourse begin to evaporate. The problem is one which British cultural studies has faced from the outset. If anything is shared between Hoggart, Williams, E. P. Thompson and indeed Stuart Hall, it has been a sense of the urgency of addressing it. While immersed within strongly empiricist intellectual traditions, they have been, at the same time, highly exposed to social diversity.

The Bruised Tentacles of Society

For Hoggart and Williams, this exposure had a strong personal dimension. As 'scholarship boys' who had come to a university education from working-class backgrounds, they had had to negotiate it as part of their own development. As Hoggart put it in *The Uses of Literacy*, the scholarship boy exemplified the 'anxious and uprooted', who could be recognized 'primarily by their lack of poise, their uncertainty' (Hoggart 1957: 291). He found it difficult to identify fully with the class from which he had come. While normally he might have been inducted into the masculine world of work, his experience was, instead, of doing homework in a space cleared on the kitchen table among piles of ironing and cups of tea: 'With one ear he hears the women discussing their worries and ailments and hopes, and he tells them at intervals about his school and the work and what the master said. He usually receives boundless uncomprehending sympathy: he knows they do not understand, but still he tells them; he would like to link the two environments' (Hoggart 1957: 296). Yet the scholarship boy was no more comfortable in the middle-class environment in which he later moved: 'He rarely feels the reality of knowledge, of other men's thoughts and imaginings, on his own pulses; he rarely discovers an author for himself and on his own' (1957: 297).

But, as Hoggart saw, the scholarship boy was not unique; he was merely one of 'the more sensitive, though now bruised, tentacles of society. The main body of the whole ignores them; but the symptoms they show refer in some degree to all' (1957: 317). In the area of education, the scholarship system was only a precursor to a wider expansion of tertiary sector and it is here that the most significant developments occurred. As Tom Steele has pointed out, all the figures most closely involved in the early development of cultural studies began their careers in the area where this expansion first occurred: in adult education or the extra-mural sector of the universities (Steele 1997: 14–16). In a late essay, Williams makes it clear that this is where, for him, cultural studies first took form:

> [I]t can hardly be stressed too strongly that Cultural Studies in the sense we now understand it ... occurred in adult education: in the WEA, in the extramural Extension classes. I've sometimes read accounts of the development of Cultural Studies which characteristically date its various developments from *texts*. We all know the accounts which will line up and date *The Uses of Literacy*, *The Making of the English Working Class*, *Culture and Society*, and so on. But already in the late forties... Cultural Studies was extremely active in adult education. It only got into print and gained some kind of general intellectual recognition with those later books (Williams 1989a: 154).

Williams is equally clear on the significance of adult education: it was a context in which modes of address could not be presumed. Like the scholarship boy, WEA or extension students often found themselves unable to 'feel the reality of knowledge on their own pulses'. This did not mean they rejected the knowledge that was offered to them, but it did mean an insistence on two conditions: '(1) that the relation of [it] to their own situation and experience had to be discussed, and (2) that there were areas in which the discipline itself might be unsatisfactory' (Williams 1989a: 156). It was out of this encounter that the new kinds of writing that became known as 'cultural studies' emerged.

The history here has often been framed in terms of relations between 'high' and 'popular' culture, particularly with reference to the confrontation between Leavisite literary criticism and new commercial forms of entertainment. But the problem of address was more general than this suggests. As Hoggart pointed out in his writing on media, it also affected communication internal to 'popular' cultural forms. It was most extreme, in fact, in television, which faced 'a vast, unknown, unassessed, varying audience which has to be *won*': 'This situation is not wholly limiting, but it can be inhibiting. How will a miner in South Wales or a woman in a North Yorkshire farmhouse or a solicitor in London take this? Will some be dangerously shocked? Dare I assume this? How far will most people go along with me if I risk this?' (Hoggart 1970: 160) Such anxieties were not restricted to middle- or upper-class elites; they were also felt by those attempting to adapt themselves from older working-class publications: 'writers in Britain are so used to working within known limits, not only of *genre* but of unconsciously assumed audience, that they feel outfaced by the imponderables within a new medium of communication' (1970: 154).

In considering the emergence, in this context, of a generalized concept of power, two factors appear particularly significant. The first was a widespread appeal, in response to the problem of address, to 'neutral' points of reference free of particular associations with any social group. As Hoggart noted, such an appeal was very marked in the new 'mass' media:

> mass communications tend to seek an 'objectivity' which can be pretty well statistically demonstrated, and, if necessary, defended against those literal-minded pressure-groups which haunt all public organs of opinion. It may be, too, that there is a general tendency among individuals ... to hold to what is semi-scientifically demonstrable in preference to that which is called 'mere impressionism' or even 'mere interpretation' (Hoggart 1970: 154).

The suggestion of a more 'general tendency' is confirmed by Anderson's diagnosis, discussed in Chapter 1, of the need in Britain for 'fundamental concepts of man and society'. If Anderson is any guide, there can be little doubt that much of the attraction of European 'theory' in Britain was, initially, its apparent universality. A more abstract analytic vocabulary, augmented by 'foreignness', promised to transcend the particular contextual references of existing class cultures.

The second factor that appears to have favoured a generalized concept of power was increasing levels of social suspicion. One of the clearest analyses of this development is in Williams's discussion in *The Long Revolution* of a common response to the loss of confidence that one's experiences are shared. This is a 'retreat into private worlds', which are set up in abstract opposition to those 'others' – the 'masses' – who belong outside one's immediate sphere of meaning and control: '[I]nevitably, by this extending process, we are all converted into masses, for nowhere, in a world so composed, can our own individuality be fully recognized by others; they are turning away from us to establish their own. This is the experience we are now trying to face and interpret, at the limit of the meanings we know' (Williams 1965: 114). The result of this tendency, for Williams, is a reduction of political options to a choice between 'romantic individualism' and 'authoritarian and abstract social thinking' (1965: 130). The individual or primary group becomes the only recognizable locus of affirmation while social involvement can be thought only in terms of manipulation for extrinsic ends: 'The image of society is then of something inherently bad: a restrictive, interfering, indifferent process, whether it claims the virtues of an established order or the creation of human brotherhood' (1965: 128–9).

It seems reasonable to suggest that generalized concepts of power were a condensation of these two factors. If Hoggart and Williams are accepted as witnesses, the pressure to develop an 'objective' social vocabulary coincided in the 1950s and 1960s with a widespread sense of social hostility – an experience which did, in fact, transcend social classes. The concepts of power that began to take form from the late 1960s have sometimes been characterized as associating power with 'badness' or negativity. This association has been criticized, particularly from a 'Foucauldian' perspective, as a preface to suggesting that power might also be thought of as 'positive' or 'productive'. But the more significant development may have been that power was *totalized*. What had previously been understood in Hoggartian terms as distinct and specific powers came to be seen merely as variants – whether 'positive' or 'negative' – of a single, objective social phenomenon.

Of Snail-eating Frenchmen

This development clearly crystallizes in British cultural studies during the 1970s. But to proceed immediately to the adoption of generalized concepts of power might give an impression that it represents the only response to the 'crisis' outlined above. I wish to begin an argument here, to be continued in later chapters, that this is not the case. If post-war developments in Britain have favoured generalized concepts of power, there have also been continued efforts to resist them or to dilute their implications. Such efforts have sometimes been identified with conservative opposition to cultural studies, but the situation has been more complicated. As I will point out in Chapter 6, the concept of power was quite well established in other disciplines and projects before being taken up by cultural studies – not all of them, by any means, identified with the 'left'. The field has not *initiated* its use so much as *responded* to its use by others. If there is any consistent pattern to the response, it has been ambivalence. For every move to engage the concept, there has been a move to back away. The history of cultural studies is as much a history of scepticism towards the concept as it is of enthusiastic embrace.

This scepticism is articulated most clearly in the early work of Hoggart and Williams. In order to understand it, we need to take seriously their reservations about the idea of an objective hierarchy of social privilege or fundamental points of social contradiction. These lie, quite explicitly, in concerns about the ethics of address in contexts of social diversity. The assumption of an objective truth about social relations, however much it seems to involve sympathy for those addressed, leads, as Hoggart and Williams saw it, to an insensitivity in observing their actual circumstances. As Hoggart put it of the 'middle class Marxist':

> He pities the betrayed and debased worker, whose faults he sees as almost entirely a result of the grinding system which controls him. He admires the remnants of the noble savage, and has a nostalgia for those 'best of all' kinds of art, rural folk-art or genuinely popular urban art, and a special enthusiasm for such scraps of them as he thinks he can detect today... Usually, he succeeds in part-pitying and part-patronizing working-class people beyond any semblance of reality. (Hoggart 1957: 16)

Williams's position was, at many points, similar. In *The Long Revolution* he rejects the assumption that class mobility from a working-class background can be seen in terms of an upward movement. As he points out, such an idea assumes a general equivalent against which class position can be measured, an equivalent which is implicitly middle class: 'We all like to think of ourselves as standard, and I can see that it is genuinely difficult for the English middle class to suppose that the working class is not desperately anxious to become just like itself' (Williams 1965: 324). The only response to this, for Williams, is to indicate that things can be imagined otherwise:

> I can only say for myself that I have never felt my own mobility in terms of a 'rise in the social scale', and certainly I have never felt that I wanted to go on climbing, resentful of old barriers in my way: where else is there to go but into my own life? ... It is ... less the injustice of the British class system than its stupidity that really strikes me. People like to be respected, but this natural desire is now principally achieved by a system which defines respect in terms of despising someone else, and then in turn being inevitably despised. (Williams 1965: 349)

The avoidance here of reference to a fundamental social injustice cannot be entirely explained by the uniqueness of Williams's personal experience; it also has a clear political motivation: To appeal to abstract measures of equality and inequality is to assume a general social norm, yet such an assumption is precisely what needs to be put in question in responding to diversity.

It was in the context of these concerns, in fact, that the concept of *culture* assumed a central importance. The significance of the concept, for Hoggart and Williams, was to *particularize*, to deny points of reference external to the limited contexts in which habits, customs and forms of knowledge have emerged. The strategy is used to exemplary effect in Hoggart's rendition of class difference in *The Uses of Literacy*:

> To live in the working-classes is even now to belong to an all-pervading culture, one in some ways as formal and stylized as any that is attributed to, say, the upper-classes. A working-class man would come to grief over the right way to move through a

seven-course dinner: an upper middle-class man among working-people would just as surely reveal his foreign background by the way he made conversation (the tempo of conversation, not only the matter of idiom), used his hands and feet, ordered drinks or tried to stand drinks. (Hoggart 1957: 32)

The position is contrasted against a view that class can be read off from objective social coordinates. Hoggart does not believe that the working class has generally thought of the highly educated as structurally dominant; nor does he see that they should: '[T]hey are on the whole just not interested in artists or intellectuals; they know of their existence, but regard them as oddities rarely seen within their orbit, like snail-eating Frenchmen' (1957: 183).

The model of foreign relations here is significant. As Williams points out in his essay on Hume, it suggests a possible solution to the impasse of empiricism when faced with diversity. Hume himself was a notable contributor to the recognition of differences in experience where they occurred between different *societies*. To quote an example cited by Williams:

In countries where men pass most of their time in conversation and visits and assemblies, these *companionable* qualities, so to speak, are of high estimation and form a chief part of personal merit. In countries where men live a more domestic life and either are employed in business or amuse themselves in a narrower circle of acquaintance, the more solid qualities are chiefly regarded. (Hume quoted in Williams 1983: 139)

One way of describing the project of early British cultural studies might be as an attempt to apply a similar principle of relativity to comparisons between moral systems *within* particular societies. As Williams puts it in *The Long Revolution*, 'we need to learn ways of thinking and feeling which will enable us genuinely to know each other in the other's terms' (Williams 1965: 117). The problem of address to those whose experiences one does not share is resolved through an appeal to models of translation and diplomacy.

Williams's much-quoted definition of culture as 'the whole way of life' is, in some ways, unfortunate, as it suggests a totalizing perspective. As applied by Williams, however, it is the opposite of totalizing. The function of the definition is to resist the application of analytic categories which suggest easy equations between different contexts and experiences:

Politics and art, together with science, religion, family life and other categories we speak of as absolutes, belong in a whole world of active and interacting relationships, which is our common associative life. If we begin from the whole texture, we can go on to study particular activities, and their bearings on other kinds. Yet we begin, normally, from the categories themselves, and this has led again and again to a very damaging suppression of relationships. (Williams 1965: 56)

To 'begin from the whole texture' is to insist on contextual specificity. To see analytic categories as limited abstractions from that texture, rather than as having a substantive or transcendental value, is to refuse a global perspective. Such a position requires an attention to 'particular activities'; relations between activities can only be seen in terms of imaginative translations.

To put the point, alternatively, in the terms I borrowed from Oakeshott in Chapter 3, the emphasis on 'culture' was, for Hoggart and Williams, an option for a politics of scepticism. The consistent refusal of a generalized concept of power is a refusal also to imagine society as available for comprehensive reform. The relevant contrast is sharply drawn by Williams in *Culture and Society* through a comparison between his own political position and Leninism. All that a socialist should wish for, for Williams, is that the 'channels of communication are widened and cleared'; what emerges as a result must be valued as 'an actual response to the whole reality'. The alternative view is that put by Lenin: 'Every artist ... has a right to create freely according to his ideals, independent of anything. Only, of course, we communists cannot stand with our hands folded and let chaos develop in any direction it may. We must guide this process according to a plan and form its results' (Lenin quoted in Williams 1958: 283). Williams's comment on the latter is an acerbic rejection: 'There is no "of course" about it, and the growth of consciousness is cheapened ... by being foreseen as "chaos"' (1958: 283).

There is clearly some common ground between this position and certain forms of conservatism. But to move from this observation to simple equations would be to reduce left politics simply to projects of social engineering. If the rigid binarisms of the Cold War often made such reductions difficult to avoid, early British cultural studies serves as a reminder of a greater complexity. A wariness of totalizing social visions – including a totalizing concept of power – has not been the sole preserve of those with substantial interests to protect; it has also been articulated with the perspective in mind of those with relatively few resources. There are good reasons, from such a perspective, to have reservations about issuing licenses for an overbearing intrusion of public agencies into everyday lives.

Good and Bad Men

Where a generalized concept of power does emerge in British cultural studies, therefore, it emerges as an alternative strand to these already-established positions. The most significant text in this development appears to have been E. P. Thompson's review, mentioned earlier, of Williams's *The Long Revolution*. Despite its slenderness and now relative obscurity, it deserves to be seen as one of the more important documents in the early formation of cultural studies. As Hall (1980) makes clear in his account of the history of the Birmingham Centre for Cultural Studies, it was an essential reference in the early 'curriculum' of the field. In many ways, it can be seen as laying the foundations, in Britain, for what is now recognized internationally as 'cultural studies'.

Thompson's differences with Williams fasten immediately on the theme of social conflict. He opens by taking issue with a line from Williams in a review for the *Guardian*: 'You can feel the pause and effort: the necessary openness and honesty of a man listening to another, in good faith, and then replying' (Thompson 1961: 25). For Thompson, this betrays a misunderstanding of communication, even in the literary tradition to which Williams so often refers: 'Burke abused, Cobbett inveighed, Arnold was capable of malicious intent...' (1961: 25). But more seriously, Williams is charged for complicity with forms of social privilege:

> What is evident is a concealed preference – in the name of 'genuine communication' – for the language of the academy. And it is easy for the notion of 'good faith' to refer, not only to the essential conventions of intellectual discourse, but also to carry overtones – through Newman and Arnold to the formal addresses of most Vice-Chancellors today – which are actively offensive. (Thompson 1961: 25)

The knife is twisted on the issue of Williams's continued respect for the English literary tradition: 'Oh, the sunlit quadrangle, the clinking of glasses of port, the quiet converse of enlightened men! ... [H]ow wide (or narrow) does an opinion have to be to be handled with such deference – does it become part of The Tradition only when it can be washed down with port?' (Thompson 1961: 25, 26–7) The reversal here of Hoggart and Williams is complete: intellectuals are to the working class not as 'snail-eating Frenchmen' but as a fundamentally oppressive social presence: 'the tone of the academy has seemed less than disinterested to those millions who have inhabited the "shabby purlieus" of the centres of learning' (1961: 25). Thompson even confirms Hoggart's suspicions of 'middle-class Marxists', casting Williams as a displaced and benighted Jude the Obscure (1961: 35).

There are many points on which Thompson's arguments might be questioned: If Burke, Cobbett and Arnold were often abusive, how can measured attempts at understanding be associated with the literary tradition? Is 'pause and effort' necessary or likely in smug conversations between class-equals over glasses of port? Is the *figure* of 'pause and effort' intended by Williams as a description of communication in general or an ideal of how it *can be*? But to raise these questions is perhaps to miss the point. Thompson's conflictual vision of the social is not developed out of an argumentative engagement with Williams so much as a reaction to the whole tenor of his writing. He himself may have come closest to the truth in admitting 'I have a real problem with Raymond Williams *tone*' (1961: 24).

What Thompson most objects to in Williams is a drift towards a kind of relativism. Williams has 'partially disengaged' from the socialist intellectual tradition (1961: 24), he has neglected the 'problems and approaches which have been the particular concern of the socialist tradition' (1961: 28), 'he has tried to take in too much, over-reached himself, and is in danger of losing some of the ground he has really gained' (1961: 32), 'he has cast loose his moorings' (1961: 34). The thought of Williams at Cambridge – possibly with a glass of port in hand! – presents a category confusion which Thompson clearly finds intolerable. The idea of a 'long' revolution is similarly unacceptable. If there is a revolution, he argues, 'then it is fair to suppose that it is a revolution *against* something (classes, institutions, people, ideas) as well as *for* something' (1961: 25). Williams fails to lead people towards 'active confrontation' (1961: 28); 'there are no good and bad men in Mr Williams' history, only dominant and subordinate "structures of feeling"' (1961: 29).

These objections anticipate a wider reaction against Williams on the part of a younger generation, a good example being Eagleton's judgement on his writing:

> an elaborately formal, resoundingly public discourse ... a conjuring of weight out of emptiness which lacks all edge and abrasiveness. Concrete particulars are offered in such a modified, mediated and magisterial a guise as to be only dimly intelligible through the mesh of generalities... It is a style which in the very act of assuming an unruffled, almost Olympian impersonality displays itself (not least in its spiralling modifications) as defensive, private and self-absorbed. (Eagleton 1976: 8)

Thompson's distinction between 'good and bad men' could be seen as responding, more generally, to a widely felt disgust at a malaise in English intellectual life – a tendency which Anderson memorably described as a 'slow, sickening entropy': 'Today, Britain stands revealed as a schlerosed, archaic society, trapped and burdened by its past successes, now for the first time aware of its lassitude, but as yet unable to overcome it' (Anderson 1964: 50). A desire to inject some structure into public debate can be found even in Hoggart:

> We can soon put ourselves in a position in which we lie back with our mouths open, whilst we are fed by pipe-line, and as of right, from a bottomless cornucopia manipulated by an anonymous 'Them'. One would be happier if the dislike of authority were more often an active dislike, implying a wish to stand on one's own feet... We are moving towards a world of what Alex Comfort has called 'irresponsible obedients'; it would be better if more were 'responsible disobedients'. (Hoggart 1957: 196)

Williams appears, in this context, to have been trapped by the very tendencies he so clearly diagnosed. In the absence of a sense of ongoing material bases for shared experience, the very appeal to experience comes to appear as mere subjectivism, lacking in any public principle.

A Whole Way of Conflict

The significance of Thompson's intervention is in offering a vigorous solution. Within the terms of this solution, themes of conflict are only a vehicle for establishing objective points of reference. An important strategy here is a deployment of figures of *violence*. Williams's history of the 1840s is accused by Thompson of ignoring jailings, deaths and tyrannical abuse: 'tens of thousands of handloom weavers starved out of their "whole way of life" at home and with millions starved out theirs in Ireland' (Thompson 1961: 29). But the point is taken further, illustrating precisely why, for Williams, reference to conflict was always fraught with difficulties: 'Suffering', Thompson argues, 'is not just a wastage on the margin of growth: for those who suffer it is absolute' (1961: 29). The clear implication is that it licenses a certain categorical absolut*ism*, dividing the world into 'oppressed' and 'oppressors', 'good' and 'bad' men.

Thompson's commitment to certain fundamentals defines an entirely different intellectual terrain, a terrain that can be outlined through a number of significant features. The first are the twin concepts of 'interests' and 'ideology'. Thompson's understanding of conflict as a strictly *social* phenomenon implies objective stakes around which positions are organized. Material interests are posited as a point of political orientation entirely independent of cultural forms: '[I]t is not clear to me how "universal participation" or a "common culture" can "dismantle the barriers of class" which are also barriers of *interest*: if improved communication enabled working people to understand better the way of life of the corporate rich they would like it less, and feel the barriers of class more' (Thompson 1961: 36). The question here is not whether Thompson sees material interests as *determining* cultural forms – whether, in Marxist terms, he sees a causal relation between 'base' and 'superstructure'. What is important is that he *abstracts* them from each other. It is only at this point that it becomes possible to ask what relations pertain between the abstracted terms. Once this question *is* asked, we are faced with the classical problem of ideology: how does culture contribute to – or how is it determined by – objective regimes of material interest? For Thompson, this is exactly the question which should be posed: '[I]t is only when the systems of communication are placed in the context of power-relationships that we can see the problem as it is. And it is the problem of ideology' (1961: 37).

A second major feature of Thompson's programme is a redefinition of the concept of culture. This follows from the effective displacement of the concept by the concepts of 'interests' and 'ideology'. If any sense is retained of culture as a 'whole way of life', then the concept comes to do double duty: it appears as both the way of life and an element *within* the way of life.[4] Williams drew attention to this

---

4. John Frow has argued that this confusion remains a basic problem in cultural studies: 'The central "anthropological" version of the concept of culture ... is a serious embarrassment... The main line of filiation here is to Raymond Williams... [C]ulture both *is* the "way of life" and is the "meanings and values" *in* that way of life; the "way of life" and the "culture" are at once identical and in an expressive relation based on some ontological distinction between them' (Frow 1995: 7–8). But to trace the problem to Williams is unfair. Frow overlooks the fact that he was the first to point it out.

problem in *Culture and Society*, as one affecting the Marxism of the 1930s. The use of the term 'culture' by Marxists was, he argued, inconsistent:

> It normally indicates, in their writings, the intellectual and imaginative products of a society; this corresponds with the weak use of 'superstructure'. But it would seem that from their emphasis on the interdependence of all elements of social reality, and from their analytic emphasis on movement and change, Marxists should logically use 'culture' in the sense of a whole way of life, a general social process. (Williams 1958: 282)

Thompson approaches the question on the assumption that a distinction between culture and objective 'interests' is a given: 'Any theory of culture must include the concept of the dialectical interaction between culture and something which is *not* culture' (Thompson 1961: 33). This means that the concept acquires the relatively specialized sense of 'the intellectual and imaginative products of a society'. It is defined as a specific instance within social totalities, losing its association with a resistance to analytic abstraction.

A third significant feature is a perceived need for general 'theory' and a turn to continental European sources to provide it. Once 'interests', 'ideology' and 'culture' are posited as objective social phenomena, then an account of their relations seems to be required. The English literary tradition could not provide such an account because it was not a sociological tradition; it was a tradition of situated argument through imaginative categories of thought. As Thompson points out, Williams is 'still' within this tradition: 'I must record my view that he has not yet succeeded in developing an adequate *general* theory of culture' (Thompson 1961: 28). The lack of a general theory is immediately experienced as embarrassing. For Thompson, Williams's cast of interlocutors were theoretical lightweights who tended to talk 'out of the top of one's head' (1961: 30):

> The Tradition (if there is one) is a very English phenomenon... If Williams had allowed himself to look beyond this island, he might have found a very different eleven Players fielding against him, from Vico through Marx to Weber and Mannheim, beside whom his own team might look, on occasion, like gentlemen amateurs. (Thompson 1961: 30)

England becomes identified with 'tradition' and a suspicion begins to form over both. Thompson is the first in a distinguished line of intellectual entrepreneurs to propose an import licence for European theory.

But the feature that draws together and thematizes all of the above is a generalized concept of power, a concept that is introduced through an appeal to Marxism. In moving from criticisms to constructive suggestions, Thompson proposes a series of transformations that would make Williams's position more acceptable:

[I]f we were to alter one word in Mr. Williams' definition, from 'way of life' to 'way of *growth*', we move from a definition whose associations are passive and impersonal to one which raises questions of activity and agency. And if we change the word again, to delete the associations with 'progress' which are implied in 'growth', we might get: 'the study of relationships between elements in a whole way of *conflict*'. And a way of conflict is a way of *struggle*. And we are back with Marx. (Thompson 1961: 33)

As Thompson goes on to summarize his argument, 'what has been left out of Mr Williams notion of "communication" is *power*' (1961: 36).

A Revolution Complete?

At a certain level, it is obvious which of the two strands in early British cultural studies has been dominant in later developments. The field, as it has come to be defined, appears thoroughly 'Thompsonian'. Culture must be placed in relation to real relations of power that are external to it; politics is defined not by dialogue but by 'struggles' in which different interests are structurally opposed; a sophisticated political understanding requires the rejection of empiricism for the universalist scope of European 'theory'. These positions have come to be so widely accepted that they rarely appear any longer *as* positions – they are taken simply to be the established ground on which work in cultural studies is able to proceed. In the formal representation of positions, the significant question is only *how* the concept of power is used: Are gender, race and sexual orientation admitted beside class as dimensions of power? Is power considered exclusively in terms of domination? What relations are posited between culture and power?

But to begin from an awareness that a generalized concept of power was not 'foundational' to cultural studies opens the possibility of quite a different question. It allows us to ask whether its introduction has succeeded in fully restructuring the field. On first impressions, the answer may appear obvious, but on closer investigation it is much less so. It is, in fact, ironic that Thompson should have been the first great entrepreneur in British cultural studies of European theoretical approaches, for he later became one of their most vociferous opponents (see Thompson 1978). But in this ambivalence, he has not been alone. The pattern of response within the British New Left to the introduction of an abstract theoretical vocabulary might best be described as a complex fracturing, finely graded by degrees of acceptance and resistance. Even those, like Anderson, who could fairly be placed at the 'far' end of the spectrum, have reached their point of reversal (Anderson 1983; Anderson 1992a: 193–301). However far debates may have shifted from the positions of Hoggart and Williams in the 1950s, it is not at all clear that the influence of those positions – and of the contexts that informed them – has been completely erased. It is to the question of this influence in later developments that I now want to turn.

–6–

The Sociological Encounter
'Power' at Birmingham

The 1970s for cultural studies might be described as the decade of the 'break'. The theme was most sharply focused in the Althusserian concept of the *coupure epistémologique* – an abrupt transformation from 'ideology' to 'science' – but contemporary accounts of the development of the field abound in references to 'interruptions', 'departures' and 'ruptures'. These are defined in two ways: at a theoretical level, in terms of the new possibilities opened up by the uptake of Marxism, structuralism and European philosophy; and at the political level, in terms of the upheavals of the late 1960s and the possibilities opened up by student activism, feminism and the 'new social movements'. For those who participated in these developments, there was little doubt that something had fundamentally changed.

The point is significant because the 1970s is also the decade in which cultural studies is often seen to have taken form. It is the decade in which Stuart Hall and the Birmingham Centre for Contemporary Cultural Studies produced their most influential work. It is the decade in which exchanges developed with and between a number of other initiatives, from London and Cardiff to Sydney and Illinois, in a way that has since allowed the field to be projected as more than a local phenomenon. And it is the decade in which something like a 'curriculum' was defined – a set of common references that have provided a basis for the undergraduate programmes and publishing industries of the 1980s and 1990s.

The conjunction of the theme of the break with the current constitution of cultural studies presents, potentially, a major obstacle to the argument I have so far developed. The problem is not so much that the account in the last two chapters of early British cultural studies may be invalidated; it is more that it may appear as simply irrelevant. If the 1970s was a historical 'caesura' (to use another term of the time), then anything preceding them might be seen as having little bearing on cultural studies as presently defined. It may be conceded that Hoggart and Williams did, indeed, resist a generalized concept of power, yet any attempt to enlarge on the significance of this may be dismissed. The intellectual formation out of which they emerged has clearly been displaced. It could be concluded that cultural studies as now practised derives from different contexts entirely.

Such a view has well-established precedents. It became common, from the late 1970s, to look for ways in which the field had transcended its early beginnings. Hall's reading of Williams is modelled, for example, on Althusser's reading of Marx. *The Long Revolution* is nominated, together with E. P. Thompson's *The Making of the English Working Class*, as a work 'of the break'. The earlier arguments of *Culture and Society* become significant, from this perspective, only in 'writing the epitaph' of the English literary tradition (Hall 1996a: 32). The break in Williams's writing is identified, particularly, in intimations of a generalized concept of power. In an essay of the late 1970s, Hall quotes a line from Williams which he takes to indicate 'a significant modification of his earlier positions': 'in any particular period there is a central system of practices, meanings and values which we can properly call dominant and effective ... which are organized and lived' (Hall 1977a: 332). The suggestion is best developed, for Hall, through Marxist theories of ideology. Althusser and Gramsci come to occupy the space left vacant by the interment of Coleridge, Ruskin and Arnold.

The line between past and present was drawn even more decisively at the political level. An influential statement here was Terry Eagleton's dismissal in 1976 of the programme set out in the *Mayday Manifesto* by Williams, E. P. Thompson and a young Stuart Hall:

> The essentially liberal conception of socialist organization implicit in the circular totality of the [first] New Left – 'connecting', 'co-operating', 'explaining', 'communicating', 'extending' – was politically sterile from the outset. Only the media could provide a provisional point of intersection between the literary academics and real politics. May 1968, the date of the Manifesto's publication in book form, signalled a political moment of rather more import than this well-intentioned offering, before which it was inevitably thrust into oblivion. (Eagleton 1976: 18)

The shift in political orientation of the Birmingham CCCS is humorously recorded in a recollection by Hoggart of receiving minutes of a meeting after his departure to become deputy-director of UNESCO: 'One of the minutes had a sentence which said "You've got to recognize that we are now a Red Cell and must have no more to do with the Hoggartian, Matthew Arnoldian literary tradition". It was wonderful. In a way, what this student was doing was pointing out the way things had leaned before I left' (Gibson and Hartley 1998: 18–19).

The dissociation of cultural studies from the early British initiatives has increased with the internationalization of the field. As I will argue in Chapter 8, the development of cultural studies outside Britain has often been identified with anti-colonialism in the ex-British Empire. In Australia, particularly, the desire to find an alternative to the elitism and inertia of academic English has had continuities with a long tradition of radical nationalism (Milner 1997; Gibson 2001). The new theoretical perspectives and political possibilities of the 1970s were embraced, in this context, as an opportunity to emerge finally from the shadow of colonialism. Exchanges with British cultural studies have generally been with the 'post-Hoggartian' CCCS and other sites of theoretical innovation which have themselves been defined in opposition to 'Englishness'.

A good index of the effect of international contexts on British cultural studies has been the changing intellectual identity of Stuart Hall. In the 1960s and 1970s, there was little question that Hall's significance was as a leading figure of the British New Left. In the 1980s and 1990s, however, he has become increasingly defined as a 'diasporic intellectual', exemplary for his negotiation of a global structure of relations between 'centres' and 'margins' (see, for example, Chen 1996b). The implications of this redefinition is made clear in a bid by Jon Stratton and Ien Ang to remove any specific reference to Britain in representing the history of cultural studies. For Stratton and Ang, the common element in the field, whatever its location, has been 'the empowering validation of the marginal, although the naming of the marginal differs greatly from one context to another' (Stratton and Ang 1996: 377–8). While Hoggart and Williams are written into this account, their work is seen as flawed by the assumption of a British frame of reference. Hall's recent writing on the politics of race is correspondingly promoted as freeing cultural studies from such a limitation.

My argument in the following two chapters is that there are much stronger continuities between the 'first' and 'second' generation of British cultural studies than all of these accounts suggest. I wish to demonstrate, in particular, that the early scepticism of Hoggart and Williams about generalized concepts of power remained very much active in what is often taken to be the 'classical' cultural studies of the Birmingham Centre for Contemporary Cultural Studies during the 1970s under the directorship of Stuart Hall.

As I have related this scepticism in earlier chapters to English political contexts, an implication of the argument is that the work of Hall and the CCCS never entirely escaped a formative 'Englishness'. This introduces difficult questions about how we should now think about cultural studies as an *international* field, but I will leave these aside until Chapter 12. My point is not that what holds of the CCCS must necessarily hold for everything which is now called 'cultural studies'. It is merely that what has been one of the most influential and widely recognized sites for the development of cultural studies has been informed as much by sceptical 'English' approaches to questions of power as it has by moves to reject them. This is to reverse the onus of proof in the question of relevance. Rather than assuming that an empiricism with respect to power has been a limited case, now only of interest to antiquarians, we can begin to ask where it has *not* had some influence. If there has been no absolute break between the early work in Britain of Hoggart and Williams and the later work of the CCCS, where *is* the rupture or departure that would allow a line to be drawn between an empiricism with respect to power and the present constitution of the field?

An Indecent Adventure

The interpretation of the 1970s that I am suggesting could certainly be taken too far. There is little doubt that those involved in the major developments in cultural studies at the time *believed* that the adoption of oppositional forms of politics and general theories of power marked a significant break with the past. This in itself needs to be respected and there is also evidence that the belief was justified. It has to be remembered that the 1970s was a violent decade in which deeply held convictions were often bitterly opposed. In this context, the development of the new positions with which cultural studies became associated required a determination and sometimes courage which should not be ignored.

Two points can be made, however, in moderating the conclusions that might be drawn. The first is that the significance of oppositional politics and general theories of power cannot be separated from the *context* into which they were introduced. I have already quoted Meaghan Morris's observation in the 1970s that Marxism had a 'local subversive potential' in a country like Australia that would be unthinkable to most European intellectuals (Morris 1988: 52). The observation suggests that Marxism in Australia must be considered as a different phenomenon from Marxism in contexts where it has been more deeply rooted in the political culture. A similar point could be made of psychoanalysis and semiotics, which have figured in much the same way as counters within English-language debates. As Morris puts it, 'Marx and Freud have had less the status of master-thinkers, and more the exhilarating effect of an indecent adventure' (1988: 52). Even in its representation as 'foreign', imported theory has been significantly transformed.

The same could be said of the political level. As Hoggart pointed out of the British student movement of the late 1960s and early 1970s: 'One would think that the political model being drawn upon had been found somewhere over the mid-Atlantic or mid-Channel, without the intervention of any British history' (1982: 54). Following observations on the subject by Colin Crouch, however, he goes on to suggest that 'in a deeper manner the British student movement, even at its most lively, was nevertheless English to the core in another sense, in that with some exceptions it showed a gentleness rarely found elsewhere' (1982: 54). Claims in relation to 'breaks' or 'departures' need, in other words, to be put in perspective. In local contexts, the adoption of new political models, as of new theoretical approaches, was clearly significant. But this does not mean that it completely displaced what had gone before.

The second point is that the struggles that took place over the new forms of theory and politics were never simply struggles between 'past' and 'present'. In some respects, the conservative defence of 'Anglo' virtues was as different from the traditions it sought to uphold as those who set out to reject them. As Perry Anderson pointed out in his essays of the 1960s, English intellectual life had been significantly transformed in the first half of the twentieth century. The shift involved its own processes of intellectual importation, through the agency, particularly, of the 'émigré intellectuals' – Ludwig Wittgenstein, Bronislaw Malinowski, Lewis Namier, Karl Popper, Isaiah Berlin, Ernst Gombrich, Hans Jürgen Eysenck and Melanie Klein. In Anderson's negative gloss:

> British empiricism and conservatism was on the whole an instinctive, ad hoc affair. It shunned theory even in the rejection of theory. It was a style, not a method. The expatriate impact on this cultural syndrome was paradoxical. In effect, the emigres for the first time systematized the refusal of system. They codified the slovenly empiricism of the past, and thereby hardened and narrowed it. They also, ultimately, rendered it more vulnerable. (Anderson 1968: 19)

While the distinction has often been blurred, the theoretical initiatives of the 1970s were articulated not so much against 'the slovenly empiricism of the past' as against the 'hardened and narrowed' attempt at systematization – particularly claims to an 'objective' basis for knowledge. To the extent that the latter developed as a complex cross-cultural hybrid, it might as well be described as 'Viennese', 'Polish' or 'Russian' as 'English'.

It is misleading, therefore, to represent divisions as occurring between 'European' theory and 'English' empiricism. They occurred, more accurately, between divergent responses to a particular historical conjuncture, both of which developed out of English intellectual culture while also appealing to intellectual imports. I will argue below that this point is particularly important in understanding the tendency in British cultural studies towards a generalized concept of power. In the case of Hall, at least, a commitment to such a concept developed not so much from criticisms of 'traditional' English intellectual culture as from a desire to resist another kind of import – a positivism with respect to power associated with American political science, sociology and mass communication theory.

The historical interpretation I am suggesting here is not entirely new. There have always been sceptics about the theme of the 'break'. One of the most interesting and persistent has been Colin Sparks. Sparks spent two years at the Birmingham CCCS in the mid 1970s, but always felt distanced from the main work of the Centre by a more thoroughgoing commitment to Marxism. In an article that first appeared in 1974 in the Centre's *Working Papers in Cultural Studies*, he expressed doubts as to whether the conversion to Marxism was more than superficial. Marxism, for Sparks, was inseparable from its historical relation to working-class political organization, particularly in Europe (Germany being the model). The latter was never seriously considered by cultural studies:

> What happened ... is that a number of thinkers, of varying degrees of ability, were lifted out of the Marxist tradition and gutted quite ahistorically for the light they could shed on other concerns. With staggering arrogance, the collective experience of millions of working people was tossed away with the label: 'profoundly residual'... There was

not, and never has been, any attempt to come to terms with Marxism as a revolutionary practice, any attempt to critically assimilate the history of that practice, any effort to understand or relate to the organizational expressions of revolutionary practice, any recognition of the historical dynamic of that practice. (Sparks 1974: 17)

Marxism, in this view, did not constitute a real departure from the early British formation of the field; a methodology was abstracted from the contexts which gave it its sense and grafted onto 'the unreconstructed problematic bequeathed by Hoggart' (1974: 16). 'It is not', as Sparks puts it, 'that nothing has changed, but that the transformations of vocabulary and methodology, and even some of the attempts to negate the Hoggartian framework, remain trapped within [the earlier] conception of Cultural Studies' (1974: 13–14).

The Logic of the Ampersand

Sparks's position on the relation between Marxism and cultural studies has remained fairly much unchanged over twenty years. In revisiting the subject recently, he restates many of the arguments of the mid 1970s with the added knowledge now that the two have increasingly grown apart. In this longer perspective, it becomes clearer still to him that the relation was never fundamental:

> [I]n the current associated with Stuart Hall, the link between marxism and cultural studies was much more contingent and transitory than it once appeared even to its main actors. The initial formation of cultural studies was in part a rejection of the then dominant version of marxism. The later elaboration of marxist cultural studies took place through the appropriation of one particular version of marxism. It was from the start beset by internal intellectual problems arising in part from the radical incommensurability between the project of cultural studies and the variety of marxism adopted. The productive life of this marxist cultural studies was very short: certainly less than a decade and perhaps as little as five years. (Sparks 1996: 97–8)

On these estimates, Marxism does indeed begin to fade in significance. If the beginnings of cultural studies are dated from the late 1950s, it can be counted as a direct influence for at most one fifth of the life of the field.

Sparks's perspective might be dismissed as idiosyncratic, betraying too pure an understanding of Marxism, but it is confirmed to some extent by no less a figure than Hall himself. Speaking at Illinois in 1990, Hall went to some lengths to set the record straight for an international audience:

> There never was a prior moment when cultural studies and Marxism represented a perfect theoretical fit... [T]he encounter between British cultural studies and Marxism has first to be understood as the engagement with a problem... It begins, and develops

through the critique of a certain reductionism and economism...; a contestation with
the model of base and superstructure, through which sophisticated and vulgar Marxism
alike had tried to think the relationships between society, economy, and culture. It was
located and sited in a necessary and prolonged and as yet unending contestation with the
question of false consciousness. (Hall 1992: 279)

If this leaves any doubt, Hall goes on to underline the point: 'the notion that Marxism
and cultural studies slipped into place, recognized an immediate affinity, joined
hands in some teleological or Hegelian moment of synthesis and there was the
founding moment of cultural studies, is entirely mistaken. It couldn't have been
more different from that' (1992: 280).

A different objection to my argument at this point might be that to question the
significance of Marxism is not, in itself, to question the adoption of a generalized
concept of power. Certainly, the two cannot simply be equated: feminist cultural
studies, black cultural studies, gay and lesbian cultural studies, postcolonial criticism,
approaches based on the work of Foucault – all have, in various ways, taken issue
with Marxism while using the concept in its most expansive sense. In Chapter 8,
I will argue that the attachment to a generalized concept of power has, in fact,
deepened with these later developments. But the historical importance assigned to
Marxism is nonetheless significant because of the way it has functioned to imply a
settled consensus on the theoretical and political orientations of cultural studies. If,
as Hall, puts it, there was a 'founding moment' at which cultural studies was simply
'Marxist', then it can be assumed that a generalized concept of power was firmly
established as a starting point on which everything else has grown. If, however,
there was no such moment, then the status of the concept begins to appear much less
certain.

Many of the 'post-Marxist' initiatives in cultural studies have been introduced,
to use terms suggested by John Hartley, according to a logic of the 'ampersand'
(Hartley 1999: 20). In the beginning, so this logic goes, the field was concerned with
power as it operated along the axis of class. It was realized, however, that such an
approach was limited, ignoring relations of power that operated along other axes.
It was necessary, therefore, to supplement class analysis with an attention to other
dimensions of social difference – first of gender, then race, then a string of other
categories of identity. Cultural studies, in this context, becomes 'analysis of (insert
object of analysis here – film, TV series, cultural form) according to questions
of class & gender & ethnicity & sexual orientation & nationality & language-
community & age & size & disability &&&' (1999: 20). Each initiative made on
the basis of this logic, has further entrenched an assumption that previous versions
of cultural studies were always already concerned with the operation of power in the
cultural domain. It is Marxism, above all, which secures the end of the chain. Even
as Marxism is rejected for its exclusive emphasis on class, its historical importance
is paradoxically inflated.

The historical importance attributed to Marxism is therefore significant well beyond an assessment of 'Marxist' cultural studies itself. What is at stake, more substantially, is whether a generalized concept of power has ever been foundational. If it has not, then the implications flow through into feminism, writing on 'race' and all the other 'post-Marxisms'. Once the imaginary anchor of an 'original' Marxist cultural studies is lost, a whole chain of associated reasoning begins to drift. The important point is that cultural studies can no longer be defined as simply 'about' power. It becomes more appropriate to see it as a field that has engaged, more or less critically, with the *concept* of power.

The Social Eye of Cultural Studies

The key figure in relation to these questions is undoubtedly Hall. Hall has always stressed the importance of intellectual cooperation and a significant amount of his work has been co-authored with others, but there is little question that his efforts were crucial in establishing an intellectual space for the work that developed during the 1970s at Birmingham. His adaptation of Marxist concepts and arguments has been more influential than any other and has been widely accepted as definitive. If there was ever a moment in which cultural studies was decisively influenced by Marxism, it is the moment represented by Hall's directorship of the CCCS. If doubts can be raised about the extent of this influence, we must begin to question whether there has ever been a fully 'Marxist' cultural studies.

It is not difficult to show that Hall had well-developed intellectual and political positions before any serious identification with Marxism. His first major publication, *The Popular Arts*, co-authored with Paddy Whannel, closely follows the examples of Hoggart and Williams in its analysis of popular culture. As Hall and Whannel put it themselves: 'They [Hoggart and Williams] have made a major contribution to this whole debate, and our debt, directly and indirectly, to them is immense' (Hall and Whannel 1964: 15). The approach adopted to popular film, television, literature, music and dance is more generally informed by the English literary tradition. Matthew Arnold's *Culture and Anarchy* is described in an appendix as setting the debate about popular culture 'in its proper perspective' (1964: 435) and Q. D. Leavis's *Fiction and the Reading Public* as 'still perhaps the best introduction to the subject [of popular literature]' (1964: 448).

The Popular Arts makes no systematic use of the concept of power, but its argument has a bearing on how the concept might be regarded. Hall and Whannel's strategy in claiming a space for the serious study of popular culture is similar to the strategies of Hoggart and Williams in gaining recognition for working-class culture. It is not to adopt an oppositional stance on behalf of the popular against 'high art', but to contextualize both to the point where they no longer appear in competition:

Popular music, for example, has its own standards. Ella Fitzgerald is a highly polished professional entertainer who within her own sphere could hardly be better. Clearly it would be inappropriate to compare her with Maria Callas; they are not aiming at the same thing. Equally it is not useful to say that the music of Cole Porter is inferior to that of Beethoven... Porter was not making an unsuccessful attempt to create music comparable to Beethoven's. (Hall and Whannel 1964: 38)

The argument is most clearly directed against the assumption of a universal hierarchy of value, but it is also inconsistent with the idea of a structural hierarchy of cultural forms. Like Hoggart and Williams, Hall and Whannel are sensitive to a condescending approach to popular culture which regards it distantly, even if sympathetically, from a presumed position of 'privilege'. The context for this sensitivity is also similar. *The Popular Arts* is embedded in a practical engagement with problems of education. Hall and Whannel are concerned with pedagogical modes of address and work from experience, as teachers themselves, of what students are likely to accept. There is a consistent effort throughout the book to think of differences in other than hierarchical terms.

It is clear from this why Hall should have had an uneasy relation with Marxism. He has described his early political position as of the 'independent left': 'We were interested in marxism, but not dogmatic marxists, anti-stalinist, not defenders of the Soviet Union' (Hall 1996d: 492). His wariness of Marxism appeared to be vindicated following the Soviet invasion of Hungary in 1956 and the ensuing crisis of the British Communist Party. In a 1958 article in the *Universities and Left Review*, he argued that the evolution of capitalism had made Marxist analysis obsolete (Hall 1958). An old sense of class was breaking up as workers began to forge their identities in the sphere of consumption. The 'base and superstructure' metaphor was now inadequate as ownership of the means of production was no longer fundamental. What was needed was an attention to patterns of fragmentation and dispersal rather than a more concentrated structural analysis. This distance from Marxism continued well into Hall's time at the Birmingham CCCS. By his own account of the early period of the Centre: 'for five or six years, long after the resistance to theory of cultural studies had been overcome ... we walked right around the entire circumference of European thought, in order not to be, in any simple capitulation to the *zeitgeist*, Marxists' (Hall 1992: 280).

There is no clear sense, then, in which Hall was 'originally' a Marxist. The important question is the nature and significance of his *turn* to Marxism in the early to mid 1970s. How complete was this turn? What were its circumstances? To what extent did it commit him, and the CCCS, to a generalized concept of power? The most useful texts to consider here are not so much the mature 'Marxist' manifestos as the more exploratory efforts that preceded them. It is possible to observe in these the points of transition where Hall is considering what to retain from his previous positions, what to leave behind and the stakes involved either way. A good example is 'The Social Eye of Picture Post', which appeared in *Working Papers in Cultural Studies* in 1972, just on the cusp of the declared 'conversion'.[5] The essay was written in homage to the popular wartime photo-magazine *Picture Post*, but Hall uses it also as an opportunity to take some distance from the 'social democratic' politics with which he had so far identified.

In writing of *Picture Post*, it is almost as if Hall cannot help but show a respectful warmth towards an old love:

> *Picture Post* captured for the still commercially produced 'news' photograph a new social reality: the domain of everyday life. The decisive impact of a *Picture Post* page lies in its ability to *look hard* and *record*... [T]here is a sort of passion behind the objectivity of the camera eye here, a passion to be *present*. Above all, to present people to themselves in wholly recognizable terms: terms which acknowledged their commonness, their variety, their individuality, their representativeness, which finds them 'intensely interesting'. (Hall 1972: 83)

The significance Hall sees in *Picture Post* has strong resonances with his own project of *The Popular Arts*. It was its ability to present popular culture and everyday life simply in its own terms rather than in terms of an abstract hierarchy of relations with other spheres: 'This clarity of attention raises the "unnoticed subjects" to a sort of equality of status, photographically, with the heroic subjects (Prime Ministers) and activities they elsewhere depict' (1972: 83). The emphasis is on social variety distributed along a continuum; ordinary lives are documented in 'cross-section' rather than sampled for 'vox pops' (1972: 82).

Picture Post's achievement is closely identified by Hall with 'Englishness'. John Hartley has questioned this identification, pointing out that the magazine was originally the creation of a Hungarian Jew – Stefan Lorant – and relied heavily on the skills of émigré German photographers (Hartley 1999: 116–17). But Hall's use of the term 'English' is not as literal as Hartley assumes. He is clearly aware of the national origins of those involved in the magazine; 'English' is used in a more abstract sense as a description of a certain field of political possibilities.

In the latter part of the essay, this sense is developed through an extended discussion of George Orwell's wartime hopes for an 'English revolution'. This was to be a non-violent revolution, though catalysed by the war, in which social contradictions were not sharpened but left to fade through no longer being observed. In Orwell's words:

---

5. My attention has been drawn to the significance of this essay by John Hartley. For Hartley's own analysis, somewhat different from my own, see his discussion in *The Uses of Television* (1999: 112–26).

It will not be doctrinaire, nor even logical. It will abolish the House of Lords, but quite probably will not abolish the Monarchy. It will leave anachronisms and loose ends everywhere, the judge in his ridiculous horse-hair wig and the lion and the unicorn on the soldier's cap-buttons. It will not set up any explicit class dictatorship. It will group itself round the old Labour Party and its mass following will be in the trade unions, but it will draw into it most of the middle class and many of the younger sons of the bourgeoisie. Most of its directing brains will come from the new indeterminate class of skilled workers, technical experts, airmen, scientists, architects and journalists the people who feel at home in the radio and ferro-concrete age. But it will never lose touch with the tradition of compromise and the belief in a law that is above the State. (Orwell quoted in Hall 1972: 106)

Hall's judgement on this is far from dismissive. '[I]t is worth pondering', he suggests, whether Orwell's powers of foresight were not greater than his reputation, or indeed his own estimate, has led us to believe' (Hall 1972: 106).

It is not in its origins or essence, then, that *Picture Post* was 'English'; it was in participating in the 'structure of feeling' described by Orwell. Williams's concept is, in the context, highly appropriate. As Hall points out, the magazine was similar to other strands of British social documentary in seeking a consistency between structure and feeling: 'The documentary style, though at one level, a *form* of writing, photographing, filming, recording, was, at another level, an emergent form of social consciousness' (1972: 100). As with the tradition of documentary film associated with John Grierson (in any case a Scot), *Picture Post* borrowed many of its techniques from continental Europe. But in Britain these techniques were 'domesticated' so that, in Grierson's words, 'an adventure in the arts assumed the respectability of a public service' (Hall 1972: 97). Whatever its weaknesses, in Hall's view, this tendency also had definite strengths. Most importantly, it 'opened up the difficult space between the "free movement" of art and the social engagement of *rapportage*' (1972: 100). The analysis is striking in itself, but is all the more significant given that it was exactly the 'difficult space' referred to which had been staked out by cultural studies.

Angled, Posed, Framed, Prettied Up or Cocooned

Yet, despite all of this, Hall's assessment of *Picture Post* is ultimately more reserved. His criticisms start from a simple observation that its momentum was not sustained. From the early 1950s, the circulation of the magazine was progressively eroded by the new 'colour supplements' until its eventual closure in 1957. The latter were a very different media form:

[T]hough ... the art of the photograph has been raised to a pitch of technical perfection, the social rhetoric on which the art is founded is *not* based on the passion to record,

> inform or document. No one in the Colour Supplements is interested in looking hard or straight: everything is angled, posed, framed, prettied up or cocooned. Men and women, in those glossy pages, *need* to be rich, glamourous, trendy, primitive or degraded. Trapped in the extremes of fantasy or poverty, to be interesting subjects for the camera. (Hall 1972: 84)

But in pointing to the demise of *Picture Post*, Hall is also moving to develop a new style of writing which is able to find a level of social engagement in the kind of media environment represented by the colour supplements. It is a style that requires him to set aside the 'passionate objectivity' of British social documentary in favour of the intellectual resources of European philosophy and aesthetics.

The latter, for Hall, are considered first in historical terms. Indicating an awareness of their context of formation, he relates European thought on the visual image to the revolution in photographic techniques that occurred, particularly in Germany, between the wars. His key witness here is Walter Benjamin: 'Benjamin observed that, in the transformation of forms and values consequent upon the revolutionary innovations in the new media of mechanical reproduction, tradition had been shattered forever, and art, in its traditional sense, had lost its "aura"' (Hall 1972: 100). The promise held out for relocating the scene of thought to this historical conjuncture is immediately indicated through a quotation from Benjamin: 'For the first time in world history, mechanical reproduction emancipates the work of art from its parasitical dependence on ritual... Instead of being based on ritual, it begins to be based on another practice – politics' (Benjamin quoted in Hall 1972: 100). It is not just politics which Hall is interested in, of course, but more specifically revolutionary politics (in the 'French' not the 'English' sense). It is the explosive heat generated by the opposition between 'tradition' and 'change' that provides him with a new point of rhetorical engagement.

Having opted in this way, Hall begins to commit himself to the consequences. The most significant of these is that the consistency of 'structure' and 'feeling' is effectively dissolved. In writing of *Picture Post*, Hall uses the term 'structure of feeling' in ways which Williams might have done, but elsewhere the usage is subtly shifted to an equivalent of either 'structure' *or* 'feeling' in the relatively abstracted sense in which their separation and formal opposition allows. An example of a reduction to 'feeling' is an interpretation of the politics of *The Mirror*: '[B]y a fortunate series of events, the paper found itself in a position, first, to overhear what was actually being said and felt among ordinary people, and then to be *converted* by this powerful, and changing, "structure of feeling"' (Hall 1972: 95). The 'structure of feeling' is identified here with 'what is said and felt among ordinary people' (feeling), which is placed in turn in an external relation to the media institution and forms of journalistic writing (structure). Hall goes on to imply that the relation is not only external, but always at some level *contradictory*; the 'authentic trends, moods and attitudes articulated among people' are 'limited', 'altered' and 'transformed' by the media (Hall 1972: 95–6). The popular voice is subverted and controlled by the fixed constraints of convention.

Where the reduction is made to 'structure', the idea of a 'structure of feeling' is overlaid with harder-edged, structuralist concepts which were just beginning to gain currency in English-language cultural criticism in the early 1970s – concepts such as 'logic' or 'code' (although not yet the Althusserian 'problematic'). Hall draws these together in the concept of a 'social eye'. The concept is a deliberate echo of themes developed out of European theories of the visual image in the work of Christian Metz, John Berger and Peter Wollen. As Hall himself observes in a later essay on the concept of ideology, these theories owe most to a quite different intellectual tradition from British empiricism – that of Kantian and post-Kantian philosophy (Hall 1977b: 11ff). Within this tradition, forms of thought and perception are considered in abstract from *what* is thought or perceived. It is this abstraction that opens up the possibility of formal 'critique'. The categories and structures of thought can be systematically considered for what they make it possible to see or prevent from being seen. In fact, this theoretical work assumes priority, as the categories and structures are regarded as a *condition of possibility* for experience.

It is inevitable, at a certain point, that Hall should use this critical perspective to reflect back on the tradition of social documentary from which he is taking his leave. Hence the 'straightness' of *Picture Post* – its simple use of commonly understood photographic conventions – begins to be interpreted as a liability. Even as Hall appreciates the magazine for capturing the texture of everyday life in a way that communicated directly to its readership, he criticizes its photographic technique as 'not yet revolutionary' (Hall 1972: 83). The tragedy of *Picture Post*, for Hall, is that it neglected the talents of John Heartfield, a founding member of the Berlin Dada group who had emigrated to Britain before the war. Heartfield's experiments in *photomontage* were explicitly designed to 'destroy the "logic" of perception which underpinned bourgeois artistic expression' (Hall 1972: 109). The use of such techniques would have offered the best hope, in Hall's view, of transforming the magazine into a vehicle for the development of a revolutionary political consciousness.

The Sociological Encounter

It might be concluded from this that Hall's own transformation was complete, that *The Popular Arts* and other early writings can safely be dismissed as juvenilia, of little relevance for the later development of cultural studies. This is perhaps how they would now appear to Hall himself, but a closer examination of the shift suggests a more complex picture.

There is certainly evidence that Hall's new emphasis on structural antagonism comes to organize his whole way of thinking. Towards the end of the essay on

Picture Post, social contradictions begin to assume the status of a fundamental truth. In this perspective, Orwell's 'English Revolution' was always ill-conceived and therefore bound to fail:

> The war *did* democratize the society to a degree, but the political meaning of the process was never taken up as a conscious strategy nor its full significance, in terms of structural change, ever fully articulated… The solid foundations of class society in Britain were never really undermined. The message and symbolism of the 'war effort' pulled the classes together in a curious way, thereby working against the necessary division and class-polarization. (Hall 1972: 108)

Taken out of context, such passages do, indeed, suggest a systematic 'conversion'. But to read them in this way is to overlook tensions between Hall's theoretical judgements and a milder *historical* mode of assessment. His essay concludes, in fact, by attributing the demise of *Picture Post* not so much to a fundamental error as to an inability to adjust to the new political divisions and more ruthless commercial competition of the post-war period: 'Squeezed by the Cold War on the one hand, and the greed and philistinism of commercial journalism on the other, *Picture Post* gave up the struggle… The era of social democracy was over' (1972: 116).

This second perspective suggests the possibility of quite a different reading of Hall. The entire shift in his thinking could be seen, in a sense, as unfolding within a continuing 'English' intellectual identity. That is to say, his recognition of social contradiction and antagonism might be interpreted in a similar way to my interpretation, in Chapter 5, of Williams's recognition of 'domination' and 'subordination': not so much as a recognition of universal social phenomena as a recognition of particular historical *experiences*. The language of 'solid foundations', 'necessary divisions' and 'structural change' would appear then not as elements of a general social theory or political programme but as a *rhetoric* appropriate to the times. Chris Rojek (1998) has made a provocative argument somewhat along these lines, but it is not quite the argument I wish to make. There is too much to suggest that Hall has really been convinced, at times, of an ontological basis for the concept of power. His differences from Williams on this point are significant. My claim is only that Hall's early formation has continued to exercise *some influence* over his later development.

There is evidence of this influence in his impatience with the use of the concept of power in recent cultural studies. An example is the quotation I placed at the opening of Chapter 1. Another is some comments, in an interview with Kuan-Hsing Chen, on the difference between the use of the concept by Foucault and the way it has been taken up in American cultural studies:

> Foucault is not a political activist in any simple sense, but when you read the Foucault interviews, you know at once that his work has a bearing on resistance, on sexual politics,

on '1968', on the debate about the West, the nature of state power, and the Gulag; it has political implications. Wonderfully agile Foucauldian studies can be produced in the American academy which invoke power all the time: every second line is power/ discourse, power/knowledge etc., whilst the actual integument of power is absolutely nowhere located in concrete institutions, as it is in *Discipline and Punish* or in the disciplinary regimes of knowledge, as it is in *The Birth of the Clinic*. (Hall 1996c: 397)

There is, again, a way of reading this that would preserve the view that Hall's own use of the concept assumes an ontological foundation. This is the implication of his reference to the 'actual integument' of power. But another reading is at least as plausible: that the concept of power only gains its *meaning* from a historical field of reference – in Foucault's case, from sexual politics, '1968', the debate about the West, the nature of state power and the Gulag. The sense of 'political implications' is similar to passages in which Hall applies the description to Hoggart, Williams and the early British New Left (see, for example, Hall 1996a: 33). What is essential to the application is not reference to power but a directness of relation between concepts, whatever they are, and the contexts from which they have been abstracted.

More substantial evidence can be found, however, in the nature of Hall's adoption of Marxist concepts and arguments. A key point here is that his negotiation of the concept of power is played out against the background of *already established* uses outside cultural studies. It is a point that needs to be emphasized. The concept has become so central to more recent definitions of the field that it is sometimes regarded almost as a unique property – the *species differentia* that sets cultural studies apart from other kinds of social or cultural enquiry. There is little, however, to support such a view. Debates around power formed a whole subset of political science well before the concept was taken up in cultural studies and also had a history in sociology. On the political 'right' there was a fully developed 'pluralist' concept of power, particularly well represented in American mass communication theory. On the 'left', a different use of the concept was readily abstracted from existing variants of Marxism – from the 'mass society' critiques of the Frankfurt School to the 'bad old' Marxism of the Communist Party – all of which Hall and the CCCS had, until the early 1970s, been determined to hold at a distance.

The Proposition of Dominance

Hall's negotiation of a position for cultural studies can only be understood in relation to these points of reference. The territory he entered in committing the field to the concept of power was not only occupied, but jealously guarded within the polarized field of the Cold War. In his 1982 essay 'The rediscovery of "ideology": return of the repressed in media studies', he sets out the options with a retrospective clarity. Given, as he takes as a starting point, that some engagement in sociological discourse was necessary or unavoidable, two major alternatives suggested themselves: the 'European' approach exemplified by the Frankfurt School, 'historically and phil-osophically sweeping, speculative, offering a rich but over-generalized set of hyp-otheses' and, significantly defined in reaction against it, the 'American' approach, 'empirical, behavioural and scientistic' (Hall 1982: 58). Each of these approaches is, for Hall, unsatisfactory; the programme he puts forward is to chart a third way which avoids the problems of both.

Of the Scylla and Charybdis of Marxist grand theory and positivist sociology, Hall is more concerned to avoid the latter. This is not, as the history has often been told, because it did not have a concept of power; it is because of the *nature* of the concept. Hall is quite explicit on this:

> Pluralism, as [Steven] Lukes has suggested, did retain a concept of power, based on the notion of 'influence'. A influenced B to make decision X. Certainly, this was a form of power. Pluralism qualified the persistence of this form of power by demonstrating that, because in any decision-making situation, the As were different, and the various decisions made did not cohere within any single structure of domination, or favour exclusively any single interest, therefore power had been 'pluralized'. The dispersal of power plus the randomness of decisions kept the pluralist society relatively free of an identifiable power-centre. (Hall 1982: 64)

Hall's objection to this is not that it was 'wrong' in some absolute sense; it is rather that an atomistic conception of power, founded on notions of individual psychology, lent itself to a narrow scientism:

> its primary focus was the individual; it theorized power in terms of the direct influence of A on B's behaviour; it was preoccupied ... with the process of decision making. Its ideal experimental test was the before/after one: its ideal model of influence was that of the campaign... [A] mixture of prophecy and hope, with a brutal, hard-headed, behaviouristic positivism provided a heady theoretical concoction which, for a long time, passed itself off as 'pure science'. (Hall 1982: 59)

Hall's preference, in this context, for the idea of a 'power-centre' cannot be read as an indication that his earlier reservations about Marxism were swept aside; it had an essentially *strategic* motivation. This is clear in his objection to attempts by 'post-Marxist' theorists such as Ernesto Laclau, to weaken the idea of a 'ruling class': 'to lose the ruling-class/ruling-ideas proposition altogether is ... to run the risk of losing altogether the notion of "dominance". But dominance is central if the propositions of pluralism are to be put in question' (1982: 84).

If Hall is less critical of Marxism than he is of pluralism, it is only because it appears to offer *some space* for a freer, more experientially sensitive use of the concept of power. Because propositions in relation to power are framed at a 'macro' level, they are less amenable to claims of scientific verification. Even so, Hall is prepared to accept them only on the evidence of major internal critique and reform. As he puts it himself, 'important modifications to our way of conceiving dominance had to be effected before the idea was rescuable' (Hall 1982: 84–5). All of these modifications are such as to weaken assumptions of a direct relation between concept and referent. In a sense, Hall's wariness of Marxist concepts of power remains quite consistent throughout his intellectual career. He moves to an accommodation with them only on condition that their claims to transparency are significantly weakened.

Hall's first softening towards Marxism follows his encounter with Althusser and the argument that the economic 'base' is determining only in 'the last instance'. From his perspective, this could be seen as much a case of Marxism moving towards cultural studies as of cultural studies moving towards Marxism. The significance of Althusser for Marxist analyses of power was the suggestion that there was no direct relation between the mode of production and other spheres – particularly the spheres in which meanings and identities were formed. This is no more than Hall had been arguing, against Marxism, in 1958. At the same time, Althusser opened the possibility for Hall of a strategic adoption of the 'proposition of dominance'. The proposition becomes acceptable because its implications are *limited*. The kinds of 'superstructural' analysis developed by cultural studies – in effect a continuation of the projects of Hoggart and Williams – could continue fairly much unaffected because of the assurance from Althusser that the superstructures are 'relatively autonomous'.

But the more significant development was Hall's adoption of Antonio Gramsci's concept of hegemony. Despite its deferral of the moment of economic determination, Althusserianism still retained mechanical assumptions and a tendency to cast itself as a 'science'. Gramscianism went much further in weakening the idea that there is any 'foundation' of power. As Hall puts it in his recent attempt to correct historical misconceptions:

> while Gramsci belonged and belongs to the problematic of Marxism, his importance for this moment of cultural studies is precisely the degree to which he radically *displaced* some of the inheritances of Marxism in cultural studies. The radical character of Gramsci's 'displacement' of Marxism has not yet been understood and probably won't ever be reckoned with, now that we are entering the era of post-Marxism. (Hall 1992: 281)

Hall may be right on the latter point, but it is worth making a suggestion here. What has rarely been recognized about Gramscianism is its implication, no less, that the most central political processes cannot be understood in terms of power. The formation of hegemonic blocks is, for Gramsci, a *precondition* for domination. As such, the process of formation cannot be explained in *terms* of domination. The crucial moments in which political alliances are negotiated are moments in which some other dynamic must be operating. If this were not the case, no distinction could be made between domination and hegemony, 'coercion' and 'consent' (cf. Carey 1997b: 277). Power is implicitly demoted by Gramsci to the status of a second order concept, describing an effect of other processes rather than a fundamental principle.

It might seem to stretch credulity, given the importance of Gramsci to British cultural studies, that this could be so and yet not have been clearly recognized. If we return to the historical context, however, there are good reasons why the 'radical' implications of Gramsci could never be fully spelled out. The first is the strategic importance, already noted, of the 'proposition of dominance' in countering the positivist tendencies of political science and sociology. In order for Hall to present a critical alternative to 'pluralism', he had to *appear* to engage in similar positive references to power. For purely pragmatic reasons, a collapse of 'hegemony' into 'domination' is an option which needed to be kept open. Probably more important, though, was the sensitivity, during the 1970s, of professions of belief or disbelief in domination. Not to affirm the reality of domination was to place oneself out of sympathy, as Williams might have put it, with an emergent 'structure of feeling'. As we have seen, this is a problem which Williams himself struggled with. I will argue in Chapter 8 that it became more acute with the development of feminism. Hall clearly decided, at some point, to make a less hedged affirmation than Williams of the new political forms that burst onto the scene in the late 1960s and early 1970s. This precluded an open scepticism about power.

But the evidence is there that Hall has consistently taken the next strongest option, *tempering* the concept of power in such a way as to prevent it ever from being used with certainty. It is not too much to suggest that the significance of 'Birmingham' cultural studies in relation to the concept is almost the opposite of that which is widely assumed. It has not been an insistence on the 'fundamental realities' of power, but a resistance to suggestions by others that such realities exist. The problems, for Hall, with pluralism and Marxism are, despite their differences, very similar: too confident a belief that the concept of power corresponds, in a simple way, to some universal or absolute reality. His determination to reject such certainty has never significantly wavered. Hall has sometimes been found theoretically inconsistent (McGuigan 1992; Chen 1996a). He has particularly disappointed his Marxist comrades of the 1970s for appearing to abandon earlier commitments. But to criticize him on these grounds is perhaps to miss the whole 'point' of his work: to maintain a space for a use of the concept which is responsive to historical experiences, yet proofed against familiar tendencies to intellectual fundamentalism. In many ways, this is still the space, adapted to a different context, which he had admired in *Picture Post* – one in which the 'free movement of art' can be combined with the directness of social *rapportage*.

–7–

A Continuing Tension
The Unresolved Politics of Cultural Studies

The account of the history of Birmingham in the last chapter may appear to have surprisingly little to say about the complex series of developments in theories of power at the CCCS. But to deal with the latter in greater detail would be to risk subverting my main argument: that these developments have been less significant *in themselves* than they are often taken to be. What has been important about them is not their positive claims so much as the kinds of openings they have offered through their neutralization of *other* claims – a neutralization, on the one hand, of positivist sociology and, on the other, of Marxist grand theorizing. In this chapter, therefore, I will attempt to indicate what these openings have allowed. I will use as examples Paul Willis's *Learning to Labour* and Dick Hebdige's *Subculture: the Meaning of Style*.

These two texts have often been taken as representative of 'classical Birmingham', particularly in critical assessments that have distanced themselves from the latter. Perhaps the most influential of these has been Angela McRobbie's 'Settling Accounts with Subcultures', one of the most widely cited feminist critiques of the work of the 1970s. For McRobbie, *Learning to Labour* and *Subculture* were exemplary of the exclusion of women in the work of the CCCS. The relative lack of interest of Willis and Hebdige in home and family is presented as typical of a New Left tendency to see them only as a temptation provided by Capital to divert workers and militants away from the 'real business of revolution' (McRobbie 1980: 40).

As I suggested in the last chapter, criticisms of this kind have played a major role in inflating the historical significance of Marxism in cultural studies. McRobbie's criticisms start from the assumption of an 'original' Marxist cultural studies. The subculture writing is reduced to an account of 'oppression' and a political programme for overturning it. It is clear from the criticisms themselves that 'oppression' is also understood in its most extended sense. The argument that women have been excluded works only on the assumption that Willis and Hebdige were concerned not with *specific* oppressions but with oppression *as such*. It is this assumption which generates an expectation that every 'form' of oppression must be equally represented.

McRobbie's feminism is 'post-Marxist' in the sense that gender differences are emphasized over those of class. 'In our daily lives', she suggests:

feminists wage a similar semiotic warfare [to male subcultures]. Knitting in pubs, breast-feeding in Harrods, the refusal to respond to expressions of street sexism, the way we wear our clothes – all the signs and meanings embodied in the way we handle our public visibility play a part in the culture which, like the various youth cultures, bears the imprint of our collective, historical creativity. (McRobbie 1980: 49)

Yet her position, paradoxically, may be more systematically Marxist than those she sets out to criticize. The idea of a semiotic warfare waged by women borrows directly from Marxist models of class analysis developed in the work on youth subcultures. At the same time, the borrowing overlooks aspects of the subculture writing that are not reducible to Marxism.

My intention here is not to make a particular point against feminism; I will argue in Chapters 8 and 10 that it has shown a similar complexity on questions of power to other forms of cultural studies. It is rather to draw attention to a tightening spiral in which exchanges are increasingly governed by the assumption of a generalized concept of power. As suggested, again, in the last chapter, the most effective way to neutralize this spiral is to question the premise of a foundational moment in which a generalized concept is always already there. To this end, I will argue that neither *Learning to Labour* nor *Subculture* are in a simple sense 'Marxist'. They clearly show strong influences of Marxist approaches to thinking about power, but there are other elements that are not only independent from, but inconsistent with these.

We Want to Stop as We Am

If we were to consider only the second half of *Learning to Labour*, all of McRobbie's criticisms might be justified. Willis's discussion of class relations here is a classic piece of Marxist sociological analysis. Cultural phenomena are conceived as a 'surface' behind which it is possible to discern a 'determinate social structure' (Willis 1980: 121). The latter is not precisely defined but is clearly taken to involve the operation of power in its most expansive sense, involving a 'system of exploitation and oppression for working class people' (1980: 120). In theorizing the relation between surface and depth, Willis proposes a distinction between 'penetration' and 'limitation': '"Penetration" is meant to designate impulses within a cultural form towards the penetration of the conditions of existence of its members and their positions within the social whole ... "Limitation" is meant to designate those blocks, diversions and ideological effects which confuse and impede the full development and expression of these impulses' (1980: 119). The distinction provides a framework for interpreting the language, behaviour and other symbolic forms of Willis's object of study: 'the lads', a self-defined group of disaffected boys at a school in an industrial conurbation in the Midlands of England. Willis attributes the counter-culture of 'the lads' with a 'partial penetration' of the system. They correctly perceive that the knowledge offered to them by the school assumes middle-class norms of behaviour and has little relevance to working-class lives. A full understanding of their subordinate position within a class society is limited, however, by a number of 'mystifications'. These are revealed particularly in their sexism and racism, which offer a false sense of superiority over others. It is here that Willis locates the mechanism for the reproduction of labour power within capitalism.

The analysis clearly suggests an indulgence towards masculinist forms of English working-class culture. Whatever their imperfections, 'the lads' are cast in heroic mode as proto-revolutionary subjects. Sexism and racism are not defined as problems in themselves, but only as 'diversions' from a political logic organized around class. At the same time, the counter-culture of 'the lads' is elevated to a level of general significance; they are attributed with the status of historical agents through which 'exploitation and oppression' are revealed and, one anticipates, ultimately overthrown.

But to concentrate only on these suggestions is to ignore the other half of the book: a detailed 'ethnography' of the school and of the fraught relation between teachers and 'problem kids'. Willis not only places this half first, but clearly expects some readers to go no further. 'A general aim of the book', he says, 'is to make its arguments accessible to audiences of social scientists, practitioners and general readers... Practitioners [teachers and careers advisers within schools] may be more interested in Part I [the "ethnography"] and the Conclusion; social theorists in Part II [the sociological "analysis"]' (Willis 1980: vii). The book is explicitly designed to work at different levels and employs different modes of address.

As suggested by Willis's advice to his first class of readers (the 'practitioners'), the 'ethnography' is an argument complete in itself, a fully developed attempt to explain 'how working class kids get working class jobs'. It is an argument which is made in very different terms from those described above. As Willis summarizes in introduction:

> I want to suggest that 'failed' working-class kids do not simply take up the falling curve of work where the least successful middle class, or the most successful working-class kids leave off. Instead of assuming a continuous shallowing line of ability in the occupational/class structure we must conceive of radical breaks represented by the interface of cultural forms. (Willis 1980: 1)

This is no less than the characteristic proposition, traceable from Hoggart and Williams to the early Hall, that values and forms of understanding are specific to the contexts in which they develop, having little direct relevance when applied to other contexts. As Willis goes on to expand:

> [T]he working class pattern of 'failure' is quite different and distinct from other patterns... And this class culture is not a neutral pattern, a *mental* category, a set of variables impinging on the school from outside. It comprises experiences, relationships,

and ensembles of systematic types of relationships which not only set particular 'choices' and 'decisions' at particular times, but also structure, really and experientially, how these 'choices' come about and are defined in the first place. (Willis 1980: 1)

Again, this proposition does not demand a recognition of objective social hierarchies, but, on the contrary, an effort of imagination which would allow us to think of relations in other terms. Willis asks us to question whether the lives of 'the lads' are 'obviously' undesirable and rejects the idea that they 'have no choice' but to take their place at the unskilled end of the labour market. As he points out, they appear in many ways to make more active and conscious decisions than the school 'conformists'; their rejection of institutional recognition and approval requires some determination and even courage. Such behaviour can only be understood if it is recognized that the informal counter-culture might actually be experienced as *preferable* to anything offered by the formal domains of school and career. As one of 'the lads' explains simply: 'we want to stop as we am' (Willis 1980: 168).

Monday Morning and the Millennium

Willis's sympathy with these life-choices is flatly at odds with the construction of 'the lads' as proto-revolutionary subjects. Yet it is not atypical of the work of the CCCS. As Tony Bennett has argued, the working-class male youth subcultures that provided the main object of study for the Centre during the mid 1970s were clearly recognized as *defensive* cultural formations. In the key text of the period, the collectively authored *Resistance Through Rituals* (Hall and Jefferson 1976), they 'are construed as essentially defensive reactions to a situation in which the accommodation between the working-class and ruling-class cultures which had characterized the 1930s and 1940s was profoundly disturbed by the intrusive invasion of the postwar ideologies of consumerism, affluence and growth into the traditional forms of working-class culture' (Bennett 1998: 172). The questions this raises are more complex than Bennett himself realizes. The conclusion he draws is that subcultural 'resistances' could never provide a focus for progressive politics: 'Such resistances may be ... factors which a politics should take into account, but they do not amount to a politics or provide an adequate basis for the development of one' (1998: 173). The argument is a useful corrective to any view that the Birmingham subculture theorists were, in a simple sense, Marxist revolutionaries, but it fails to explain why the subculture writing was widely *perceived* as having political implications.

Like McRobbie, Bennett pays attention too exclusively to positive claims about power, missing a different sense in which intellectual work may be 'political'. This is the sense which Hall had recognized in Orwell's idea of an 'English revolution', where radicalism consists precisely in *denying* a structural foundation for social antagonism, in refusing to construe social relations as necessarily competitive. In

Learning to Labour, as in *Resistance Through Rituals*, it is a sense that is eclipsed at a formal level by general theories of power, yet without it whole passages of argument can only appear confused or obscure. This is particularly the case, in fact, where Willis comes to draw out the implications of his research at what he calls the 'practical/political level' (Willis 1980: 185).

In a final chapter, titled 'Monday morning and the millennium', his address returns to the teachers and careers advisers, taking up the question of how they might better respond to the problems posed in the classroom by 'difficult' working-class kids. Some influence remains here from the sociological analysis: 'We cannot now naively return to discrete cultural forms and independent cultural initiatives to yield a full and effective programme' (Willis 1980: 186). But the main thrust of Willis's argument runs entirely the other way. In an impassioned moment of reversal, he points out that practitioners cannot avoid the problem of 'Monday morning':

> If we have nothing to say about what to do on Monday morning everything is yielded to a purist structuralist immobilising reductionist tautology: nothing can be done until the basic structures of society are changed but the structures prevent us making any changes... To contract out of the messy business of day to day problems is to deny the active, contested nature of social and cultural reproduction: to condemn real people to the status of passive zombies, and actually cancel the future by default. To refuse the challenge of the day to day – because of the dead hand of structural constraint – is to deny the continuance of life and society themselves. (Willis 1980: 186)

Political action is actually *opposed* here to the analysis of social relations of power. The latter comes to signify abstraction and removal, a 'contracting out' of day-to-day problems and the 'active, contested nature of social and cultural reproduction'.

Willis's 'practical/political' suggestions return, in short, to the terms of the 'ethnography'. They centre on proposals for a kind of cultural diplomacy, a set of protocols for engagement between teachers and 'problem kids' that might allow relations to develop more constructively. The key element of this diplomacy is an open recognition of cultural difference and the granting of certain rights to those disaffected with the school system to relate to it on their own terms. Some of the specific recommendations for teachers which flow from this are:

* be sensitive to the double coding of class and institutional meanings so that teaching responses and communications are not mistaken as insults to *social* class and identity
* ...Try to limit the scope of the inevitable vicious circle which develops in post-differentiated [antagonistic] relationships.
* use where possible small classes ... and techniques of group discussion and collective work. Such techniques ... move towards some kind of organizational unit which might be homologous to the collective processes and forms which are to be explored.
* take cultural forms, basic transitions, social attitudes sometimes as the basic texts for class work. (Willis 1980: 190–1)

None of these suggestions are revolutionary in the sense of proposing a comprehensive programme of social transformation. They do not even seek to question
established authority: where antagonism is openly expressed, Willis recommends 'a
tactical withdrawal from confrontation but which avoids any simplistic expression
of sympathy and maintains a degree of institutional authority' (1980: 190). Such
authority is necessary, he argues, 'in order to maintain any initiative at all in the
particular direction of class[room] activity' (1980: 191).

Yet the argument is far from a defence of an authoritarian *status quo*. The effect
of the 'ethnographic' argument is to remove the school system and working-class life
from the familiar interpretative grid of social hierarchy, creating a corner from which
they might begin to relate to each other in different terms. As Willis concludes:

> The recognition of commonality in cultural forms and the understanding of their own
> processes is already to have strengthened an internal weakness, to have begun to unravel
> the power of the formal [the school system] over the informal [working-class life] and to
> have started a kind of self-transformation. This may not be the Millennium but it could
> be Monday morning. Monday morning need not imply an endless succession of the *same*
> Monday mornings. (Willis 1980: 192)

What is 'political' in this position – perhaps even 'radical' – is not so much what it
actively seeks, as what it is prepared to *allow*. The 'self-transformation' envisaged
by Willis might be compared to a process of de-colonization, although its outcome
is not even fixed by an ideal of 'autonomy' set up in advance. While the teacher has
access to institutional and governmental resources which might determine certain
directions, they are enjoined to limit the way these resources are deployed, merely
playing 'a sceptical, unglamorous real eye over industrial, economic and class
cultural processes' (1980: 190). Opportunities are kept open but it is left to others to
decide what they want to do or be.

The Meaning of Style

Hebdige's *Subculture* is a somewhat different text in that it seeks greater consistency
between the 'cultural' and 'sociological'. Although published only three years later
than *Learning to Labour*, it shows signs of quite significant shifts in the intellectual
space of the CCCS. Even in the earlier text, there is a sense that this space is under
pressure. Willis's 'ethnographic' argument is still possible within the formal structure
of a 'Marxist' analysis because of the Althusserian alibi that the cultural level is
'relatively autonomous', but there are a number of points at which this alibi appears
in danger of giving way. It is only because the 'cultural' and the 'sociological'
analyses are kept so distinct that the problems do not become more acute than
they are. Once 'culture' is conceived as a particular sphere within a wider social

totality, questions inevitably arise about its linkages with other spheres. If the social reality is a 'system of exploitation and oppression for working class people', it is implausible that the cultural level could be insulated from it to the extent which Willis's 'practical/political' suggestions require. The understanding of differences as specifically 'cultural' is eroded in a way that the relative autonomy clause is not sufficient to prevent.

Much of the theoretical development at the CCCS during the mid to late 1970s can be understood as an attempt to address this problem. In a 1977 essay, 'Culture, the Media and the "Ideological Effect"', Hall admits that the concept of culture continued to have an 'ambiguous and unspecified relation' to the models of power and ideology which were being entertained at the time: 'There seems to be a theoretical discontinuity between the problematic in which the term "culture" has been developed and the terms of classical Marxist theory' (Hall 1977a: 321). Echoing earlier comments by Williams (1958: 282) on the English Marxism of the 1930s, he points out that culture is made to fit into Marxist models in two different ways: it is sometimes conceived as a general pattern of social organization (in Williams's terms, a 'whole way of life'), at other times as a distinct level of reflection *upon* such patterns (the level associated with language and consciousness) (Hall 1977a: 322). The latter sense assimilates culture to ideology, requiring everything to be referenced to 'real relations' at the social level. In so doing, it is quite incompatible with a specifically 'cultural' politics of the kind suggested by Willis. But so long as the idea of 'real relations' remains, it cannot easily be avoided.

Hall experiments with a number of solutions to the problem.[6] The most significant, however, is an attempt to conceptualize culture as, itself, a sphere of 'real relations'. Theoretical support for this is found, particularly, in V. N. Volosinov's (1986) idea of the 'materiality of the sign' which licenses a transposition of Marxist concepts of 'production', 'labour' and 'struggle' to the cultural domain. As Hall outlines the significance of the idea in 'The rediscovery of "ideology"':

> Meaning, once it is problematized, must be the result, not of a functional reproduction of the world in language, but of a social struggle – a struggle for mastery in discourse – over which kind of social accenting is to prevail and to win credibility. This reintroduced the notion of 'differently oriented social interests' and a concept of the sign as 'an arena of struggle' into the consideration of language and of signifying 'work'. (Hall 1982: 77–8)

The argument removes the need for cultural studies to adopt the kind of defensive posture taken by Willis in relation to sociology. The space for considering 'cultural' relations in their own terms is cleared of the threat that it may be closed down in the light of other approaches more committed to naming the 'real'.

---

6. Another, which I will not discuss here, is the suggestion that culture might be thought of as the 'form' of social existence while the social might be though of as the 'content' (Hall 1977a: 318).

It has to be admitted that the implications of this move are paradoxical. In a certain sense, the concept of culture is retained only at the cost of being 'sociologized'. All the concepts and models which had previously been defined as sociological – above all, a generalized concept of power – are imported into 'cultural' analysis. To transform Thompson's charge against Williams – that in fighting the bourgeoisie he became bourgeois (Thompson 1961: 28) – one might suggest of Hall that in fighting sociology he became a sociologist. But to draw this conclusion would be to fail to recognize the complexity of 'Hallism'. Hall's mediations and compromises can certainly be read as an absorption of the concept of culture within sociological models, but they can also be read the other way: as a site where sociological concepts are 'culturalized'. The abstraction of the concept of power from Marxist analyses of economic relations does not leave it unaltered. The dissociation of the concept from its original points of reference leaves is relatively 'theatricalized', opened to metaphorical or figurative interpretations which weaken the suggestion of a simple referential meaning.

This is the intellectual space of *Subculture*. Hebdige opens not in theoretical but in *literary* mode, quoting extracts from Jean Genet's *The Thief's Journal*. In Genet's conflict with police and prison wardens, trivial details assume a symbolic significance. As banal an object as a tube of vaseline takes on a highly charged meaning as evidence of his homosexuality and a counter in his struggle. The example is worked into a general social vision: 'I was astounded by so rigorous an edifice whose details were united against me. Nothing in the world is irrelevant: the stars on a general's sleeve, the stock-market quotations, the olive harvest, the style of the judiciary, the wheat exchange, the flower-beds... Nothing. This order ... had a meaning – my exile' (Genet quoted in Hebdige 1979: 18). The passage is clearly suggestive of a generalized concept of power, but even allowing for a certain justifiable paranoia on Genet's part, it is difficult to believe that this is not, in its original articulation, an *imaginative* vision. In the way it is taken up by Hebdige, its status as such is further confirmed. It is quoted in the context of a discussion of the concept of culture in which he also cites T. S. Eliot's famous definition: 'all the characteristic activities and interests of a people. Derby Day, Henley Regatta, Cowes, the 12th of August, a cup final, the dog races, the pin table, the dart-board, Wensleydale cheese, boiled cabbage cut into sections, beetroot in vinegar, 19th Century Gothic churches, the music of Elgar...' (Eliot quoted in Hebdige 1979: 7). The differences between Eliot ('culture') and Genet ('power') should not lead us to overlook their similarities. In both quotations, the incongruity of the listed objects breaks down any sense that a substantive phenomenon is being invoked. Attention is drawn instead to the creative act of association. The literary quality of Hebdige's own writing carries this emphasis over into his descriptions of punk, reggae, Rastafarianism and the complex exchanges between different fractions of British working-class youth.

It is by no means the *only* emphasis. Hebdige shows that he is also able to write in a sober, 'sociological' mode. The first chapter of *Subculture* presents a condensed summary of the state of theoretical debate at the CCCS. Here the concept of power is introduced more explicitly:

> [I]n highly complex societies like ours, which function through a finely graded system of divided labour, the crucial question has to do with which specific ideologies, representing the interests of which specific groups and classes will prevail at any given moment, in any given situation. To deal with this question, we must first consider how power is distributed in our society. That is, we must ask which groups and classes have how much say in defining, ordering and classifying out the social world. (Hebdige 1979: 14)

The passage shows the influence of Hall's theoretical initiatives discussed above and similar passages appear at various points throughout the text. The transitions between them and the more 'literary' mode are eased by the fact that both appear to address questions of power. The contradiction felt by Willis between the perspectives of 'Monday morning' and the 'millennium' are, as a consequence, more smoothly negotiated.

Translating Figures of Power

Nonetheless, a tension remains. It is a subtler tension than in Willis and therefore easier to miss, but is no less important to Hebdige's arguments or to the political implications of his work. The more empirically oriented sections of his text are, again, actively subversive of his formally stated theoretical positions. While the latter suggest an interpretation of culture in terms of power, the former suggest an interpretation of the *concept* of power in terms of culture. What Hebdige develops in his study of British youth subcultures comes very close to a cultural history of the concept in popular music, fashion, street-level class relations and symbolic representations of colonialism. The effect of this is that the concept becomes absorbed within the kind of 'cultural' understanding that can be traced continuously from Hoggart and Williams.

The key word in Hebdige's empirical analysis is 'dialogue'. His central argument is that youth subcultures in post-war Britain have been the site of a concentrated cross-cultural exchange between the white working class and black immigrants. Musical styles, elements of dress, speech and movement were exchanged particularly between punk and Rastafarianism. With its origins in Jamaica, Rastafarianism introduced potent figures of rebellion and utopian possibility which were given widespread currency through the popularization of dub and heavy reggae:

> All these developments were mediated to those members of the white working class who lived in the same areas, worked in the same factories and schools and drank in adjacent pubs. In particular, the trajectory 'back to Africa' within second-generation immigrant

youth culture was closely monitored by those neighbouring white youths interested in forming their own subcultural options. (Hebdige 1979: 43)

The intensity of this experience sensitized British youth culture to other traditions of cross-cultural exchange, particularly the 'subtle dialogue between black and white musical forms' in American imports (Hebdige 1979: 50), a dialogue which had earlier gone largely unnoticed. In increasing the range of available cultural perspectives, it also made possible new kinds of reflexive awareness within the white working class:

> Ironically, those values conventionally associated with white working-class culture (the values of what John Clark calls the 'defensively organized collective') which had been eroded over time, by the relative affluence and by the disruption of the physical environment in which they were rooted, were rediscovered embedded in black West Indian culture... The skinheads, then, resolved or at least reduced the tension between an experienced present (the mixed ghetto) and an imaginary past (the classic white slum) by initiating a dialogue which reconstituted each in terms of the other. (Hebdige 1979: 57)

The result was an explosion of cultural possibilities as various class and ethnic fragments interpreted their own positions in each other's terms: 'Just as the mod and skinhead styles had obliquely reproduced the "cool" look and feel of the West Indian rude boys and were systematically placed in the same ideal milieux (the Big City, the violent slums), so the punk aesthetic can be read in part as a white "translation" of black "ethnicity"' (Hebdige 1979: 64). It is impossible to ignore the fact that some of the key cultural elements being 'translated' here are figures of power. The black youth cultures that developed in post-war Britain have a similar status, for Hebdige, to Genet's vision of 'an edifice whose details were united against me'. They drew on histories of colonialism not as a direct experience but as a symbolic resource and were articulated in the language of myth and religion. The use of their terms to re-code white class relations was in turn an imaginative achievement. In his final chapter, Hebdige makes this point explicit:

> Much of this book has been based on the assumption that the two positions 'Negro' and 'white working-class youth' can be equated. This equation is no doubt open to dispute; it cannot be tested by the standard sociological procedures ... it is there as an immanence, as a submerged possibility, as an existential option; and one cannot verify an existential option scientifically. (Hebdige 1979: 131)

The subversive implication of this is clear: no formal equivalence can be drawn between concepts of power. The concept which emerges from the history of black experience does not refer to the same 'thing' as the concept which emerges from the experience of class relations in Britain. The relation between them must be understood not in 'scientific' but in 'cultural' terms.

The political implications of this are similar to Willis's recuperation of the 'cultural'. Hebdige removes us from an intellectual space in which the social appears bound by some 'underlying' principle and is therefore available for comprehensive reform. This is a consistent effect, more generally, of the 'subculture' corpus of the CCCS. Its full significance can only be understood in the context of the times. The whole debate about the direction of British society in the 1970s was pervaded by a sense of 'crisis', widely taken to call for major 'action'. On the political right, such action was envisaged as authoritarian, a determined effort to return Britain by force to an imagined former 'greatness'. On the left, it was envisaged as libertarian, a collective struggle to overturn established institutions conceived as uniformly 'bad'. Within the terms of this conflict, those on the right won out as Thatcherism set the political agenda throughout the 1980s. But the debate itself never accounted for all political possibilities. There was always a more moderate left position, not so far from certain forms of conservatism, which questioned the whole idea of a crisis and the political forms, whatever their political colour, which organized themselves around it. If the work of the Birmingham Centre had any 'default' setting, it was always this latter position.

–8–

'An Impossible Politics to Live'
Gender, Race and the Calculus of Oppression

I suggested at the beginning of the last chapter that it was not so much with Marxism that a generalized concept of power was installed as fundamental to cultural studies as with the *critique* of Marxism. The effect of this critique, first developed in the British case by feminists such as Angela McRobbie, has been to project a 'pure' Marxist moment, which never in fact existed. It is at this point, more than in the 'Marxist' writings of Hall, Willis or Hebdige, that an assumption begins to form that cultural studies is, and always has been, concerned with power.

Feminism has not been the only contributor to this development. As I pointed out in Chapter 6, what has been significant about post-Marxist initiatives for the concept of power is not so much the specific alternatives to class analysis – gender, race, sexual preference, geopolitical location, age, etc. – as the 'logic of the ampersand' according to which they have been introduced. Each addition of another axis of power has consolidated the assumption that earlier work in cultural studies was always already reducible to an analysis of power. The more 'dimensions' of power which are identified, the more attention has been given to considering the relations between them and the more a conviction has grown that the single common concern is, to recall Tony Bennett's terms, 'a commitment to examining cultural practices from the point of view of their intrication with, and within, relations of power' (Bennett 1992a: 23). Critical work on race, sexual preference and all the other 'dimensions' have contributed to this in much the same way as the early feminist interventions.

But for historical reasons feminism has become particularly associated with the 'full-blown' concept of power that developed from the late 1970s. This has embroiled it more centrally than most other strands of cultural studies in the 'culture war' debates reviewed in Chapter 1. As Meaghan Morris has remarked, there was an increasing tendency in reflections on left cultural criticism during the 1990s to 'make feminist arts and histories an object of tacit criticism, or even direct attack' (1998: xxii). What is most troubling for Morris is that these criticisms cannot be entirely dismissed as a conservative backlash. They have come, in many cases, from

> Marxist and liberal critical traditions nominally in sympathy with feminism... Some, like David Harvey's influential book *The Condition of Postmodernity*, associate feminist

aesthetics with 'nostalgic' ethnic nationalism and religious fundamentalism; in this view ... feminism can be potentially fascist. Others, like Christopher Norris's *Spinoza & the Origins of Modern Critical Theory*, passionately defend the possibility of truth and Reason against a 'postmodern' *pragmatist* history; for this view ... feminism has not yet happened. (Morris 1998: xxii)

Morris admits that she has even found it difficult, herself, at times to give a sympathetic reading to early second wave feminist texts.

There has been a marked tendency to caricature in recent portraits of 'seventies' feminism. As Morris points out, criticisms of the latter have generally overlooked a deep vein of scepticism in feminist writing. I will argue in Chapter 10, through the example of Morris's own work, that feminism has made one of the strongest contributions to cultural studies in finding ways to *resist* the tendency to dogmatism which flows from a commitment to a generalized concept of power. Precisely because feminist cultural studies has been so closely associated with the concept, it has been acutely sensitized to its dangers and particularly engaged in finding ways to overcome them.

In this chapter, however, I want first to examine why the association has arisen in the first place. Before a sceptical feminism can be properly recognized, it is important to understand the pressures that have operated against it. There is little doubt, in reviewing the history, that the emergence of feminism in cultural studies coincided with a significant inflation of the concept of power. My argument in what follows is that feminism cannot be held *accountable* for this inflation; it has been as much a *response* as a cause. But it would be difficult to deny that the inflation itself has produced tendencies that have been the opposite of sceptical. The fully generalized concept of power has provided a ground for sweeping theoretical claims much less concerned with local contexts and experiences than was characteristic of the early work in cultural studies. It has also allowed a simplification of political understanding, bringing with it less qualified forms of political rhetoric – not quite calling for a revolution 'in which there is shooting and hanging', but certainly for more vigorous confrontation.

My example here, again, will be Birmingham. This allows a continuing cross-reference with previous chapters, but the narrowness of focus is somewhat problematic. The period now under consideration was one in which cultural studies was increasingly defined in an international frame and Birmingham was probably not the most significant site for the development of feminist initiatives – or those which followed, around race and other axes of power. I will attempt to correct for this in following chapters by pulling back to consider other sites and to reflect on the present international constitution of the field.

As the Thief in the Night

In a 1990s' account by Stuart Hall, the emergence of feminism at Birmingham was 'ruptural':

> As the thief in the night, it broke in; interrupted, made an unseemly noise, seized the time, crapped on the table of cultural studies. The title of the volume in which the dawn-raid was first accomplished – *Women Take Issue* – is instructive: for they 'took issue' in both senses – took over that year's book and initiated a quarrel. (Hall 1992: 282)

In a response to Hall's description, as one of those who, herself, 'took issue', Charlotte Brunsdon admits to having been at first shocked by its implication:

> When I first read this account, I immediately wanted to unread it. To deny it, to skip over it, to not know – to not acknowledge the aggression therein. Not so much to deny that feminists at CCCS in the 1970s had made a strong challenge to cultural studies as it was constituted then and there, but to deny that it had happened the way here described. (Brunsdon 1996: 280)

But Brunsdon recognizes that there was, in this immediate reaction, something of a desire 'to have my feminist cake and eat it – to have drafted discussion documents, contributed to presentations and made arguments that attacked "men at the centre", but not to have contributed to feelings of betrayal and rejection' (1996: 280).

Morris suggests that much of recent unease about feminism might be related to its particular emphasis on *experience*. In the case of Birmingham, however, it would be difficult to argue that this emphasis was any greater than what had gone before. One of the examples given by Hall of how the debate around feminism was actually played out is a conflict between himself and women at the Centre over whether Raymond Williams should give way on the reading list for the MA programme to Julia Kristeva (Hall 1996d: 500). However such a substitution might be viewed, and however appropriate it may have been at the time, it cannot easily be represented as introducing an attention to experience where there had previously been none. Williams, if anyone, was the writer who had established an intellectual credibility for the concept of experience. Yet it was also Williams whom feminists at Birmingham sought to displace.

It is not even true to say that feminism introduced an attention to *women's* experience. According to Hall, the first collective project of the CCCS was concerned with women's magazines, although the manuscript which resulted was somehow lost: 'We took on fiction in women's magazines. We spent ages on a story called "Cure for Marriage", and all those papers, which were supposed to be written up into a book, then disappeared; which means that moment from the history of cultural studies is lost. That was the Centre's "pre-feminist" moment' (Hall 1996d: 499). In the light of my argument in Chapter 4, this early 'pre-feminist' interest in questions of gender is not surprising. As Hall points out, the interest of cultural studies in class was, initially, 'in Hoggart's and Williams's sense, not in the classic marxist sense' (1996d: 498–9). Classes were not conceived in terms of structural principles, but as cultural complexes embracing a 'whole way of life'. A 'class perspective' did not, therefore, subordinate gender to the level of secondary considerations. As Hoggart argued in *The Uses of Literacy*, there was if anything a tendency for working-class intellectuals to *over*emphasize the domestic, 'feminine' aspects of working-class life because of their alienation from the public, workplace culture which had traditionally defined working-class masculinity (Hoggart 1957: 295). It is not an accident that the figure he himself chose in order to problematize the relation between intellectual culture and working-class life was the kitchen table, strewn with piles of ironing and cups of tea.

The respect in which feminism *did* differ from what had preceded it was in its particular emphasis on questions of power – an emphasis clearly underlined by the subtitle of *Women Take Issue*, 'Aspects of women's subordination'. As Hall puts it, cultural studies had previously been 'sensitive to the gender question ... but not very sensitive to feminist politics' (Hall 1996d: 499). What distinguished 'feminist politics' was, above all, 'the radical expansion of the concept of power, which had hitherto been very much developed within the framework of the notion of the public, the public domain' (Hall 1992: 282). This development had implications well beyond considerations of gender itself: after feminism 'we could not use the term power – so key to the earlier problematic of hegemony – in the same way' (1992: 282). It is clear that the expansion of the concept of power was also the key factor in a series of shifts which Hall identifies as accompanying it: 'the opening of the question of the personal as political, and its consequences for changing the object of cultural studies'; 'the centrality of questions of gender and sexuality to the understanding of power itself'; 'the opening of many of the questions we thought we had abolished around the dangerous area of the subjective and the subject, which lodged these questions at the centre of cultural studies as a theoretical practice'; and '"the reopening" of the closed frontier between social theory and the theory of the unconscious – psychoanalysis' (1992: 282).

A certain reading of the history at Birmingham might, in fact, draw the opposite conclusion from those suggested by Morris about the relation between feminism and the category of experience. Feminist criticisms of existing approaches within cultural studies coincided with the effective abandonment of the detailed attention to 'lived experience' that had characterized work on subcultures and working-class youth. The new theoretical problems associated with feminism – particularly the 'dangerous area of the subjective' and the 'theory of the unconscious' – initiated a turn to much more theoretical concerns. Feminism also increased levels of anxiety about fundamental premises, intensifying the need for theoretical excursions. This is clear, for example, in a defence by Hall in 1980 of the increasingly abstract tone of debates in cultural studies:

> If this has appeared, at times, a form of theoretical self-indulgence, we would simply point to the elegant studies and sophisticated theorizing in our own areas of work which have elaborated their protocols, done their field work, questioned their respondents, read their documents, produced their accounts and results – and all on the unexamined premise that the world, for all practical purposes, is 'masculine'. (Hall 1980: 42)

Nor did feminist work at Birmingham achieve notable success in developing new ways of connecting with experience. It is significant that in Brunsdon's retrospective assessment of *Women Take Issue*, the sections which came closest were those which had *not* made the shift from the 'gender question' to 'feminist politics', from an older 'culturalist' emphasis to an emphasis on questions of power: 'We remained too caught up in the dialogue with the particular form of marxism dominant in CCCS at the time – in self-justification. The most successful chapters seem those which anticipate future reports of empirical investigation, rather than the attempts to theorize women's subordination at a general level' (Brunsdon 1996: 283).

It is arguable, finally, that the extension of the concept of power associated with feminism was related to an increasingly 'mythic' sense of history. Hall's blanket description of the diverse range of theories, protocols and empirical investigations of pre-feminist cultural studies as 'masculine' is typical of a tendency at the time towards a sweeping characterization of positions – a tendency which became more pronounced with the extension of similar arguments to questions of 'race'. The logic of the argument is revealed, for example, in an attack on 'white feminism' by Hazel Carby only two years after *Women Take Issue* in *The Empire Strikes Back*: 'Feminist theory in Britain is almost totally Eurocentric and, when it is not ignoring the experience of black women "at home", it is trundling "Third World women" onto the stage only to perform as victims of "barbarous", "primitive" practices in "barbarous", "primitive" societies' (Carby 1982: 222). The significance of the accusatory tone which appears in much feminist and post-feminist cultural studies is not only that it clearly favours an abrupt rejection of the past (Carby admires 'explosions' in debates in the United States, scorning the reaction in Britain as 'more akin to lighting a damp squib' (1982: 221)). It is also that it obscures histories of sceptical alternatives. In the terms I established in Chapter 7, only the 'millennial' aspirations of earlier positions are brought into focus and criticized while the attention to 'Monday morning' disappears from view.

Two Strong Handsome Men

But it would also be a mistake to invert Morris's suggestions, charging feminism with terminating an uncomplicated, sceptical vision of cultural studies and setting the field on a course towards totalizing criticism and defensive system-building. This would be to abstract it too much from the context in which it took form. Hall's metaphor of a 'thief in the night' may be useful in capturing a sense of disruption and trauma – the assault on positions and ideas that had previously been valued – but it is also misleading in characterizing feminism as an autonomous development. The 'radical extension of the concept of power', which Hall attributes to feminism was, in fact, extensively prefigured in his own work of the mid 1970s. It is true that this work was framed by Marxism, but it was a Marxism modified precisely *not* to limit the understanding of politics to the classical public domain. If, following Volosinov, signification is intrinsically defined by 'struggle', then power must be conceived as coextensive with meaning. The implications may not all have been drawn explicitly, but the 'public'/'private' distinction had already effectively been breached.

The clearest confirmation of this is that gender had begun to be politicized at the CCCS before the development of feminism. *Women Take Issue* was not the first themed issue on women of *Working Papers in Cultural Studies*. While it is rarely mentioned in histories of feminism at the Centre, the 1974 issue was titled 'Women in Sport'. The two papers written to the theme, by Charles Critcher and Paul Willis, were transcriptions of presentations to a symposium organized by the Department of Physical Education at Birmingham University in 1973, more than a year before the formation of the Women's Studies Group within the CCCS. Critcher's paper makes what he calls a 'controversial' suggestion: 'It is that by and large female sport is not taken too seriously in our society. This is a general impression gained from various sources, especially masculine ones. It seems to be crystallized in the press treatment of women in sport' (Critcher 1974: 15). In presenting the argument, Critcher admits: 'It is incidentally ironic that I should be doing this analysis. It is a product of the situation I'm describing that a man should be giving this talk at all: lecturing is a very masculine activity' (1974: 7). He justifies the exercise, however, by claiming to examine an objective structuring principle which exists independently of individual positions and intentions:

> [I]f we're honest with ourselves, we know that we habitually designate certain types of activity as more appropriate for one sex or the other ... I've culled a list of ... habitual expectations from what is a very good college text on the subject of sex roles. The male characteristics come out as: clever, ruthless, logical, competitive, rational, handsome, strong, tall, powerful, aggressive, loyal to friends, making swift decisions, good with money, mechanically minded. Female characteristics come out as: emotional, kind, intuitive, pretty, small, soft, quiet, weak, tender, gentle, good with children, given to malicious gossip, imaginative but impractical, dithering, feather-brained, no head for business and silly about money. (Critcher 1974: 7)

The paper is followed by a discussion – also transcribed – which provides interesting insights into the context of formation of feminism at Birmingham. A number of women express annoyance at what they see as patronizing assumptions. A response by a sportswoman in the audience, Diana Wilkinson, is illustrative:

> Being a rather dithery, feather-brained female I find it rather difficult to follow such an academic talk by such a strong, handsome man good with money, but I would at least like to begin really with a denial of the characteristics you give in the first part when you say you claim these for all sports, because I feel quite strongly that it depends on the sport and on what level. (Wilkinson quoted in Critcher 1974: 14)

The objection is endorsed by another contributor to the discussion, Susan Hilliam: 'Charles Critcher said that female sport is not taken seriously. I'd like to ask by whom? Is it by the public at large? Is it by the participants?' (1974: 15)

Wilkinson and Hilliam were not members of the CCCS, and were not significantly involved in the development of feminism, but the form of the encounter complicates a simple understanding of feminism as arising from a desire by women to extend the concept of power to questions of gender. Many of the early moves to suggest such an extension appear to have been made by men. In addition to Critcher and Willis, Hall and others also made efforts to sponsor the development of feminist arguments (Hall 1996d: 499). When women at the Centre themselves 'took issue', it was not over a failure by men to include gender within considerations of power; in some cases, it was almost the reverse – over the ease and apparent complacency with which such an extension was *admitted*. In a presentation on behalf of the Women's Studies Group at the time, Brunsdon identified what she called a 'peculiarly oppressive form of sexism' in which 'people individually agree that "women are oppressed", but where there is no collective effort to do anything about it, or even to examine how it operates in practice' (Brunsdon 1996: 283). The criticism is typical of feminist arguments at the CCCS: it was the *response* to the extension of the concept of power which was in question, not the extension itself.

An Impossible Politics...

There are obvious reasons why the prehistory of feminism at Birmingham may have been relatively ignored. Since *Women Take Issue*, there has been a general embarrassment about the early attempts by men at the Centre to relate gender and power. Hall, for his part, describes his own efforts in the area as 'patriarchal' and endorses the move by women to claim feminism as their own: 'Of course, they had to do it. They were absolutely right to do it. They had to shut me up; that was what the feminist political agenda was all about' (Hall 1996d: 499–500). Hall's sense of the inappropriateness of speaking for or on behalf of supposedly subordinated others is consistent not only with the objections to Critcher by Wilkinson and Hilliam, but also with Hoggart's suspicions in *The Uses of Literacy* of 'the middle class Marxist':

'Usually, he succeeds in part-pitying and part-patronizing working-class people beyond any semblance of reality' (Hoggart 1957: 16). But whereas the response of Hoggart, Wilkinson and Hilliam was to resist the implication of generalized concepts of power, the solution within post-feminist cultural studies has been more often to insist that 'domination' and 'oppression' be named and criticized only by those who are themselves identified as dominated or oppressed. The interest in questions of subjectivity has been accompanied by a greatly increased sensitivity to the propriety of 'speaking positions'.

This sensitivity has established important ethical principles for the conduct of highly politicized debates. But it has also obscured much of the complexity of the development of feminism, making it particularly resistant to historical understanding. The problem is significant not only for the ability of cultural studies to reflect upon its approach to questions of gender; it is also significant for the field more generally. The emergence of feminism coincided with early signs of a dissatisfaction and loss of confidence in the project of cultural studies which has since become more widespread. It is telling that it was the point at which Hall found himself unable to continue at Birmingham. By his own admission:

> the question of feminism was very difficult to take ... [I]f I had been opposed to feminism, that would have been a different thing, but I was for it. So, being targeted as 'the enemy', as the senior patriarchal figure, placed me in an impossibly contradictory position ... I couldn't live part of the time being their teacher, and being their father, being hated for being their father, and being set up as if I was an anti-feminist man. It was an impossible politics to live. (Hall 1996d: 500)

There is some suggestion in this that the problem related specifically to Hall's own position, but there are indications that it was much more general. The contradictions he faced equally affected women at the Centre – they were, in many ways, the reason *why* they 'took issue'. On the one hand, they were encouraged to participate in a collective intellectual enterprise – an enterprise which assumed an equality of status; on the other hand, they were casually referred to as an 'oppressed group'. As this tension developed, it became increasingly unsustainable.

The problem in allowing feminism to appear as an autonomous development is that it contains, rather than substantially addressing, some fundamental problems which emerged concurrently with the extension of the concept of power. The humility of Hall's abdication – 'they needed to shut me up' – is, in a certain sense, admirable, but it also places too much of the responsibility for the complex of changes which occurred around feminism with feminism itself. In the case of the CCCS at least, it is not quite true that the feminist agenda was to 'shut men up'. There is an intense ambivalence in feminist texts of the time about the withdrawal of men from an engagement with what became identified as 'women's issues'. The editorial introduction to *Women Take Issue* expresses strong reservations about the model of autonomy – or as it was described, of 'the "woman question" claimed by, and relegated to, the women' (CCCS 1978: 10). The model was not so much enthusiastically embraced as accepted as a least worst option: 'Sporadic attempts to argue against the "hiving off" of the woman question ... were viewed as double-binding other CCCS members – either we had something to say and we should say it, or else we didn't, and so we should stop making everyone feel guilty' (CCCS 1978: 10). It is significant that despite the obvious difficulty of relations between men and women at the Centre, two of the eleven authors of *Women Take Issue* – Steve Burniston and Frank Mort – were men.

The evidence suggests that no one at the CCCS was particularly satisfied with the compromises developed in response to the politicization of gender and other forms of identity. For Hall, the tendency towards fragmentation coincided with a drift, on his own part at least, towards academicism in the bad sense: 'I thought to myself, "You're becoming a typical disenchanted academic, you must get out"' (Hall 1996d: 500). This is particularly significant given that the intellectual generosity of the Centre had been one of its greatest strengths. It has remained, for Hall, one of the achievements he most wants to remember: 'We tried to do something innovative ... at Birmingham, institutionally. I don't think anybody has come close to the Centre, in terms of producing knowledge through collective working practices' (Hall 1996c: 398). For women at the Centre, the formation of specific 'women's studies' groups was only a marginal improvement on the difficulties of participating in wider forums: 'we assumed an illusory shared feminist position, which ... meant the atmosphere was rather tense, although still easier for women to work in than other CCCS groups' (CCCS 1978: 14). And similar problems arose in the collective address to questions of 'race'. As Paul Gilroy laments in the preface to *The Empire Strikes Back*, 'it has been sad to watch the numbers of our group dwindle as we put our ideas on to paper and real conflicts began to emerge' (CCCS 1982: 8).

Perhaps the most significant effect of the model of autonomy is that it requires the extension of the concept of power to be represented according to a simple narrative of enlightenment. Feminism, black cultural studies, and later postcolonial criticism, are made to appear as having 'revealed' or 'brought to light' timeless phenomena which had previously been invisible or concealed. While this narrative was clearly important in providing fresh inspiration to cultural studies from the late 1970s through the 1980s, it has also contributed to a radical de-historicization of the concept of power. Particularly in the more theoretical discourses which developed or consolidated in the field during the 1980s, the concept is presumed to refer transparently to a universal or quasi-universal phenomenon, specified at most with reference to 'patriarchy', 'modernity' or the historical mission of 'the West'. This de-historicization makes it impossible to consider problems in relation to the specific circumstances in which they arose. While increasingly elaborate theories of power have emerged, little attention has been paid to the way the concept has been formed by the social, political and cultural contexts of the 1970s.

Moments of Intense Subjectivity

There is an interesting suggestion in the editorial introduction to *Women Take Issue* of alternative possibilities. One of a number of 'paths not taken' by the Women's Studies Group was a historical analysis of the politicization of gender during the 1960s and early 1970s. It was a path which was considered precisely in response to limitations perceived in more abstract theoretical approaches – specifically, the theorization of patriarchy in Juliet Mitchell's influential *Psychoanalysis and Feminism* (1974), which imposed a strict analytic distinction between questions of gender and questions of class: 'It was ... because of that separation within theory that we next tried to understand the contradictions of femininity as "lived" (at the same time holding to class specificity) through a study of the particular historical conjuncture which saw the emergence of the Women's Liberation Movement' (CCCS 1978: 13). That the project collapsed may be an indication not so much that it was weak or ill-conceived as of the *difficulty* at the time of sceptical, historical modes of enquiry. The reasons for its abandonment were, themselves, contentious, but they were clearly related to the problems discussed above. Relations within the Group became fraught by the antinomies of 'solidarity' and 'individualism' and energies were increasingly absorbed in defining external relations with other work within the CCCS (CCCS 1978: 14).

There are, however, other texts from the time that offer at least some insight into the historical formation of the generalized concept of power associated with feminism. Two which were widely referred to in work of the CCCS are Juliet Mitchell's earlier book *Women's Estate* (1971) and Sheila Rowbotham's *Women's Consciousness, Man's World* (1973), both first hand accounts of the emergence of the women's movement. As Brunsdon suggests, feminism might be seen as 'one of the bridgeheads into CCCS of the new social movements of the late 1960s and the 1970s, of the "new" identities and identity politics' (Brunsdon 1996: 282). I want, in what follows, to take this somewhat further and suggest that feminism might also be seen as one of the bridgeheads into cultural studies of a new understanding of power. It would be too strong to suggest that Mitchell and Rowbotham were fully reflexive on the formation of the concept of power at the time, although at points they come very close. There is, in both their texts, an often contradictory mixture of contextual analysis and appeals to universal principles. But the immediacy of their writing in relation to the political and cultural developments which inspired the women's movement is more revealing of historical specificities than more recent material, even if (or perhaps rather *because*) the latter is more theoretically elaborated.

It is illuminating to compare Mitchell and Rowbotham with the early work of Hoggart and Williams. The similarities between them are, in many ways, striking. Like Hoggart and Williams, Mitchell and Rowbotham are concerned with an expanding interface between the institutions of government, education and the media and groups (in this case women) who had not previously been represented within them. Like Hoggart and Williams, their thinking on the problems of this interface developed in the context of an interest in education. Rowbotham had taught in technical and further education colleges and for the Worker's Education Association, while Mitchell had taught English literature at Leeds and Reading Universities. Rowbotham's analysis of the problems facing women within an expanding education system could almost have been written as an extension to Hoggart's analysis, sixteen years earlier, of the problems of the 'scholarship boy':

> The clash between home values and university or college is extreme for all students from families where higher education is unfamiliar. This is especially true for female students. Girls who go to university encounter capitalism in one of its most sophisticated forms, but their socialization in the family has prepared them for marriage and motherhood, traditional production at home. Temporarily co-workers with boys in the knowledge industry, the contrast between their traditional feminine role and competitive academic life is extreme. (Rowbotham 1973: 90–1)

There are also remarkable resonances with Hoggart in Rowbotham's appeal to 'culture' in developing her own response to this disjuncture:

> I defended myself implicitly by distinguishing myself in my head from other girls who seemed to accept their fate without resistance. It was easy to develop this sense of separateness because most of the people I was at school with left to go on typing courses. They all became much more smart and confident than those of us who stayed on. I consoled myself by retreating into an intellectual inner world of mysticism and reverie; I read everything I could find which would help me to build an important little private sphere of 'culture'. (Rowbotham 1973: 13)

But there are also differences here from the writing of the 1950s. It is significant that Rowbotham associates culture with 'mysticism' and 'privacy'. The emotional and political intensity of her writing reflects a corresponding withdrawal from established institutions and cultural forms:

> I acquired wild and dangerous notions about sex and marriage which were in marked contrast both to what everyone around me thought and to my own total ignorance in practice... Only moments of intense subjectivity seemed to have any honesty or authenticity. All removed ways of thinking appeared to me as necessarily suspect... Every rock record simply was. The words were subordinate to the rhythm and the music went straight to your cunt and hit the bottom of your spine. (Rowbotham 1973: 13–14)

That this could not have been written by Hoggart or Williams is not *only* a function of gender; it is equally a function of generation. Rowbotham explores, more fully than Hall or Hebdige, the consequences of the separation examined in Chapter 6 between 'structure' and 'feeling'. For Hoggart and Williams, the negotiation between working-class and middle-class cultural domains was always a matter of translating between sites which had associations both of structure *and* feeling. For Rowbotham, by contrast, the terms – represented now by 'removed ways of thinking' and the libidinal intensity of rock music – are relatively abstracted and opposed.

The Model of Representation

As I argued in Chapter 6, this opposition is as much a product of historical circumstance as of choice. If there is a site of 'women's culture' which might provide a similar intellectual resource for Rowbotham to the tenements of Leeds for Hoggart or the Welsh border country for Williams, she provides a number of indications of why it can no longer serve quite the same function:

> New ways of processing, preserving and selling food, new ways of storing food by refrigeration, mean that the nature of housework has become increasingly a service operation... There is a rather hopeless last-ditch stand in home-baked bread and health foods. It is evident that such work is a matter of choice, not necessity. It assumes the character of a quaint pursuit, almost a hobby. (Rowbotham 1973: 108–9)

The risk of descending into sentimentality or nostalgia, always incipient for Hoggart and Williams, is, for Rowbotham, much more urgent. The intensification of the interface between government, education and media and 'traditional production at home' exposed the latter in quite new ways to the instrumental rationality of public institutions, particularly to those of capitalist enterprise. This exposure opens up a distinction between 'choice' and 'necessity', reducing attempts to articulate the value of social activities not already recognized by public institutions to subjectivity and privacy. As Rowbotham identifies the problem herself: 'Chased out of the dominant mode of production where there is no room for emotion, such characteristics as love, tenderness and compassion assume a mawkish guise from confinement. The family is thus in one sense the dummy ideal, the repository of ghostly substitutes, emotive fictions which dissolve into cloying sentimentality or explode into thrashing, battering, remorseless violence' (Rowbotham 1973: 59).

The differences might also be considered in terms of the organization of social space. The model of relations between cultural domains for Hoggart and Williams might be described as an 'ambassadorial' one. It is significant that Hoggart always referred to the 'scholarship boy' in the singular; he was an individual who, while he may share experiences with others, was also unusual in moving between collective forms of life that were still clearly distinct and relatively stable. In a middle-class milieu, he was able to represent the background from which he came. In an adult education class, he was able to represent a middle-class intellectual heritage to those for whom it was not their own. But it never appeared that there might be a single space of representation or a perspective from which one might consider representation in general terms. The context for the emergence of feminism is quite different. As Mitchell commented of the social movements of the late 1960s: 'An essential and dominant aspect of the common context for these movements seems to me to be the vast expansion in higher education in the first half of the sixties' (Mitchell 1971: 28). The experience of those entering higher education as a result of this expansion was not individual but generational. The ambassadorial model is replaced, for Mitchell and Rowbotham, by a model of *representation* within a newly defined homogeneous domain.

Joshua Meyrowitz has traced similar developments, in America but during the same period, in relation to media. Meyrowitz points out that the emergence of feminism coincided closely with the maturing of the first television generation – a coincidence, he suggests, which is far from accidental. Irrespective of the particular content of programming, television created 'a greater sense of informational and experiential unity' than was ever possible within a print-based culture (Meyrowitz 1985: 224):

> Unlike *McCall's* magazine or the women's page of newspapers, television brought the same information and the same 'outside world' to men and women. And by 1960, television had penetrated nearly 90% of American households... Television exposed women to many 'male topics' that they might not have chosen to read about in print... Further, men and women often watched television together, so that it became almost impossible for women and men to pretend that women were ignorant of certain worldly affairs. (Meyrowitz 1985: 211)

The last point here is particularly important. The significance of television as a cultural technology is not only in making information available to populations who did not previously have access to it; it is also in radically increasing knowledge of what others know. If cross-demographic exchange of information by print media has similarities to the 'ambassadorial' model of exchange between cultural domains – crossing between sites within a relatively segmented space – television corresponds more closely to mass higher education. The possibility of conceiving relations in terms of translation or dialogue is weakened as information and experience are redefined as belonging to a common domain.

As Tony Bennett has argued, there is a close relation between the politics of representation and generalized concepts of power. Using the example of the modern museum, Bennett points out that demands for representational adequacy appeal implicitly to 'a principle of general human universality in relation to which, whether on the basis of the gendered, racial, class or other social patterns of its exclusions and biases, any particular museum display can be held to be inadequate and therefore in need of supplementation' (Bennett 1995: 91).[7] Power is represented in this context as an undifferentiated institutional resistance to demands for greater inclusiveness within a putatively universal forum. If combined with the insights of Rowbotham, Mitchell and Meyrowitz, Bennett's analysis may help us to understand the tendency in the 1960s and 1970s towards generalized concepts of power. If social, cultural and technological developments of the period were such as to produce new spaces in which questions of representational adequacy could be posed, they would also have created the conditions for such concepts to take form.

But the context for the reconceptualization of power was not only in internal developments within Britain, America or other countries in which the women's movement emerged; it was also the external relations of these countries within the highly charged international space of the Cold War. As Mitchell points out of the social movements of the late 1960s: 'These home-based, home-directed fights took over from a preoccupation with world peace and Third World struggles – Algeria, Cuba, Vietnam – yet have never lost the predilection for internationalism which their original inspiration provided' (Mitchell 1971: 20). The originality of intellectuals in the women's movement was to combine the *extensive* reference of the concept of power that had developed in the context of the Cold War and anti-colonial struggles with the *intensive* reference suggested by changes within advanced capitalist societies. As Mitchell puts it:

> The Third World revolutions and guerrilla warfare provoked new analyses of oppression and new methods of struggle... The Women's Liberation Movement is, in a sense, a summation of so many tendencies which mark these slightly earlier formations... The wish to concentrate on specific oppression in one's own country and yet link up with a universal predicament (a reaction to the scope of imperialism?) finds perfect expression in the situation of women... Women are the most 'international' of any political group, and yet their oppression is experienced in the most minute and specific arena – in the home. (Mitchell 1971: 21)

In recent reflections on the period, Mitchell gives a striking account of an occasion in which she herself attempted to establish these connections: 'I remember sitting at the table with all the men of *New Left Review*, and going round the table with people saying "Well, I will think about Algeria", "I will think about Persia", "I will think

---

7. Bennett, in fact, goes further than this, making use of Foucauldian arguments to associate generalized concepts of power with a merely 'rhetorical' politics. It could be argued that this association tends towards the kind of 'tacit criticism' of feminism that Morris observes. But it is possible to take the more limited point about the relation between the politics of representation and concepts of power without such an extension. I will discuss Bennett's general position in detail in Chapter 11.

about Tangyanika", as they then were, and I said, "Well, I'll think about women" – and there was silence' (Mitchell 1995: 124).

The Origins of 'Totalism'

This silence might be construed as a sign of a resistance to the inclusion of women. But there are other reasons why there might have been discomfort. The unlimited reference of the concept of power when taken to extend from the global to the 'most minute and specific' implies a new kind of politics, one which Mitchell herself described at the time as 'totalism':

> 'Totalism' ... is the expression of the protest against all oppressed conditions in the form of an assertion of complete liberation involving the overthrow at one blow of the whole capitalist society. In 'totalism' the oppression of one group stands for the oppression of all. Within its undifferentiated inclusiveness there is only place for tactics, not overall strategy. (Mitchell 1971: 24)

Even in this description, there are suggestions of instability, contradiction and a potential for political despair. Everything appears to be staked on 'overthrowing capitalist society', yet the 'undifferentiated inclusiveness' of the concept of oppression also makes this seem highly unlikely if not impossible. The Marxist internationalism of 'the men' at *New Left Review* was still, in Mitchell's terms, 'strategic'. While the reference of their concept of power was extensive, it was nevertheless limited (to questions relating to regulation of the mode of production and the role of the state), allowing the scope of political action to be specified. In 'totalism', by contrast, strategy becomes unthinkable. Any attempt to engage with power can no longer be specifically directed.

It is clear from Mitchell's account that 'totalism' was associated both with political generosity and serious intellectual ambition. The principle according to which 'the oppression of one group stands for the oppression of all' provides a basis for cooperation between extremely diverse projects, connecting the otherwise remote experiences of Third World guerrilla fighters and suburban 'housewives'. The idea that questions of power might be pursued in the intensive as well as the extensive dimension also suggests the possibility of quite new ways in which they might be addressed. But 'totalism' also produces a number of problems that were widely sensed within feminist writings themselves. The most serious is that while power is seen negatively, it is also conceived in such a way as to appear intractable. As Mitchell has said recently of her motivations for turning to psychoanalysis:

> By the end of the decade [the 1960s] there seemed to be something so entrenched about patriarchy..., that where we had been seeing through the work of Fanon and others that one could have multiple differences, there seemed to be some *absolute* difference

that was socially or culturally constructed between men and women, and was more entrenched... And there was something in psychoanalysis that spoke about the depth of patriarchy, and the really difficult question of eradicating it. (Mitchell 1995: 125)

By Mitchell's own account, *Psychoanalysis and Feminism* was written substantially as a response to the perceived failure of the revolutionary movements of the late 1960s. The diagnosis of failure is, however, ambiguous. The implication of the concept of power that began to form at the time is that they could not possibly have 'succeeded'. This is not so much because any specific power could not have been displaced or overthrown; it is rather that power was no longer conceived *as* specific. It was understood in such a way as to appear not only as omnipresent but also as necessarily omnitemporal. The significance of the term 'patriarchy', for Mitchell, was not only that it identified the oppression of women; it was also that it introduced a new understanding of power as transcending any particular historical or cultural formation. The emphasis is explicit in her use of a definition of the term from Kate Millett: 'a universal (geographical and historical) mode of power relations' (Mitchell 1971: 65).

Contemporary unease about the direction of cultural politics in the 1970s has since been eclipsed by highly developed criticisms of the period – some of which I will review in Chapter 11. Many of these criticisms are, however, historically insensitive. It is worth drawing attention to Mitchell's parenthetical question in describing the universalism of the social movements of the 1960s and 1970s: 'a reaction to the scope of imperialism?' The new emphasis on an 'undifferentiated inclusiveness' was not a theoretical proposition put forward in a vacuum, but a response to complex and disturbing developments. Many of the tendencies within left politics of the time can also be observed in other fields. As Mitchell points out in *Women's Estate*, much of the political rhetoric of the social movements was carried over from mainstream discourses of the Cold War:

> A great deal of the radical protest has taken the form of a demand for the realization of the gifts we are supposed to be enjoying anyway... If the society says we are so lucky, so mature, etc. let's see it... Of course, freedom, equality and the rights of the individual are fundamental ideologies of a 'free enterprise' economy. (Mitchell 1971: 176–7)

A similar argument has been made recently by P. G. Knight about the theme of 'conspiracy' within many of the early American second wave feminist texts. An example used by Knight is the concept of 'brainwashing' in Betty Friedan's *The Feminine Mystique*. The emergence of the concept in American public discourse can be traced quite specifically to Cold War contexts, in the attempt by authorities to explain why American troops in Korea had apparently succumbed to an enemy programme of propaganda and indoctrination. 'In developing an account of a conspiracy to brainwash American women into domesticity, Friedan draws on one of the key terms of cold war politics' (Knight 1997: 42).

The totalist extension of the concept of power, itself, does not appear to be any more unique to left cultural criticism than the concept of freedom or the theme of conspiracy. There are very clear shifts in usage associated with the Cold War. The emergence of superpower confrontation brought an effective end to the pluralist understanding of international politics, deriving from an older European response to modernity, as a web of rivalries and alliances between the 'Great *Powers'*. While a binary system still has two poles, it is unlike a multi-polar system in the ease with which one pole can be characterized simply as the complement or 'negative' of the other. The logic of superpower confrontation was always such as to suggest a substantial consistency of power – a potential, at least, to be conceived as a single global phenomenon. With the loss, after Hiroshima and Nagasaki, of a distinction between military and civilian space, there was an obvious context for an extension of a totalizing use of the concept beyond the 'public' domain. It is easy, from a position of historical distance, to criticize or deride Mitchell's hope of 'overthrowing at one blow the whole capitalist society', but in a context where entire societies were held to ransom against the threat of nuclear annihilation, such apocalyptic suggestions belonged to a discursive field with points of reference which were all too real.

But the strongest argument against too easy a dismissal of 'seventies politics' is that the most important intellectual shift in the cultural politics of the period has not been extensively questioned or revised. It is true that there has been a widespread rejection of the original form in which 'totalism' was articulated, particularly its inflection towards apocalyptic or revolutionary themes. But the most common usage of the concept of power in cultural studies remains 'totalist' in much the sense that Mitchell outlines. Even the strongest critics of the revolutionary political models of the 1970s have generally assumed that power is a universal phenomenon extending from the global to the particular and substantially consistent however diverse its 'forms' or 'modalities'. As I will argue in Chapter 11, one of the most developed lines of criticism – a line associated with an appeal to Foucauldian arguments – has, in fact, only consolidated the universalism in relation to the concept which first emerged in the social movements of the 1960s and 1970s. While an insistence that there is nothing 'outside' power is often represented as a definitive break from the revolutionary aspirations of the latter, it might equally well be represented as a formalization and logical extension of their central intellectual innovation.

–9–

The Trans-Atlantic Passage
'Power' in America

If the origins of 'totalism' – a concept of power as universal and all-pervasive – can be traced to the new social movements and the Cold War, it is often associated in cultural studies with the *Americanization* of the field. As noted in Chapter 1, Stuart Hall's criticisms of tendencies in the use of the concept in the 1990s were directed particularly at *American* cultural studies. It is with the emergence of the latter, for Hall, that the concept of power has become inflated – that we have become able 'extensively and without end, to theorize power', that power has become 'an easy floating signifier' (Hall 1992: 286).

Hall is not alone among external observers in his reservations about the form taken by cultural studies in the United States. In a postscript to the proceedings of the conference generally seen as marking the 'arrival' of the field in the American academy – at Illinois, in 1990 – Angela McRobbie confessed that, on first reading many of the papers, she was 'gripped by panic': 'Where have I been for the last five years? Much of this kind of cultural studies does not at all tally with what I teach, with what I find useful in understanding the everyday world and everyday culture around me' (McRobbie 1992: 721). The problem is often attributed to a loss of connection in American cultural studies with contexts outside the academy. Ioan Davies has argued, for example, that the field in America has been 'taken everywhere as an academic development, rather than a political or educational one, forgetting that many of the debates in Britain took place in the pages of *New Left Review*, *Marxism Today*, and a host of non-academic magazines and journals' (1995: 158).

Hall is also not alone in pointing specifically to problems in the concept of power. A notable example is the rejection by Tony Bennett of what he calls 'the libertarian formulations that have been the worm in the bud of American cultural studies ever since it made its trans-Atlantic passage' (1998: 5). This is more than an occasional aside; much of Bennett's work since the early 1990s can be seen as formed in critical response to the direction of cultural studies as it has been taken up in America. The initiative for which he is best known, which I will discuss further in Chapter 11, is often described as 'Foucauldian' and set in the context of theoretical developments around the idea of 'governmentality'. But it can also be considered in more geopolitical terms. Like a number of other initiatives over the last decade, it has been animated, at least in part, by a reaction to a perceived deformation of the concept of power following the expansion of cultural studies in the United States.

There is a question whether these criticisms are entirely fair. Many of the tendencies projected onto American cultural studies can also be found elsewhere. One might ask, for example, whether the theoretical 'fluency' that troubles Hall in the United States was not pioneered, to some extent, at Birmingham. Equally, an academicization of the legacy of the New Left can also be found in Britain and other sites where cultural studies has emerged. It may be more appropriate, on this question, to compare different *periods* than national locations. The term 'cultural studies' gained currency in the America somewhat later than in Britain. When it began to announce its presence in the 1980s and 1990s, it was as an academic field, but this is also how British cultural studies, by this time, had largely come to be defined.

It is also important to recognize that cultural studies in America is not a simple object. As Lawrence Grossberg has warned, any attempt even to give a descriptive overview of the field is likely to be struck by its 'truly enormous diversity': 'I think it is impossible to find any consistency or commonality in politics, theory, or methodology that might enable us to cut across the diversity to find the "truly American inheritance"' (1997: 295). There is no question that within this diversity there is a significant amount of work that engages with contexts outside the academy. The journal *Social Text*, which provides a reasonable index of current work in cultural studies in the United States, has included articles over the past five years on the politics of transnational adoptions, the use of the rhetoric of 'fiscal crisis' by city governments, Palestine and American foreign policy in the Middle East, corporate corruption, access and inclusion in the new digital public sphere, the 'war on terror' and the implications for homeless people of policies on crime prevention. Much of this work is based on dialogue or research with community organizations, activist groups, media workers and government agencies and is often associated with various forms of political involvement.

But the reactions of Hall, McRobbie, Davies and Bennett nevertheless point to something. The concept of power in American cultural studies has been a particular node of controversy. The most active sites of this controversy have not, in fact, been in cultural studies itself, but in the 'culture wars' debates reviewed in Chapter 1. However strong the desire to avoid or ignore them, these debates have affected the way the field is projected and received. *Social Text* is a good example. For all its contributions to cultural politics in the United States, the journal is probably still most widely known for its entanglement in 1996 in the 'Sokal Affair'. The stakes in this affair were somewhat muddier than many others that have besieged cultural studies since the 1990s. The central provocateur and antagonist, professor of physics at New York University Alan Sokal, identified himself as on the left, pointing out that he taught in Nicaragua following the Sandinista revolution. But the point he hoped to make in publishing a hoax article in *Social Text* was very similar to those of the conservative culture warriors: that cultural studies is so mired in 'politically correct' orthodoxies that it has abandoned serious intellectual standards or respect for evidence: 'The results of my little experiment demonstrate, at the very least, that some fashionable sectors of the American academic Left have been getting intellectually lazy' (Sokal 1996).

As I indicated in Chapter 1, the 'culture wars' have had some resonance beyond America. The Sokal hoax drew a certain interest, for example, in Australia (Hodge 1999; Franklin 2000). There is no doubt, however, that the *centre* of these debates has been the United States. Where they have flared elsewhere, it has usually been with reference to American precedents, and positions taken, on all sides, have tended to follow American models. This is not to suggest by any means that, within the United States itself, such positions account for all or even most of the work that is conducted in the name of cultural studies. Many practitioners have regarded the culture wars as little more an irritant, a background clamour of media hype and hysteria, not a framework in which they would want to position their work. But the heat around the concept of power in America suggests that there is something about the way it has circulated there and the meanings it has gained, which requires particular consideration.

I want to suggest in the following that much of this heat might be explained by a central contradiction. On the one hand, the United States has strong traditions of scepticism about generalized concepts of power – stronger, even, in some respects than those I have identified in Britain. The doctrine, for example, of the 'separation of powers', with its insistence on maintaining a sense of powers as discontinuous and discrete, is embodied in the Constitution. At a less formal level, the idea, to recall Oakeshott's terms, of a 'multiplicity of semi-independencies' is also central to a number of broadly 'republican' political traditions with deep roots in the political and cultural life of the United States. On the other hand, however, the USA has also produced some particularly abstract or crystalline concepts of power. A generalized *discourse* of power – 'politics, race, class and gender, subjugation, domination, exclusion, marginality, Otherness etc.' – is, as Hall suggests, more fully developed in America than anywhere else. There are, I suggest, a number of contexts for this: the distinctive character of the American New Left, the historical legacy of slavery, the status of the United States as a military and economic superpower and processes of abstraction in the translation across the Atlantic of European political and cultural theory.

The intensity of this contradiction makes it difficult to approach the concept of power in American cultural studies without being drawn to extremes. It often appears that the options are either to denounce it as a sign of ideological fanaticism – in the style of Sokal and the conservative culture warriors – or to rally to its defence as identifying a fundamental social 'truth', the simple 'reality' of power relations. My response to this, as it has been in previous chapters, is to propose a third alternative: to historicize.

American Cultural Studies 'before Power'

A useful starting point here, as it was in the British case, is to recognize that the concept of power has not always been fundamental to cultural studies in the United States. While the field is widely seen as an academic offshoot of the new social movements and as drawing, at some level, on European Marxist or post-Marxist theory, there is, as in Britain, an important tradition independent of both. As Joli Jensen and John Pauly have pointed out:

> Not every intellectual path of the 1960s and 1970s led to a Paris café ... At that moment, as French intellectuals were transforming their disenchantment with the failed revolution of 1968 into cultural theory, James Carey and his students at the University of Illinois (and, for a time, the University of Iowa) were fashioning an American cultural studies ... (Jensen and Pauly 1997: 162)

The analysis is tinged with 'culture wars' hostilities, but is nevertheless valuable in drawing attention to early work in the field which is now often forgotten or overlooked. 'Illinois' cultural studies, as Jensen and Pauly call it, did not borrow its central problematic from Marxism. It understood itself, rather, as building on the efforts of 'a strange collection of visionaries and outcasts loosely associated with the Chicago School of Sociology – John Dewey, Thorstein Veblen, Jane Addams, Robert Park, Lewis Mumford, and Harold Adams Innis' (1997: 162).

Power was not a central term in this tradition. As explicated by James Carey, the leading contemporary interpreter and exponent, its central objective was to counter the growing dominance in American intellectual life of positivism and the behavioural sciences. Positivism is understood by Carey not as a doctrine of the facticity of empirical observations, but as a confinement of the public use of reason to instrumental calculations: 'The assumption is the following: the ends or goals of human action are random, unknowable or, more technically, exogenous. We cannot gain rational knowledge of human ends or purposes; rational action and knowledge is necessarily confined to the fitting together of ends and means' (Carey 1997a: 8). This assumption leads, in Carey's analysis, to an evacuation of political thinking and an inability to conceive of anything other than the most abstract and formal kinds of collective life:

> Politics ... should not try to form the character or cultivate the virtue of its citizens, for to do so would be to legislate morality ... [I]nstead the state and other collective forms should provide only a neutral framework of rights, the means, within which people can choose their own values and ends. (Carey 1997a: 8–9)

Where questions arise about how values and ends are actually formed, they are attributed either to individual desires or to some external influence – genetics, environment, society or ideology. The problem with this, for Carey, is that people are conceived as 'so driven by individual need and desire or so determined by external forces as to be in principal incapable of participating in democratic life' (1997a: 9).

The early project of American cultural studies was, as Carey saw it, to counter these tendencies and reinvigorate 'the idea central to republican theory, namely that liberty depends on sharing in self-government' (1997a: 9). The very motivation for the field was to nurse into being a sense of shared involvement in, and responsibility for, forms of public life. Working from within communication studies, Carey and his collaborators found a strategic opening in the 'niche of language and meaning' (1997a: 9). This appeared to be the area where it was most easily demonstrated that social forms were not simply instrumental but also expressive and normative; it represented an opportunity 'to attack the behavioral sciences on the ground they were weakest – the analysis of culture' (1997a: 10). The approach is probably best known from Carey's 'ritual model' of communication, most fully developed in *Communication as Culture* (1989a), which shifts attention from the simple transmission of information to shared experience, active participation and creative expression. But the ambition of his general argument is much broader than this. Its ultimate horizon is that all forms of social life, even those like science and technology which appear most material and functional, should begin to be understood in similar terms.

Carey has always situated his work within American traditions and contexts. His major influences have been the pragmatism of John Dewey and the sociology of the Chicago School, but he has also maintained a conscious connection with more main-stream points of reference. In a 1991 essay on the conditions for republican politics, he takes his bearings from no less than Benjamin Franklin and Thomas Jefferson. The essay reflects on the particular circumstances of the United States in the 1990s – the political climate at the end of the Cold War, the closure of debate in Congress due to the organization of campaign finances – but is also, in many ways, a classical articulation of democratic republican principles:

> Only when citizens can speak and act with some promise that their fellows will see and hear and remember will the passions that are true and lasting grow. And, therefore, unless we can create or restore what Tocqueville called the 'little republics within the frame of the larger republic,' within political parties and trade unions, within local communities and workplaces, within places that can aggregate public opinion and sustain public discourse, political objects must remain indefinite and transient and political action short-lived and ineffective. (Carey 1991: 127)

Carey has generally been a dissenter from the dominant tendencies of his time: in the essay cited, he criticizes an increasingly legalistic, 'rights based' interpretation of the first amendment to the US Constitution. But he has done so by rearticulating some of the central themes of American political culture.

There are, at the same time, clear resonances between this 'Americanness' and the 'Englishness' I identified in early British cultural studies. As Carey makes clear, there was, in fact, significant exchange between the latter and the work at Illinois:

> I had read the usual suspects, Raymond Williams and E.P. Thompson, corresponded with Richard Hoggart and was following the early work of the Centre for the Study of Contemporary Culture [*sic*]... The Birmingham Centre had worked through the scholarship of the Chicago School, particularly in 'labeling theory', and found it useful in its early formulations of central issues in the analysis of subcultures and deviance. (Carey 1997a: 4)

Illinois cultural studies had a number of distinctive American characteristics. It defined itself, because of local circumstances and opportunities, not in relation to English literature but the field of communication studies. But it shared with early British cultural studies in its central attempt to bring attention to collective social forms as not just functional but normative and dialogic. Carey's 'ritual' model of communication bears close comparison, in this respect, to Williams's 'structures of feeling'.

Carey is sensitive, in his recent reflections, to suggestions that the Illinois project was incapable of addressing questions of power: 'I should declare what I hope is obvious: the emphasis on language, culture and meaning does not exclude issues of power and conflict; instead, it attempts to locate them' (Carey 1997a: 10). But it is clear, as with early British cultural studies, why the relation to these issues might be an awkward one. If the concept of power is given a theoretical centrality, it threatens the attempt to counter positivism in Carey's sense. To the extent, at least, that culture is reduced to a field in which certain groups gain an advantage over or struggle against the dominance of others, we are returned to the instrumentalist conception of social life that both early British and American cultural studies had sought to displace. The normative or expressive aspects of cultural forms come to be discounted as merely apparent, masking more fundamental calculations of interests or positions of advantage.

This is, in fact, fairly much what Carey now believes has actually occurred: 'Indeed, cultural studies by and large incorporated the most basic and troubling assumptions of the positivist tradition into its own thinking' (Carey 1997a: 9). The criticism is sharply drawn in relation to the model of textual analysis that developed following the importation of British cultural studies to the United States:

> The emergence of the text ... reduced the entire domain of culture to ideology and all social relations into surrogates of power, a vicious self-fulfilling prophecy. The complex culture of a people ... was exhausted by grasping one limited part of its formulation... [P]olitical culture was reduced to the most managed and instrumental parts of life and the common-sense understandings of politics were completely evacuated. (Carey 1997a: 17–18)

But the strongest criticisms are reserved for the influence of Foucault: 'A particular misfortune was the encounter with Michel Foucault... [I]n Foucault's rendition, power is simply another name for culture, for the webs of significance and meaning, in which the self is suspended, but that web is one of intrinsic cruelty. This is where the conversion of culture into ideology and power inevitably leads (Carey 1997a: 18–19). Questions might be asked about the generosity of this view of Foucault – given, as I have argued, that he was dealing with somewhat similar problems. Carey's position in recent essays has increasingly converged with conservative criticisms of cultural studies, including occasional notes of paranoia about foreign theoretical influences. But his analysis is nevertheless useful in the clarity with which it draws attention to the stakes involved, generally, in centralizing the concept of power.

An Invitation to Care

If there are similarities in the early formations of American and British cultural studies, there are also similarities in the way they have tended to be submerged. A good example here is the work of Lawrence Grossberg, a central figure in the later development of the field in the United States and widely recognized as one of its most authoritative commentators. In the same essay, cited above, insisting on the 'diversity' of cultural studies, Grossberg suggests that there has always been a fundamental commonality: 'Power is there for cultural studies from the very beginning' (Grossberg 1997: 260); 'Cultural studies is *obviously* a set of approaches that attempt to understand and intervene in the relations between culture and power (1997: 344, emphasis mine). These statements are particularly curious given the relation between Grossberg and Carey. It appears similar, in many ways, to the relation in Britain between Perry Anderson or Terry Eagleton and Raymond Williams. The generation of the 1960s (Grossberg, Eagleton, Anderson) were well aware, in both countries, of the general bearings of what I have been calling cultural studies 'before power'. As Eagleton was to Williams, Grossberg was a student of Carey's and has continued to recognize him as a major influence (Grossberg 1997: ix). He also spent time at Birmingham in the 1960s, when seminars were still being conducted by Richard Hoggart as exercises in 'reading for tone and value' (1997: 24). But there is little obvious sign of these influences in his many commentaries and reflections on cultural studies. Even more than his British counterparts, his intellectual identity has been built around a conviction in the use of the concept of power, a conviction that leads to a significant departure from the earlier project.

The terms of this departure are most clearly articulated in a 1983 essay, 'Cultural Studies Revisited and Revised', which also reveals some of Grossberg's investment in British cultural studies. His differences with the Chicago School tradition are developed through a comparison between its 'founding discourse' in the writings of

John Dewey and the work of Raymond Williams. While noting strong similarities between the two, Grossberg sees a divergence in their approach to questions of power:

> The two traditions to which they give rise differ significantly because of Williams's eventual incorporation of the problem of politics into the moment of signification or culture. Thus, rather than understanding power as an external intervention into the process of culture, the British school of 'cultural studies' argues that power is a struggle within and over meaning. As a result, cultural studies have drawn upon contemporary theoretical developments in marxist theories of ideology and semiotic theories of signification. (Grossberg 1997: 142)

There is something of an irony in this schema. Where, from the current perspective, American cultural studies seems more focused on power – even, as Hall and Carey suggest, *obsessed* with power – the emphasis is attributed by Grossberg to Britain.

This paradox suggests one context for differences in the concept of power in American cultural studies – the effect on the concept of processes of abstraction. As it is imported by Grossberg from British cultural studies, it is transformed from merely an element in a set of responses to post-war British society to an essential distinguishing feature. As we will see below, this can be seen as part of a wider pattern in American borrowings of European Marxist and post-Marxist theory. While concepts of power can clearly be found in the latter, they have also been thoroughly embedded in concrete considerations of working-class movements, relations of production, processes of commodification and the character of particular state formations. Their removal from these contexts is not entirely unique to America. As we saw in Chapter 6, commentators such as Colin Sparks observed similar tendencies at Birmingham in the 1970s. But the American uptake of Marxist and post-Marxist theories, often *via* Birmingham, can be seen as a further stage in the process – one in which they have come to be framed essentially as theories of power.

If the alternatives, for Grossberg, are an American cultural studies 'before' power and a British cultural studies 'after' power, the choice between them is clear: 'Despite its impeccable humanistic credentials, the American culturalist tradition seems a less fruitful alternative than the British school of cultural studies, which attempts to link signification and social processes, communication and miscommunication together' (Grossberg 1997: 149). The discussion has close parallels with Stuart Hall's discussion of 'culturalism' and 'structuralism' in British cultural studies and was probably influenced by it. Like Hall, Grossberg gives a sympathetic rendition of culturalism, but there is never any doubt that he sees the more 'structuralist' approaches which followed as superior. The necessity of centralizing the concept of power appears to him simply as obvious.

The differences between Grossberg and Carey do not appear to have developed into open disagreement. It should be noted that Carey's analysis has only developed over time. His recent pessimism about the state of cultural studies appears to have taken form in the context of the 1990s' debates around 'political correctness'. The readiness of many in the field to accept the terms of these debates – pitting reverence for the 'Western tradition' against attempts to unmask it as cover for racism, sexism and exploitation – revealed, for Carey, the narrowness of the emphasis on ideology and power. As he puts it in a 1992 essay, 'the America imagined in the political correctness debate is disconnected from the experience of the majority of its citizens, historic and contemporary' (Carey 1997b: 276):

> Both the left and the right seem to believe that the raison d'être of education is to serve as a site on which to conduct a political struggle. The public generally, parents specifically, are not particularly enamoured of this view… They are less worried about whether the curriculum is Eurocentric or has some other focus than about whether there is any kind of curriculum at all. (Carey 1997b: 284)

Carey's evident disgust at this outcome seems to have hardened views that may previously have been only mild reservations. It is doubtful, however, that this outcome itself could have been foreseen. Referring to the British debates, he suggests that when the culturalism–structuralism divide was reached 'the wrong road was taken and the price was the abandonment of the progressive programme developed by Williams and Hoggart' (Carey 1997a: 15). But it is only in retrospect that the point is made.

From Grossberg's perspective, the departure involved in centralizing the concept of power has probably never seemed as great as Carey now represents it. He would almost certainly reject any equation between the move and a simple return to an instrumentalist conception of social relations. Indeed, any such equation would be very much open to argument. As we saw in Chapter 6, the danger that cultural studies might collapse back into positivism was acknowledged in Britain by Hall. The problem is clearest, for Hall, in 'post-Marxist' work, such as that of Ernesto Laclau, which abandons the notion of dominance. Without some idea of dominance, he suggests, the concept of power loses its distinction from the pluralist notion of 'influence' in American mass communication theory, converging again with a narrowly instrumentalist view of the social. But the very fact that such a development was recognized as a danger suggests that, even after Laclau and Foucault, it may never have been fully realized.

In the introduction to *Bringing It All Back Home*, his collection of essays on cultural studies, Grossberg confesses that his writing sometimes has a 'sermonic' tone (1997: 32). There are certain problems in this, problems which, in naming it, Grossberg himself is amiably aware of. But they are almost the opposite of the problems Carey identifies in the dominant instrumentalism of American intellectual life. Rather than restricting himself to a narrow 'objectivity', Grossberg – at least by his own analysis – tends, to a fault, to 'conflate *is* and *ought*' (1997: 32). As it is actually articulated, the discourse of power appears quite consistent with the earlier Illinois project of revivifying shared cultural forms, running strongly counter to the privatization of judgements concerning ends. Grossberg's work is, in his own words, 'an invitation to care and to join in the collective labor of cultural studies' (1997: 32). Carey's vision of shared participation in public forms seems, here, to remain very much alive.

Even so, it needs to be asked why the decision to opt for the concept of power is, for Grossberg, so straightforward. It is clear that he understood, and was influenced by, the early projects at Illinois and Birmingham. Yet even in comparison with his British counterparts, there is relatively little sense of a cultural studies 'before power' as a continuing tension in his work. Part of the answer might be found in the fact that Grossberg was a student in the United States in the 1960s, a moment in which the salience of concepts of power did appear 'obvious'. But to pursue this line it is important to consider some of the *differences* between American and British cultural politics of the time, particularly the distinctive concepts of power which emerged from the high tide of American radicalism, from the civil rights movement and demonstrations against the Vietnam War through to the rise of the new social movements.

Twenty-two-year-olds set out to Change the World

There is an immediate problem, in making this suggestion, which needs to be addressed: a widespread view that *no* concepts of power have emerged from within the United States itself. There is a tendency, on all sides of debates about American cultural studies, to project the concept as 'foreign'. Despite their differing assessments of the *value* of theories of power in cultural studies, both Grossberg and Carey see them as imported, without strong roots in local contexts or intellectual traditions. At a certain level, this seems justified. Formal discourses of power, most notably Marxism, have been relatively undeveloped in America, prompting those who are interested in them to look abroad – as in Grossberg's case, to 'Birmingham'.

There is a real question, however, whether the imported concepts have carried their meaning with them, or have served rather to articulate meanings whose origins are more local. In an illuminating essay on the emergence of cultural studies in America, David Shumway (2004) asks a similar question for the field more generally. Questioning a common assumption that cultural studies was simply imported from Britain, he draws attention to its conditions of formation in the American New Left. It is not even, for Shumway, that we should look to a *parallel* history of cultural studies in America – one independent from, but similar to, that in Britain. As he points out, there are important differences between New Left formations in the two countries, differences that bear significantly on the development of cultural studies.

The analysis is suggestive and can be extended to examine differences in the concept of power.

The New Left in America was more radically 'new' than in Britain – at least in its own understanding. Some background was shared in common, particularly the rapid expansion of higher education and collision between new popular cultural sensibilities and established institutional forms – the context discussed in Chapter 8 as a background for feminism. But whereas the British New Left grew out of the Old Left and continued to engage with it intellectually, the American movement developed 'in the vacuum that resulted from the McCarthy era repression of the Old Left' and sought, from the outset, to dissociate itself from the sectarian battles of organizations such as the League for Industrial Democracy (Shumway 2004: 241). It found a potent model of a new form of politics in the civil rights movement, which began to claim victories against racist legislation and practices in the South from the 1950s. Its leading organization, Students for a Democratic Society (SDS) was 'made up mainly of undergraduate students and focused on activism' (Shumway 2004: 240). As Todd Gitlin puts it in his study of the Sixties: 'Because the Old Left had suffered political defeat and moral collapse in the Fifties, the New Left resolved to be a student movement and a left at the same time. Twenty-two-year-olds set out to change the world' (1987: 8).

As a result of this, the American movement lacked institutional articulation. In Britain, as Shumway (2004: 240) points out, the New Left was founded by academics and teachers. Its major work was intellectual, finding an outlet in two influential journals, the *Reasoner*, later the *New Reasoner* and *Universities and Left Review*, later the *New Left Review* – both of which were widely taken up in the academy. No comparable organs existed in the United States. In the early 1960s, when Raymond Williams was establishing himself at Cambridge, Richard Hoggart was appointed to a professorship at the University of Birmingham and a number of New Left figures were acting as policy advisers or participating in establishment forums of debate, the American movement was being defined by student sit-ins and anti-war demonstrations led by an organization (SDS) which, at one point, seriously contemplated the abolition of all office-holding positions (Gitlin 1987: 189). The strength of one was the weakness of the other: the British New Left had little mass base; the American had little institutional presence which might give it stability and a capacity to exercise influence when the immediate passions of the moment had passed.

The American New Left was, as Shumway puts it, 'very much something which happened in the media' (2004: 245). It was formed, particularly, in and through musical expression: '[Bob Dylan's] lyrics would provide ... more of its rhetoric and slogans than all Marxist writing put together' (2004: 247). The result was an emphasis on expressive culture. The movement developed more through theatre, performance, gesture and style than through systematic argument or organization. A good example, if perhaps an extreme one, is the Weathermen, a breakaway faction of

Students for a Democratic Society, which took its name from an obscure line from Dylan's 'Subterranean Homesick Blues': 'you don't need a weatherman to know which way the wind blows'. As Gitlin describes them, with some bitterness at their betrayal of the broader movement, they 'didn't recruit through force of argument so much as through style. Their esprit was undeniable. They were good-looking. They had panache' (1987: 385).

The relative institutional weakness of the New Left in America meant that its legacy was stabilized largely around categories of identity. As the broad movement fragmented at the end of the 1960s, the two arms best positioned to claim an enduring space in the academy were feminism and the movement for black rights. These became established during the 1970s in the form, respectively, of Women's Studies and Black or Afro-American Studies. When cultural studies eventually took off in America in the 1980s, it did so as a relative latecomer to a field already organized around academic forms of identity politics and drew on them for ideas and personnel. American cultural studies has been particularly defined by the contributions of feminists. An indicative list might include Tania Modleski, Donna Haraway, Judith Butler, Teresa de Lauretis, Gayatri Spivak and Eve Kosofsky Sedgwick. This is the reverse of the order in Britain. To recall Hall's description, feminism and politics around race were experienced there as 'interruptions' to cultural studies, even as 'thieves in the night' threatening its very existence. The difference has had significant consequences for the constitution of the field in the United States. It has meant, particularly, that categories of race and gender have tended to be seen as foundational.

The Figure of Slavery

A consequence of this is that the forms of politics associated with them have also been seen as foundational. These are quite different from those that informed the development of British cultural studies in the 1960s and 1970s. As I pointed out in Chapter 8, there has been a tendency to project post-feminist concepts of power backwards onto early British cultural studies. An attention to gender – and then to race, sexual preference and other kinds of difference – has often been presented as merely filling out the analysis of power by drawing attention to other 'axes' along which it operates. The implication is that cultural studies was always already concerned with power, an assumption which has deepened with the expansion of the field in the United States. It is an implication, however, which is misleading. The concept of power was not central at the origins of cultural studies in Britain and even during the 'Marxist' period, at Birmingham in the 1970s, it existed in tension with older 'Hoggartian' impulses.

The importance of recognizing this is not only, as I have argued in previous chapters, that it deepens our understanding of British cultural studies; it is also that it draws attention to the particularity and originality of the concepts of power which have emerged from the United States. There are a number of similarities with Britain in the contexts informing these concepts, but there are also significant differences. The opposition between 'structure' and 'feeling', to recall my discussion of Williams's terms, is much more marked. The drama of confrontation between the US military and political establishment and fresh-faced student demonstrators, so engraved in the iconography of the 1960s, has no real parallel in Britain and created the conditions for much harder-edged representations of the 'system' or the 'dominant paradigm'. The 'newness' of the New Left in America is also important, strengthening the conviction that to adopt the perspective of power relations is to stage a revolution against previous ways of seeing. This establishes the conditions for a more systematic commitment to the concept of power.

But probably the strongest statements of a specifically American context for thinking about power are those that have drawn attention to the salience of *race*. As Cornell West put it at the 1990 conference in Illinois: 'the U.S. begins with the dispossession of Native American lands. And the continuing racial encounter is there from the very beginning, with Mexican peoples and African peoples. America starts in part with the expansion of European empire and these racial encounters. The country commits civil suicide over the issue in the 1860s' (West 1992: 694). West is careful not to deny other contexts, wanting only to point out that race has had a depth of lived experience in America which it has not quite had in Britain or in other locations where cultural studies has taken form: 'I don't necessarily mean to privilege it exclusively; I simply mean it has a lot of weight and gravity in any story that you tell' (1992: 694).

There can be little doubt of the importance of race, and above all the cultural memory of slavery, for concepts of power in America. Its potency is captured by West in the 2001 preface to his bestselling book *Race Matters*: 'Black people in the United States differ from all other modern people owing to the unprecedented levels of unregulated and unrestrained violence directed at them... The unique combination of American terrorism – Jim Crow and lynching – as well as American barbarism – slave trade and slave labor – bears witness to the distinctive American assault on black humanity' (West 2001: xiii). This history was crucial to the formation of the American New Left. The movement was largely galvanized by the emergence of the civil rights movement in the 1950s and the image of black confrontation with white authority continued to provide a key point of reference in the development of positions and ideas. As Gitlin writes of the late 1960s, 'Nothing made the idea of revolution more vivid to the white Left than the Black Panther Party.' (Gitlin 1987: 348)

There is a richness and historical density to these contexts and to the concepts of power they have produced. Some sense of this can be gauged from a series of snapshots offered by Gitlin of the Black Panthers and their impact on the New Left:

Image: Eldridge Cleaver writing in *Ramparts* how he fell for the Panthers when he saw Huey P. Newton hold a shotgun on a San Francisco cop in front of the *Ramparts* office, and face him down. *Image*: Rally after rally, on the steps of the Oakland courthouse where Newton was held without bond on the charge of killing an Oakland policeman, the paramilitary teenagers in black berets and leather jackets chanting 'The Revolution has co-ome, it's time to pick up the gu-un,' with 'Off the pig?' tossed in on the back beat … *Image*: Police bulletholes in the window of the Panther office, the photos circulating widely. (Gitlin 1987: 348)

It is arguably in and through such images that concepts of power have gained depth and meaning. It must be admitted, at least, that there have been volatile contexts in the United States in which these concepts may have developed, mutated or reformed.

Why then is the concept of power often seen as lacking an organic connection with American histories and political forms? One reason, perhaps, is that the United States has offered *such potent* figures of power that they have lent themselves to a kind of instant abstraction, an abstraction in which their origins are paradoxically erased. In relation specifically to slavery, such a tendency might be traced back well before the 1960s, or any of the immediate contexts so far discussed, to the appropriation of the figure of the slave in European political philosophy, its fusion with concepts of power developed, after Hobbes, in the formation of the modern state. The obvious urtext here is Hegel's early nineteenth-century theorization of the 'master/slave dialectic' in *The Phenomenology of Spirit*. It would be too much to suggest that Hegel was responding in any direct way to race relations in the United States, but there is a strong case that he was responding at some level to the actual institution of slavery. As Susan Buck-Morss (2000) has pointed out, *The Phenomenology of Spirit* was written in 1805–6, shortly after the Haitian revolution, an event that was widely reported in the European press and of which Hegel would certainly have been aware.

If placed in this context, the significance of Hegel for the history of the concept of power may not be so much in his particular account of human desire, inter-subjective relations and structures of domination; it may be more in the simple fact that these terms are brought together within a single theoretical frame. The intimate, the psychological, the closely interpersonal, are articulated to universalist concepts of power previously restricted to discourses on sovereignty. The latter context is still clearly dominant: Hegel's political thinking is very much organized around the observation of state formations, from ancient Greek polities to the European settlement following the Napoleonic wars. At the same time, however, the universalism of discourses of sovereignty is transferred to the conception of interpersonal relations. We are invited to think of the power of the master not just as *a* power, but as an instance or expression of a universal phenomenon 'power'.

If, as Buck-Morss suggests, this more theoretical understanding has been abstracted in part from the actual historical experience of slavery, it has continued to interact with contexts where that experience has been more immediate. It has been central to the politics of race in the United States, allowing particular struggles to be written into a wider narrative of human emancipation. As Paul Gilroy (1993: 54) points out, Hegel has been the favourite philosopher of a number of black American intellectuals, including W. E. B. DuBois and Martin Luther King. A further line of influence can be traced through the adaptation of the Hegelian schema to colonial contexts, most notably by Franz Fanon. In this form, it found its way into the manifestos of the student movement of the 1960s, in its solidarity with anti-colonial movements and opposition to the war in Vietnam (Gitlin 1987: 263). It was also a major inspiration in the development in the 1980s of postcolonial theory, through the work of Edward Said, Homi Bhabha and Gayatri Spivak – all of whom have been significant figures in the formation of American cultural studies.

But there is a danger here, again, in attributing too much to the influence of European theory. The abstraction of the concept of power can also be traced independently to discursive strategies of the American New Left. The most important of these was probably the borrowing of figures of domination and oppression in one context to metaphorize another. The practice was particularly common in feminist writing, as in Kate Millett's 1970s' classic *Sexual Politics*:

> What goes largely unexamined ... in our social order, is the birthright priority whereby males rule females. Through this system a most ingenious form of 'interior colonization' has been achieved. It is one which tends moreover to be sturdier than any form of segregation, and more rigorous than class stratification, more uniform, certainly more enduring. However muted its present appearance may be, sexual dominion obtains nevertheless as perhaps the most pervasive ideology of our culture and provides its most fundamental concept of power. (Millett 1970: 25)

In each comparison here between gender, class and colonial relations, the concept of power is further removed from particular contexts in which it might previously have been embedded. In each comparison, we are encouraged to think not of this power or that power, but power in general. As I argued in the last chapter, feminism has not simply 'applied' the concept of power to thinking about gender; it has also significantly reworked it. Much of this reworking has clearly occurred in America.

There is no question that British or European theories of power were important in the formation of cultural studies in the United States. But as Shumway argues, the idea of a field produced entirely from external influences is simply implausible:

> If Cultural Studies 'exploded' between 1984 and 1990, it was not because the Birmingham model became newly influential and suddenly transformed old-fashioned humanists into politically committed critics of mass culture. Rather, we need to understand the emergence of Cultural Studies in the United States as coalescing trends in progress since the late 1960s and early 1970s around a concept and a name that gave them a specific identity. (Shumway 2004: 50)

What needs to be examined in the case of the concept of power specifically is the resonance or connection between imported concepts and those emerging from distinctive American circumstances.

Marxism in America

A useful text in examining this exchange is *Marxism and the Interpretation of Culture*, edited by Cary Nelson and Lawrence Grossberg (1988) and proceeding substantially from an earlier conference at the University of Illinois in 1983. The central focus of the collection, as indicated in the title, is Marxism – or, more precisely, Marxist theories of culture. There are contributions from a number of leading European Marxist or post-Marxist thinkers, including Henri Lefebvre, Chantal Mouffe, Étienne Balibar, Armand Mattelart, Oskar Negt and Franco Moretti. But the volume is also very much a product of its American time and place. Local inclusions, particularly from feminism and black cultural studies, establish a context of reception quite different from those from which the European contributions are drawn and Marxist theoretical perspectives are as much transformed by the encounter as they themselves transform.

The importance of a prior context for the emergence of Marxism in the United States, is recognized, in fact, by Nelson and Grossberg, who draw attention in their introduction to the background of the New Left: 'A loose, partly organized, partly fragmented configuration of varied political commitments and intellectual projects, the New Left helped establish the intellectual networks and shared urgencies that would later energize debate within Marxist theory' (Nelson and Grossberg 1988: 5). The collection is significantly organized around these networks and urgencies: 'we felt we had to recognize certain standard … subject areas – popular culture, Latin America, feminism – so as to be certain that relevant constituencies were guaranteed a forum and a chance to work together' (1988: 2). Marxism is conceived, in this context, not so much as a definite body of theory as a *medium* through which the different positions which have precipitated from the New Left are able to represent themselves to each other. It is, as Nelson and Grossberg put it, 'a place where competing theories work out their similarities and differences and articulate their challenges to one another' (1988: 10).

Central to this process is the concept of power. It is clear that the 'similarities and differences' which Nelson and Grossberg have most in mind are in ways of understanding power, particularly the 'axis' – gender, race or class – which is taken to be the major theoretical focus. For Marxism to provide a 'place' or 'territory' where these issues can be negotiated, they suggest, its own particular biases have had to be recognized and opened to critical scrutiny. It has had to interact with 'analyses of how power is exercised in terms of hierarchical structures of difference and otherness that are not reducible to the model of class exploitation', to 'rethink its understanding of racism, sexism and colonialism' (Nelson and Grossberg 1988: 10). The 'Marxism' which emerges from this is defined not by theories of capitalism and class but, at a more abstract level, by an attempt 'to find more sophisticated models of the relations between culture and power, more reflective understandings of its own position within these relations, and more politically insightful and relevant tools for the analysis of contemporary structures of power' (1988: 11).

As we have seen, almost identical formulations are later used to define cultural studies, not just in the United States but internationally. From one perspective, this might suggest that, as an international phenomenon, the field has been fundamentally formed by European influences. Certainly, the 'tools for the analysis of contemporary structures of power' have been overwhelmingly drawn from European Marxism and post-Marxism. From another perspective, however, it suggests strong American influences. The abstraction of the concept of power as used by Grossberg and Nelson can be traced quite directly to the general tendency towards such abstraction in the American New Left. There is even a certain Americanness in the very idea of convening a range of European thinkers for what they have to say, in general, about 'relations between culture and power'. It presupposes a context of reception in which their particular projects as political activists or public intellectuals have little resonance and where interest will focus on questions of power in its most generalized sense.

Grossberg has often been critical of the loss of contextual reference – to specific traditions or empirical bases – in discourses around power. In *Marxism and the Interpretation of Culture*, he worries, with Nelson, that Marxism may lose any real definition: 'Discursively, Marxism threatens to collapse into criticism with a political edge' (1988: 12). More recently, as Marxism has indeed been displaced by a vaguer 'criticism with a political edge', he has expressed similar concerns about the indiscriminate use of the term 'cultural studies': 'when the range of material being described as cultural studies is expanding exponentially, I believe that cultural studies can be and needs to be defined or delineated' (Grossberg 1997: 245). He has also resisted a tendency for theoretical models to be discussed without reference to actual processes or formations to which they might be applied: 'If one's theory tells one the answers in advance, because one's theory travels with one across any and every context, I do not think one is doing cultural studies' (1997: 262).

What is not often considered, however, is whether these problems may be intrinsic to the very way in which cultural studies has been constituted. Once a field is defined by a concern with power in the abstract, it becomes almost impossible to regulate in the way that Grossberg suggests. Any intellectual position that addresses questions of power, any power, appears ripe for inclusion. Given the diversity of positions that can be construed as doing so, the field that results will inevitably be eclectic, lacking in any common tradition or base of reference. Equally, to conceive of power in general, erasing any residue of association with particular *powers* (class power, the power of specific European political formations, etc.), is to develop a concept, if not quite a 'theory', which is precisely *designed* to 'travel with one across any and every context'. The desire to limit the field in which discourses of power are employed, or to embed this field in specific contexts, runs up against the very way its central concept has been defined.

I want, in the next chapter, to consider some further problems that have followed from the abstraction of the concept of power. But I should close here by saying that it has not been my aim in this chapter simply to pin this abstraction as a 'bad tendency' on cultural studies in the America. It has been, on the contrary, to situate and contextualize distinctive features of the concept of power so that they might be understood more sympathetically. If there is peculiar disturbance around the concept in America, it cannot be attributed, as Alan Sokal might suggest, to the ideological fanaticism or irrationalist tendencies of the postmodern left. It cannot be attributed to murky agents of French theory who have planted it unnaturally in American soil. Nor can it even be attributed to the sometimes machine-like character of a highly professionalized American academy. Even when offered in good faith, such explanations quickly degenerate into little more than accusations against supposed enemies. The significance of the concept in the United States can only seriously be approached if it is considered as a complex cultural artefact, thrown into relief against the background of particular political traditions, gaining affective force through histories of race relations, inflected by the specific character of political movements and given form through translations of theory. It should, in short, be less an object of ideological skirmishing and more an object of cultural history.

–10–

The Shoals of Banality

Living with the Concept of Power

Although I consider myself to be a student of cultural studies ... I am frustrated by the mounting tendency to turn [it] into a vacuous methodology for reading cultural texts that has no real political grounding.

> Ben Agger (1992), *Cultural Studies as Critical Theory*, 1

[T]he voxpop style of cultural studies is ... offering us the sanitized world of a deodorant commercial where there's always a way of redemption. There's something sad about that, because cultural studies emerged from a real attempt to give voice to a much grittier experience of class, race, and gender.

> Meaghan Morris (1996 [1988]), 'Banality in Cultural Studies', 161

Cultural studies remains fixated on theoretical and textual orientations which provide little purchase in seeking to equip students with knowledge and skills for citizenship and employment in the 1990s.

> Stuart Cunningham (1992), *Framing Culture*, 177

It is here that we encounter the impoverished condition of cultural studies in that its ability to theorize questions of identity and difference is limited by the all-too-familiar 'race, class, gender' mantra, which is really only a weak version of liberal multiculturalism.

> Kobena Mercer (1992), '"1968": Periodizing politics and Identity', 425

[T]he question for cultural studies is whether ... it has survived into middle-aged respectability with many of its youthful prejudices intact. If so, any apparent innovations that are associated with [it] as it gains a firmer foothold in academic institutions, may not be so bold and radical and new after all, but merely the beginning of a spoilt, arrogant, *pouting* phase for a discipline which has abandoned its 1960s' idealism and commitment to social change in favour of a belated discovery of its own 'me generation' selfishness.

> John Hartley (1992), *The Politics of Pictures*, 16

From the around the early 1990s, one of the dominant modes of reflection on cultural studies became a discourse of discontent. I have already cited Stuart Hall's reservations about the direction of American cultural studies at the time. The above selection of comments from others gives some indication of wider concerns

The volume of internal criticism of cultural studies makes it difficult to sustain a picture of the field sometimes suggested by external critics as self-satisfied, unreflective, convinced of its own rectitude. As one of its sharpest recent critics, Thomas Frank, is compelled to admit: 'If cultural studies had a unique intellectual virtue, it was a willingness to admit its own failings, and in this chapter [vigorously criticizing the field], I have made liberal use of the work of several of the discipline's most prominent critics.' (Frank 2002: 303)

It would be misleading to give the impression that there is any consensus in the quotations above that the problems identified can be traced to the concept of power. In some cases, indeed, it appears the reverse. Ben Agger's criticisms of a 'lack of political grounding' and Meaghan Morris's concerns about the 'sanitation' of cultural studies might easily be read as calling for greater emphasis on power, not less. Others have made this line explicit. Writing, also in the early 1990s, of 'an unease that something is being lost in the contemporary movement of cultural studies', Martin Barker and Anne Beezer suggest that 'However colleagues may phrase it, it is a worry about the *disappearance* of power as a central concept' (Barker and Beezer 1992: 18, emphasis added).

What can fairly be said, however, is that the increasing abstraction of the concept of power in cultural studies has coincided with something of a crisis of confidence in the field. This is particularly striking as, on the face of it, one might expect the reverse. The generalized definition of the field as concerned with 'relations between culture and power' suggests a clear and distinctive focus – an identifiable set of concerns that sets the field apart from others. The refinement of theories of power might seem to provide a basis from which to project itself with increasing authority. At some levels, perhaps, the promise here has been fulfilled. Cultural studies has continued to attract students and has 'sold' well as a publication category. But an increasing amount of energy has been absorbed since the 1990s in internal criticisms, and a worrying tendency has emerged for some of those most central to its formation to declare a loss of faith.

I want, in this chapter, to examine this development through the example of Meaghan Morris. As suggested by the range of voices above, there are a number of leads that might be taken, but Morris's contribution is particularly illuminating. Her 1990 essay 'Banality in Cultural Studies' is one of the earliest and most influential in crystallizing reservations about the field. Beyond this, however, Morris allows us – both through her analysis and her own example – to establish a longer and more complex genealogy than is often acknowledged for recent concerns. This stands as a counter not only to the often cartoon-like representations of cultural studies in external criticisms of the field. It also challenges easy criticisms from *within* cultural studies of earlier approaches in the field – what Morris herself has described as 'the self-promoting fairy tales of cultural studies today (once upon a time in the seventies, the story goes, feminists had a monolithic view of the media as repressive...)' (Morris 1997b: 244).

It is not an accident, I want to argue, that some of the most acute observations of problems around the concept of power in cultural studies should come from one who has consistently identified as a feminist. As I argued in Chapter 8, feminism has been closely implicated in the emergence within the field of an abstract, universalist concept of power. This has meant that it has often been placed under particular suspicion by those who are uneasy with such a concept. There is often an assumption here that only those who are clearly distanced could be expected to have any insight into the problems it generates. Morris's case suggests the reverse: that it is precisely those who have been *closest* to the generalized concept of power who have been most sensitive to its dangers and who have gone furthest – beyond simple denunciations – in an effort to address them.

Not the Sort of Revolution in which there is Shooting and Hanging

In the introduction to her 1998 collection of essays *Too Soon Too Late*, Morris engages these themes herself in quite a direct and unsettling way, through a review of the life and work of Claire Johnston, 'one of the first and most visionary of British feminist theorists working with film in the 1970s' (Morris 1998: xiii). Her relation to her subject is characteristic in its complexity. One of the reasons she first returned to Johnston's writing in the early 1990s, she confesses, was to understand 'why I found it hard then to read [her] essays (along with most other early "second wave" feminist texts)'. The idea of a blockage in relating to 1970s' feminism crystallizes around the fact that Johnson took her own life in 1987, after writing an essay (never published) on why, in Thatcher's Britain, it was impossible to go on. At the time of her death, it was difficult, Morris says, not to read her work 'as though to find out what had "gone wrong"' (1998: xiv). The question is allowed to hang briefly as one that might be asked of feminist cultural criticism more generally.

But against this moment of doubt, the argument Morris develops in rereading Johnston is one of measured optimism. She finds in her work something she did not quite expect to find:

> For as time passed, a more complex, less mythical sense of how texts work in history, over time – *her* critical sense, in fact – began to assert itself. Johnston's writing, always historical, nervous of myth, became more a part of my present than it ever had been of my past. It began to be important, not something to disavow, that I was actually reading many of her texts for the first time in my life. (Morris 1998: xiv)

The discovery of 'another 1970s' suggests, for Morris, the possibility of writing a history of feminism as a discourse of *scepticism*. It is true, she admits, that 'most of the dreams of historicism, from bloody revolution to the millenarian community, have been taken up, at one time or another, by some form of feminism'. But there has always been, beside this, a 'basic skepticism about History' which has made feminism 'at once resilient in surviving its own failed experiments and resistant to modes of argument that base their claims on necessity' (Morris 1998: xv). It is the resources for such scepticism that are still valuable in the early feminist criticism of writers such as Johnston. The legacy of this work has not been one of defeat but rather of *survival*.

The idea of second wave feminism as animated by a fundamentally sceptical impulse runs counter to the way it is now often regarded – and by no means exclusively by conservative critics. There is, however, considerable evidence to support it in the way feminism emerged from the wider political context of the 1960s and 1970s. As Morris reminds us, one of the clearest motivations of the early women's movement was to resist a tendency on the left at the time to heroic conceptions of 'revolution'. She cites as an example Ann Curthoys and Lyndall Ryan in one of the foundational texts of Australian women's liberation: 'we see women's liberation as working for revolution, but not the sort of revolution which is an event that takes two or three days, in which there is shooting and hanging' (Morris 1998: xiv). Feminism emerges in this picture as having a similar position to the one I have argued has been most characteristic of cultural studies. While certainly within the orbit of generalized concepts of power, it has sought to temper them in such a way as to moderate their simplifying force.

Morris's perspective is also consistent with my reading of the emergence of feminism at Birmingham. Feminism is widely seen as responsible for the expansion of the concept of power at the CCCS in the late 1970s, but I argued in Chapter 8 that it might as well be seen as a *response*. There is clear evidence of the expansion having preceded the formation of the Women's Studies Group. However dramatic feminist interventions may have been, they only crystallized a set of tendencies that had been gathering for some time. If the result was, in Stuart Hall's terms, an 'impossible politics to live', the roots of this needs to be traced back before feminism to an increasingly abstract conception of social relations as 'relations of power'. This development had already begun to cast relations between members of the Centre in instrumentalist terms, threatening the collectivist ethic which had made its work so distinctive. As in the politics of the new social movements, feminism can be seen as both condensing out a transformation in concepts of power and as first bringing a conscious attention to its consequences.

As Morris points out, the tensions played out around feminism have placed considerable stresses on those involved: 'To act, as I believe feminism does, to bring about concrete social changes while *at the same time* contesting the very bases of modern thinking about what constitutes "change" is to induce intense strain, almost a kind of overload, in historical articulation – and sometimes, in feminists' lives' (Morris 1998: xv). But if there is clearly a dimension of tragedy here, there are also resources of hope. As Morris writes of Johnston, she always resisted a capitulation to simplifying abstractions, maintaining a sensitivity to experience, a sense of 'eventfulness': 'I think that this, more than anything to do with "postmodern" pragmatism, describes the activating principle of Claire Johnston's feminist film history, and provides me with a starting point today' (1998: xxiii).

Antipodean Theory

Morris's reflections on Johnston could be seen as reacting to an increasing hostility to feminism in the 1990s, at least to its 'second wave' form. But the attempt to define and hold a sceptical space can also be traced back, well before this, to internal debates *within* feminism in the 1970s and 1980s. As she puts it in the title essay of *The Pirate's Fiancée*: 'Feminisms both past and present have run into some solid brick walls through trusting too lightly to "the obvious", assuming a continuous and evenly distributed, consistently significant, oppression of the eternal natural object "woman" or "women" through the ages' (Morris 1988: 54). The attempt to negotiate a way around these brick walls has involved Morris in what might be described, to recall Juliet Mitchell's term, as an internal critique of 'totalism'. To emphasize the positive dimensions of this project, it might be read alternatively as an extended attempt to *make* the space defined by a generalized concept of power habitable, to *prevent* its politics from becoming 'impossible to live'.

Morris has not, of course, been alone in this project. Many of the problems she has worked to address were identified in the women's movement by writers such as Mitchell and Sheila Rowbotham, whose work I discussed in Chapter 8. Mitchell was concerned, for example, with the dangers of the concept of experience as it was posited in the new social movements as an abstract opposite of structures of power:

> The aspect of the ideological revolution that has enabled the promotion of 'feelings' to the ranks of political action (the 'politics of experience', propagated above all by the Hippies) has certainly had important liberating effects... However, while being a crucial initiator of Women's Liberation itself, sometimes it has also boomeranged back in a way that has been highly detrimental... Here, as with all the other radical movements in which they initially participated, women have found their inspiration and their desolation. (Mitchell 1971: 38)

Rowbotham was more concerned with the emergence of a fatalistic notion of 'anatomic destiny': 'the different possibilities for men and women are held to be biological and psychological in origin, and thus the need to transform the social relations between all human beings is ignored' (Rowbotham 1973: xii). Feminist writing since the late 1960s constitutes, more generally, a rich archive of practical and theoretical responses to such problems – problems that have been closely associated with a generalized concept of power.

But Morris has been particularly successful in projecting feminist insights into broader debates. There is an important context here in the fact that she has written, until recently, from Australia. A consistent strand in her work has been a suspicion of metropolitan intellectual presumption. In *Too soon too late*, she describes British film theory, for example, as a kind of 'Latin': 'a mythic Latin saying "I am an instance of rigorous scientificity"; as [Lesley] Stern says, the effect can be "sombre, not to say tyrannical"'. One of the reasons she admires Johnston is that she regarded this discourse irreverently: 'she had a way of using that Latin to make it sound like a fart in church' (Morris 1998: xvi). There is a similar irreverence in Morris's own work – a strategy of 'enunciation', to use her own preferred term, that mobilizes an ex-centric speaking position to puncture accumulated pieties.

McKenzie Wark (1992b) has suggested that the more appropriate description might, in fact, be 'speaking trajectories'. Morris's writing is mobile, elliptical; she rarely sets out a straight line of argument, but surrounds her subject with a series of acute observations while resisting the usual academic convention of building towards a 'conclusion'. Many of her sharpest points are deflationary, removing the ground beneath simplifying conceptual schemas and overblown theoretical claims. But this is not to say that her contributions have merely been negative. The other side of her vigilance against the grand and heroic has always been a more affirmative project of coaxing into more public view the blunt edges and ordinary textures of everyday life, particularly those which affect women. If there has been, in Foucauldian terms, a 'Morris effect', it has been in a continuing surprise and interest in the way this terrain is engaged.

Morris's style is distinctive, but as Wark suggests it can also be situated in a wider body of 'Antipodean theory'. An important element in this formation has been an unusually direct connection, for Anglophone cultural studies, with the major source of new theoretical ideas through the 1970s and 1980s in France. As Morris has said of herself: 'I was lucky to be a student in French at the time when most feminist debates were unquestioningly "English" or "American" in orientation; I got to read a lot of stuff and think about it years before it was translated' (Morris 1997b: 244). There were others in Australia who were similarly 'ahead' in this way in international debates, particularly those associated with the Sydney-based Feral Publications, which published some of the earliest translations and discussions of a number of significant French texts (see particularly Morris and Patton 1979).

Part of the significance of French theory in Australia, probably going a long way to explaining why it was absorbed so rapidly, is that it was not British. As Andrew Milner has argued, a major context for the early formation of Australian cultural studies was the attempt to develop a fully postcolonial identity. Where the initial problematization of the old literary conception of culture was developed in Britain in relation to *class*, it developed in Australia in relation to *nation*:

From at least as early as the 1890s, Australian radical nationalisms had sought to relocate the national community and a putative national literary canon away from the past and toward a liberal-democratic or even socialistic future, away from England and toward Australia. Despite the attenuation of the *Bulletin*'s more generalized republican political nationalism, a structural opposition persisted thereafter between the more Anglophile forms of academic literary criticism, on the one hand, and radical nationalist non-academic criticism on the other. (Milner 1997: 138)

This opposition crystallized in the 1940s and 1950s, particularly in writing associated with the journals *Meanjin* and *Overland*. It is here, for Milner, that many of the political orientations of Australian cultural studies first took form.

One of the implications of this, it could be argued, is that 'theory' has been received quite differently in Australia than it has in Britain. As we saw in Chapter 3 in the discussion of Perry Anderson and *New Left Review*, the introduction of theory in Britain was associated with a 'crisis' in the established intellectual culture, a sudden and profound loss of confidence which could only be remedied by letting down the barriers to imports. This crisis was generally experienced as painful and its persistence as a long-running sore had significant implications for British cultural studies. In Australia, by contrast, it could be regarded as an *opportunity* – the weakness of the old metropolitan centre could be grasped as an opportunity to assert greater intellectual independence. Where in Britain, the appeal to European ideas was associated with a sweeping rejection of local institutions and histories (including, importantly, those of the left), it could be associated in Australia with a much more *affirmative* project of nation building.

Morris is too sophisticated a thinker to subscribe to a simple nationalism, particularly given its association in Australia with a white masculine paradigm of explorers, settlers and sporting heroes. But there is in her work a consistent suspicion of Englishness. It is evident, for example, in an interview from the late 1990s in which she indicates a certain sympathy with past expressions in Australia of anti-intellectualism:

I can see why hostility to academics became so strong. From back in the 1890s when Henry Lawson snarled 'Get out of the tracks we travel' to his 'Cultured Critics', the Australian literary academy has largely been so British-oriented, so timorous, dull and mediocre – you get the odd, strange comet like H.M. Green flashing through the sky, but mostly this thick grey pall of Anglophile gloom that we had no literature, no history, no culture... Anyone with any vitality would want to get away from an atmosphere like that. (Morris 1997b: 249)

Much of the excitement of Morris's work in the 1970s and 1980s was in offering a real possibility of 'getting away'. It had an intellectual daring to match that of Perry Anderson and *New Left Review*, but avoided the angst, divisiveness and hysteria that infused the British debates over the 'peculiarities of the English'. Without the same need to mount attacks or build defences, it was able to explore the new intellectual directions of the time in a more open, flexible mode. There is a lightness in Morris's writing; even in addressing serious issues, she has maintained a disarming directness and sense of humour.

Mary, You're Not Speaking to *Me* ...

Morris's basic commitment to feminism and wariness of systematic theorizing makes it easy to overlook the sharpness of her observations on problems afflicting left political positions formed around generalized concepts of power. More recent external critics of these positions, such as the conservative culture warriors, have had considerable success in claiming credit for their diagnoses as 'bold', 'new' or 'original'. What has generally been lost in this is a recognition of the *internal* analysis that preceded them. Yet, Morris's comments on the weaknesses of left cultural politics are as uncompromising on many points as any of the conservative culture warriors. Her closeness to her object means only that they are more precisely calibrated and more sensitive to context and nuance.

In a 1985 essay, 'Politics Now', for example, Morris gives full recognition of authoritarian tendencies in the movements that emerged from the 1970s. Addressing an audience of fellow veterans in Sydney, she bluntly rejects the idea that problems of the left at the time could be blamed on the desertion by a younger generation of an earlier cause:

> We're the ones ... who installed a ruthless surveillance system monitoring every aspect of style – clothing, diet, sexual behaviour, domestic conduct, 'role-playing', underwear, reading matter, 'accessibility' versus 'obscurantism' in writing and art, real estate, interior decoration, humour... And this monitoring process functioned constantly to determine what styles, which gestures, could count as good ('valid', 'sound') politics, and which ones could not. (Morris 1988: 178)

The only major difference here from 1990s' conservative tracts on 'political correctness' is that Morris includes herself ('We're the ones') *within* the problem she describes. It is a crucial difference, because it prevents the analysis from becoming a denunciation – a form that only reproduces the intolerance and moral absolutism it claims to oppose. It allows the problem to figure, rather, in documentary mode simply as something to be recognized and addressed. But it would be difficult to argue that the problem itself is not clearly identified.

Another problem Morris has pursued with a particular clarity and insistence is that of repetition. In 'Banality in Cultural Studies' she describes a feeling in the late 1980s that 'somewhere in some English publisher's vault there is a master-disk from which thousands of versions of the same article about pleasure, resistance, and the politics of consumption are being run off under different names with minor variations' (Morris 1996: 156). As noted above, the observation provided an important jolt to cultural studies at the time. But again, the general order of concern can be traced back to earlier debates within feminism. As Morris puts it in *Too Soon Too Late*, feminism has always lived in danger of becoming 'cruelly bound by repetition, confined by the terms that we are contesting'. Without a continued and active scepticism, a vigilance against hardening orthodoxies, 'feminist criticism ties its own hands and finds itself, again and again, bound back home for the same old story'. (Morris 1998: 92)

One of Morris's most acute analyses of the problem of repetition is, in fact, an essay from 1982, 'A-mazing Grace', on the influential work of American feminist Mary Daly. She is careful not to present her argument as a 'case' against Daly (Morris 1988: 29). One of the things which disturbs her most about Daly is her black-and-white division of the world between the enlightened and the unenlightened, between 'big strong women' who have freed themselves from the patriarchy and 'other women' – 'painted birds' and 'fembots' – who remain trapped within it. It is important, for Morris, not to replicate the same kind of opposition by casting Daly herself as a betrayer of the cause. But this does not prevent a searching examination of the ways in which feminist concepts of power can become a trap in which the same familiar points are made and remade.

Daly's practice is, for Morris, repetitive in just this way. The significance of this is not that it is boring or irritating. As Morris indicates, repetition can function 'as a reminder or – in an ancient tradition of both academic and priestly discourse – as a ritual and pleasurable reaffirmation of what has already been said before; an *act* of repetition of shared statements which – like the Communion Service – ritually reunites both speaker and hearers in an affirmation of their common identity' (1988: 39). It is more that such ritual forms are, by their nature, inflexible, incapable of recognizing or responding to change. Morris cites as an example an interjection of a woman at a Mary Daly lecture: 'Mary, you're not speaking to *me* ...' Daly's response was to refuse dialogue with the interjector: 'she could stay (ie. accept the speech) or go (ie. reject it altogether)'. This response amounts, for Morris, to 'a refusal to change rhetorics, or to change the mode of *énonciation* to deal with this new "I" that had emerged...' (1988: 39).

This refusal, in Morris's analysis, is structural rather than incidental. Although highly elaborate, Daly's system is premised ultimately on a simple division of the world between different kinds of being. At the most obvious level, the division is biological – between women and men. But at a secondary level, it is also spiritual – between 'less-damaged' women with 'Woman-Identified ears' and those who are lacking, without the inner qualities to respond to the call. This fundamental order determines the possibilities of discourse:

> This is why it is possible to *see through* deceptive discourse to reveal who the speakers
> really 'are'... This is why discourse can be a recognition ritual for finding out who people
> are (or rather, who *women* are – since a male is a male is a male): and for separating 'we'
> women from Other women. And I think this is probably why discourse itself ... cannot
> be a site of experiment...: the mode of *énonciation* must be relatively fixed, since it is
> the means by which 'the *multiply mobile*: the movers, the weavers, the Spinners' (p.xiv)
> may find themselves identified, and identify each other. (Morris 1988: 41–2)

Daly's system involves a view of language and representation which Morris describes as 'romantic': it 'implies a doctrine of Self-expression – in which the qualities
of the "self" in a sense, can be held to determine qualities of language' (1988: 41).
The function of language, like the function of art, is not to communicate or persuade,
but is 'dealt with by such notions as "identification" and "empathy"' (1988: 41).

The danger in this, as Morris has seen from at least the early 1980s, is an inability
to address anyone who is not already fully convinced, or who wavers even marginally
from the cause. As she puts it in 'Politics Now' of similar intolerances in the broader
cultural left:

> When I think of the resulting loss ... of so much goodwill, enthusiasm, commitment and
> activist energy coming from quarters not necessarily immediately recognizable as 'ours',
> a loss often directly attributable to the Left's own conservatism, inertia and punitive
> style-scrutineering, the fact that some stylish young kid might be striking nihilistic poses
> in the latest art-exhibition catalogue is quite frankly the least of my worries. (Morris
> 1988: 178)

To put it simply, if faced with Daly's choice – of 'staying' or 'going' – many will
choose to 'go'. By 1986, the evidence, for Morris, was clearly showing. To fail
to communicate with those who do not immediately share a cosmology formed
around left political discourses on power is a recipe for increasing isolation and
irrelevance.

Banality in Cultural Studies

The problem Morris finds in cultural studies is related to this but also different.
Consistent with my own view in previous chapters, she sees the field as structured
in critical counterpoint to simple or dogmatic applications of the concept of power.
This places it, in important ways, in an *opposite* camp to Mary Daly. Where Daly
sees social identities as more or less fixed by their relation to structures of power
(the patriarchy), cultural studies generally makes the case for greater fluidity,
indeterminacy and individual agency. But precisely because it is so structured,
Morris suggests, the field tends towards an inverted form of repetition. Where Daly
and other 'orthodox' left positions repetitively invoke generalized forms of power,

cultural studies repetitively insists that these phenomena are *not* fully determining, that social agents are able to 'negotiate', 'resist' or 'oppose' them.

This is the 'banality' Morris refers to in 'Banality in Cultural Studies'. The article is significant in revealing the complexity of the pitfalls put in place by generalized concepts of power. Even those who seem most critical of simple, unreflective uses of such concepts can end up replicating them in a mirrored form. Cultural studies is not the only position which runs this risk. Morris considers the field alongside the work of French media theorist and philosopher Jean Baudrillard. Baudrillard and cultural studies cannot be simply identified: as Morris recognizes, they 'are not *a priori* related, let alone opposed ... They involve different kinds of events. "Baudrillard" is an author, British Cultural Studies is a complex historical and political movement as well as a library of texts' (Morris 1996: 146). But there are significant commonalities between them in a desire to question the authority of 'orthodox' left discourses of power. There are also commonalities, for Morris, in the way this desire produces tendencies towards simplification and repetition.

Baudrillard's position on discourses of power is openly dismissive. As noted in Chapter 2, he is notorious for declaring that 'power is dead', that it no longer exists. The position rests on a wider argument about the triumph, in a media saturated society, of 'simulation' over 'the real'. The error of naïve forms of political radicalism, for Baudrillard, is an assumption that political strategies are still played out around real stakes, objective interests, where in fact any such stakes have disappeared following a collapse of the distinction between media representation and a reality preceding it. A 'banal' order, in which social agents compete over objects and productive resources, has been supplanted by a 'fatal' order, governed by artifice, seduction, challenge and sacrifice. Baudrillard sometimes suggests, alternatively, that the banal and the fatal have always contaminated each other in a continuing spiral of exchange and reversal. But in either case, left discourses on power are discredited, their authority undermined by the revelation of their blindness to fatality and seduction.

Cultural studies has generally been more respectful of 'orthodox' left positions, even as it sets out to distance itself from them. It has not usually questioned the *validity* of discourses of power, seeking only to *qualify* them. As Morris sharply characterizes it, the field has tended towards a 'yes, but...' discourse, one

> that most often proceeds *from* admitting class, racial and sexual oppressions *to* finding the inevitable saving grace ... And in practice the 'but...' – that is to say the argument-ative rhetoric – is immediately directed not to the hegemonic force of the 'dominant classes', but to other critical theories (vulgar feminism, the Frankfurt school) inscribed as misunderstanding popular culture. (Morris 1996: 160)

The structure of argument is particularly characteristic, for Morris, of British cultural studies, the authors she uses to illustrate being John Fiske and Ian Chambers. The 'but' for Fiske and Chambers – the qualification that always needs to be made to any claim in relation to power – is that 'the people' have a capacity to escape it, to '"negotiate" readings, generate new interpretations, and remake the materials of culture' (Morris 1996: 158).

If Baudrillard's vision is dark, apocalyptic and drawn to extremes, cultural studies is cheerful, democratic and interested in everyday experience. But despite their differences, Morris argues, they share something in seeking to displace or silence 'an unequivocally pained, unambivalently discontented, or *aggressive* theorising subject':

> It isn't just negligence. There is an active process going on of discrediting – by direct dismissal (Baudrillard) or covert inscription as Other (cultural studies) – the voices of grumpy feminists and cranky lefists ('Frankfurt School' can do duty for both). To discredit such voices is, as I understand it, one of the immediate political functions of the current boom in cultural studies... (Morris 1996: 160)

It is the polemical form of this project of discrediting which produces simplification and repetition. Baudrillard's fatal strategies 'keep returning us to his famous Black Hole', a scenario that is 'grim, obsessive, and in its enunciative strategies, maniacally over-coherent' (Morris 1996: 26). Cultural studies keeps returning us, by contrast, to a cheerful vision of the redemptive potential of popular culture – in short, 'the sanitized world of a deodorant commercial'.

As Morris goes on to argue, the problem here is not just emotional simplification – an inability to admit the 'pained', 'discontented' or 'aggressive'. It also affects the analytical power of cultural studies. Much of Fiske's and Chambers's case for the resistive potential of popular culture is built on an argument about the relative independence of the sphere of consumption. The position is pitched implicitly against an orthodox Marxism which insists that social relations are always determined by structures of domination in the sphere of production – the 'boss'/'worker' relation. The theoretical interest for Fiske and Chambers in television, shopping, popular music and other 'practices of consumption' is that they offer a terrain on which this doctrine can be disproved. Any instance of autonomy, creativity and agency among ordinary consumers can be taken as further evidence against the orthodox view – as proof that their identities are *not* fixed by relations of production.

It is not so much that this is wrong: Morris has no desire to defend an orthodox Marxism. It is rather that the structure of argument requires a radical simplification of the terms 'production' and 'consumption'. In setting up a counter-position to their own, Fiske and Chambers effectively concede the orthodox position on economic relations, despite the fact that it is derived from a nineteenth-century analysis of factory production. It may be true that 'you can't derive your analysis of what people make of a record from finding out that capitalists own the factory': 'But in an era of deindustrialization and increasing integration of markets and circuits alike, the problem of theorizing relations between production and consumption (or thinking 'production' at all) is considerably more complex than is allowed by the reduction of the effort to do so to anachronistic terms' (Morris 1996: 162). The desire to define cultural studies in opposition to naïve applications of generalized concepts of power compromises its own credibility and relevance.

Why 'Power'?

The clarity of Morris's perceptions of problems arising from generalized concepts of power has been, to summarize, exemplary. It is significant, however, that she has never sought to question these concepts themselves. Indeed, in more recent work, she has shown some defensiveness towards any suggestion that they might be. In a 1997 essay, for example, she responds with irritation to criticisms of cultural studies by Australian newspaper columnist Beatrice Faust as obsessed with 'capitalism, elitism, racism, sexism'. The problem for Morris is not with this characterization itself; she amplifies it, in fact, by extending Faust's list to 'imperialism and colonialism as well'. She takes issue, rather, with the idea that it is anything to be troubled by: '[It] is hardly a scandal; after all, what area of the humanities capable of sustaining a skerrick of interest in the great human conflicts of our time is not deeply concerned with these things' (Morris 1997a: 39).

Morris takes Faust to be arguing from a naïve premise that discourses of power commit the speaker to a narrow and dogmatic range of views. On this reading, the objections are readily countered with an elementary lesson in Foucault:

> Cultural studies does *not* [...] treat power relations as intrinsically or uniformly bad, and it does not construe power only as an oppressive property that *other* people 'have'. Power is not necessarily a bleak and paranoid concept, and cultural studies is not a discourse of powerlessness. Power is understood positively as a productive and consequential capacity to act, and power relations are defined not only in terms of a distribution of boundaries, prohibitions, and constraints, but also in terms of the processes of empowerment and disempowerment involved in even the most ordinary forms of engagement with a specific power structure. (Morris 1997a: 40)

This gesture to complexity, in which critics are inscribed as simply misinformed, has become a common response in cultural studies to scepticism about the concept of power. At a certain level, it is convincing. Faust is by no means the harshest or least sympathetic critic of discourses of power in cultural studies – as a founder of the Australian Women's Electoral Lobby, she actually shares with Morris a background in 1970s' feminism. But, like most journalists who write on the subject, she probably has little knowledge of the actual history of cultural studies, or the twists and turns of theories of power. It is fair, given the strength of the attack, to ask that it be supported by evidence.

But there is also a certain evasiveness in refusing, as Morris does, to negotiate a commitment to the concept of power itself. A generous reading of Faust's objection might be that it is an objection precisely to the insistent thematization of diverse phenomena under a generalized rubric of 'power'. There are ways of developing this objection that cannot easily be dismissed as naïve. As I have argued in previous chapters, a generalized thematics of power is a relatively recent development in English-language cultural criticism and can be traced to quite specific contexts. It is, in fact, a recent development even within those 'progressive' intellectual projects such as cultural studies that have emerged from the New Left since the 1950s. And, as Morris herself has been among the first to recognize, it is a development that has produced significant problems – not least, for feminism.

Why then the brittleness of Morris's response to questions posed over the concept of power itself? The answer must be somewhat speculative – the point is precisely that her investment in the concept is never openly articulated – but a couple of reasons suggest themselves. It is clear, firstly, that Morris has tended to identify moves to question discourses of power with a hostility to feminism. It has to be admitted, there are some grounds for doing so. There has been, as I have pointed out, a close *historical* association between feminism and the emergence in cultural studies of a fully generalized concept of power – an association with 'totalism'. If the relation is more contingent than necessary, critics of the concept have not generally made the distinction. As Morris points out in 'Banality in Cultural Studies', attempts to displace the concept of power in the field have often set their sights implicitly on feminism. In this context, a defence of the conditions for articulating women's experience in the public domain appears to require a defence also of the concept of power.

But perhaps more importantly, Morris has tended to consider any question over the concept of power in Baudrillardian terms, as a question over the 'reality' of the phenomena it claims to identify. This framing of options can be seen not only in her engagement with Baudrillard himself (Morris 1984; 1996), but also in wider interventions into debates on postmodernism. In an essay on the property boom in Sydney in the 1980s, for example, she criticizes popular discourses which seek to deflate corporate claims over urban space as merely a projection of petty male egos. Such a response, she argues, 'misses the point about the role of the "urbanization of capital" in creating economic and social inequalities, precisely at a time when its operation in our cities are reaching new heights of intensity and savagery' (Morris 1998: 128). The criticism is extended to the theoretical work of Robert Venturi, Paul Virilio and Robert Somol. The articulation of the concept of power in this work is not entirely straightforward, but the veridical reference of, at least, certain classical figurations of power is clearly in question. The danger in this, for Morris, is that it deprives criticism of its ability to point out exploitation, social inequality or hardened indifference to the effects of economic change.

Morris never really considers the possibility that there may be other positions on the concept of power than this stark either/or: either it identifies a 'real' phenomenon or it does not. This stands sharply at odds with the way she regards other concepts. The general principle of the sceptical, historical approach she brings to 'culture', 'woman', 'the nation' or 'the left' is that they should *neither* be attributed with an absolute ontological status *nor* regarded as insubstantial or illusory. Concepts do not work in a pure philosophical void, but in practical, historical circumstances. They are not arbitrary, weightless – they have a cultural inertia and material bearing; but nor are they fixed for all time. The concept of power appears here as the signal exception. This is not to say that Morris regards the *form* of power as fixed: she is on this point a good Foucauldian. But, like Foucault, she tends the regard power as simply 'real'. Notwithstanding qualifications, the concept is assumed to be delivered outside history, offering itself to be universally applied.

With Respect to the English?

An important context for this is Morris's early dismissal of 'Englishness'. Through most of her career, her fluency in European, particularly French, theoretical references has given her a distinct intellectual edge. In 'Banality in Cultural Studies', she runs rings around Fiske and Chambers – notably positioned as 'British' – in the sophistication of her understanding of the implications of generalized concepts of power. Playing with figures which have circulated historically in intellectual engagements with popular culture – particularly the identification between 'mass culture' and the 'bimbo' – she suggests that it is now the *white male theorist* who has emerged, almost wilfully, as the bimbo. The description is not pressed too seriously and is balanced by generous recognition of the humane intentions of Fiske, Chambers and 'British Cultural Studies'. But it also crystallizes an assurance, running through most of Morris's work, that there are few real insights to be gained from 'Anglo' traditions and perspectives.

But this assurance also involves limitations. One that immediately appears, in the light of my discussion in previous chapters, is Morris's oversight of another dimension than simple populism in the 'British' engagement with questions of power. She assumes, admittedly with most others who have written on the subject, that the problematization of power in British cultural studies has been a problematization only of the reach and saturation of power. Her attention falls entirely on the themes of 'agency' and 'resistance', themes that only come into view once the general rubric of power has already been accepted. But there has always been something else in play in British cultural studies, even if in an oblique and subterranean way: a problematization of the concept of power itself. As I argued in Chapter 3, it comes close to the surface in Fiske's distinction between 'imperializing power' and 'localizing *powers*'. Implicit in this is quite a different drama than the confrontation between 'the people' and the 'power bloc'. It is a drama played out over the very validity of a generalized rubric of power.

In fact, Morris herself may owe more to this 'English' perspective than she has wanted to admit. There is a strong *empiricist* dimension to her work. In a 1990s' essay, for example, she describes her approach to textual analysis as one which 'assumes that the objects we read can provide, through their own material "resistance" to our acts of abstraction, terms for questioning and revising the models we bring to bear' (Morris 1998: 143). The principle bears comparison with Dick Hebdige's statement of respect, quoted in Chapter 3, for the 'incandescence of the particular'. It invites speculation on whether Morris may owe a similar debt to an 'English' intellectual inheritance as Hebdige reluctantly diagnoses in himself. Hebdige's account of his relation to Englishness – 'I tried to escape the English tradition, to find my own "elsewhere"' – has clear echoes with Morris's flight from the 'thick grey pall of Anglophile gloom' of 1950s' Australia. Might it be for Morris as for Hebdige that 'the legacy of an English education (however poorly assimilated, however badly understood)' nevertheless 'shows through'?

There are a number of obvious ways that such a connection might be denied. Morris has sometimes suggested a specifically *feminist* provenance for empiricist themes in her work. In the preface to *Too Soon Too Late*, she claims 'experience', for example, as a 'feminist category' (Morris 1998: xxii), setting it against the dominant concerns of Anglo-American cultural theory. Elsewhere, characteristics that might be identified in Hebdige's sense as 'English' are denominated by Morris as *Australian*. In the introduction to *Australian Cultural Studies*, she pays tribute with John Frow to the early work in adult education of autodidact and film enthusiast John Flaus. If placed in the British context, Flaus would probably be seen as falling with Richard Hoggart and other early figures who emerged from adult education on the 'English' side of the divide between an 'indigenous' practice and continental 'theory'. But for Frow and Morris, his very significance is that he was not English but Australian.

At a certain level, these points might be taken: 'experience' clearly *has* been a central category in the development of feminism; the formative influence in Morris's work of figures like Flaus probably *was* greater than any from early British cultural studies. But it is doubtful whether they can be extended, as Morris sometimes implies they might be, to a defence against any association with Englishness. In relation to the first, 'experience' has a venerable history from Bacon, Locke and Hume as one of the key distinguishing categories of English thought. The connection to this tradition of the feminist use of the term needs at least to be discussed. In relation to the second, it is surely no accident that it is possible to find Australian parallels with the early British pioneers of cultural studies. A common context in adult education and an enthusiasm for the democratizing potential of popular cultural forms is only one aspect of shared political histories and institutional forms. However much

Australia has taken its own distinctive course, some relation to Britain must again be recognized.

It may seem oddly obsessive to press this point so far, but it has significance for the argument which I want to make in the next chapter: that some of the most interesting responses to problems of power in cultural studies in recent years have begun to reactivate connections with English intellectual traditions. I do not wish to suggest that it is necessary, in appreciating these, to assign them a simple positive value. But a condition for the argument is a more complex understanding of 'Englishness' than as something simply to be disavowed.

–11–

Beyond Power? The 'New Pluralism' and the Turn to Ethics

Can the story of the concept of power in cultural studies have anything other than a depressing conclusion? As we saw at the beginning of the last chapter, there was a moment in the 1990s when, for many at least, it seemed not. Whichever way it turned on the concept, the field seemed to be confronted with unattractive options. To emphasize the determining significance of power relations was to be exposed to increasing suspicions of dogmatism, paranoia and political authoritarianism. As potential readers or audiences became alienated and as radical tendencies themselves fragmented with the discovery of multiple dimensions of identity, it was also generally to play a losing game. But to argue that power is *not* determining, or at least not entirely determining – as cultural studies has more often done – also appeared unsatisfactory, pointing the way of populist 'banality'. The blithe optimism of this option, and the anodyne celebration of 'agency' and 'resistance', put at risk the hard-earned respect which the field had earlier gained.

But where is cultural studies on questions of power today? Have the pessimistic assessments of the 1990s proved to be justified? As I suggested in Chapter 1, the picture is somewhat confused. There has been relatively little direct reflection on concepts of power in recent years, the last really significant development – at the level, at least, of theory – being the reception and absorption of Foucault. While many have seen Foucault as offering deliverance from problems in previous uses of the concept of power, his work was already well known in the 1990s and was not sufficient to immunize cultural studies either from internal dissatisfaction or external criticisms. There would be some justification for thinking, therefore, that little has changed. And indeed, the form of arguments developed in the 1990s continue to be widely deployed. Cultural studies is criticized on one side as 'populist' and on another, paradoxically, as authoritarian and dogmatic.

But I want to suggest in this chapter that there is another story to be told. There is a danger here of responding to pessimism with simple optimism, but I would like rather to suggest open possibility. The options for the use of the concept of power are not as tired and familiar as many would have us believe. Something *has* changed; cultural studies is *not* condemned to an endless oscillation between asserting or resisting generalized discourses of power; alternatives *have* been found both to a Thompsonian insistence on power and Fiskean themes of popular 'agency'. At the same time, the shift is, in a sense, not a shift at all: it is rather a reconnection with a way of thinking about questions of power that has always, at some level, been there. This is the way of thinking I identified in early British cultural studies and traced to broadly 'Anglo' patterns of political development – an understanding of powers as plural.

The two cases I want to discuss in what follows may appear at first oddly chosen. The first is the so-called 'policy' intervention into cultural studies in the 1990s, the second what I will call a 'media republican' position which developed at around the same time. Both were clearly engaged in debates around power (in the singular) and, more than that, were defined by strong, often polemical, positions. Both also drew, to differing degrees, on continental European authority. The policy advocates proposed a rigorous Foucauldianism in which nothing, even 'resistance', was allowed to escape explanation in terms of power. The media republicans proposed almost the opposite: a deliberate *displacement* of the concept of power – at least for most practical purposes – by concepts of democratic participation, pleasure, beauty and desire. In short, both could easily be seen as playing out the familiar antinomies which have plagued cultural studies since the emergence of generalized concepts of power – and playing them out, if anything, in somewhat exacerbated forms.

But to rest on such a conclusion would be to overlook the more interesting effects of the two initiatives. Precisely because they did explore extremes, they destabilized generalized concepts of power in significant ways. This is perhaps clearest in the case of media republicanism, which constructed an account of social and political relations in which such concepts appeared to have little place. But a destabilization of the concept of power can also be seen in the policy arguments. The insistence in these arguments that there is nothing outside power, that everything is formed in and through it, has a paradoxical effect. The concept loses any capacity for discrimination – a basis from which to say 'this is an effect of power', 'this is not' – thereby becoming emptied of meaning. Despite their obvious differences, the two developments share a significant commonality: they both engineered a recession in the real effectiveness of generalized concepts of power. It is in this space that a 'new pluralism' in relation to power has been able to take form.

A Contrived Appearance of Ineffable Complexity

The sharpest statement of the policy position came in two essays by Tony Bennett, 'Putting Policy into Cultural Studies' (1992a) and 'Useful Culture' (1992b). A later, more developed, statement of Bennett's arguments can be found in his 1998 book *Culture – A Reformer's Science*. But the position also had considerable breadth, figuring for a time as nothing less than a comprehensive 'movement'. Part of its strength was in its capacity to play both at the level of practical considerations of cultural policy (for example, Cunningham 1992) and at the level of high intellectual reflections on a 'Kantian' legacy in the humanities and on the relations between government, aesthetics and ethics (Hunter 1992; 1994). It also achieved some international reach. While most prominent in Australia, it developed in close dialogue with a substantial body of British work inspired by Foucault's writing on governmentality (notably Rose 1990; Miller and Rose 1992) and also found some influence and response in North America (Bratich, Packer and McCarthy 2003).

The policy intervention was quite explicitly remedial. It was pitched as a way of rescuing cultural studies from the kinds of problems considered over the last few chapters. As Bennett puts it in 'Putting Policy into Cultural Studies':

> [I]t is only by using the kinds of correctives that would come from putting 'policy' into cultural studies that cultural studies may be deflected from ... those forms of banality which, in some quarters, have already claimed it while also resisting the lure of those debates whose contrived appearance of ineffable complexity makes them a death trap for practical thinking. (Bennett 1992a: 32–3)

In *Rethinking the School*, Ian Hunter writes, in a similar vein, of a need for a kind of 'intellectual therapy' (Hunter 1994: 172). The object in need of reform, in this case, is not quite identical with cultural studies, but it is clear that Hunter is thinking most immediately of Marxist and feminist positions in educational theory, which have, at least, a close affinity with the field.

Bennett's reference to 'banality' invokes Meaghan Morris's criticisms, discussed in the last chapter, of populist tendencies associated particularly with 'British' cultural studies. But the policy intervention was in fact much more focused on the other problem he identifies – the 'contrived appearance of ineffable complexity'. The objects of criticism here are more often American, coming into view in the context of the inflation of the concept of power discussed in Chapter 9. One of the major contributions of the policy intervention was in offering a searching analysis of conceptual problems arising from this development. While never presented in quite these terms, the central point of this analysis was that when the concept of power is generalized to a certain point, any claim to speak against power becomes driven to a kind of irrationalism. 'Opposition' or 'resistance' can only be spoken from a position of radical otherness, completely removed from the field of analysis. The problems with this are not only analytical but ethical: oppositional discourses become literally unaccountable.

An exemplary development of the argument is a critique by Bennett of Michel de Certeau's theorization of popular resistance through the influential distinction between 'strategy' and 'tactics'. The discussion has a context in the increasing eclipse by de Certeau of earlier perspectives on resistance in cultural studies, such as the Birmingham Centre's *Resistance Through Rituals* (Hall and Jefferson 1976). As Bennett points out, this eclipse can be related to the increasing internationalization of the field. In the Birmingham work, bases of resistance were understood as local and particular. What was being resisted was not 'power' as such, but an identifiable post-war project of moulding and transforming English working-class life. Resistance was understood as similarly specific, being an attempt to maintain aspects, at least, of older working-class culture. In de Certeau, by contrast, the terms are thoroughly abstracted, becoming, in the process, much more transportable between contexts. Power is associated with a generalized 'system' and resistance with an unspecified and somewhat mysterious 'other'.

The disappearance of any idea of a stable position independent of the functional requirements of power is articulated by de Certeau in an extreme literalization of Foucault's analysis of the disciplinary society. In Bennett's paraphrase:

> Panoptic power … is ubiquitous and all-triumphant: there are no longer any spaces outside it capable of nurturing the cultural resources through which it might be resisted or counter-attacked. All of the fortifications and barriers behind which the subordinate might have developed cultural spaces of their own are down; all of the ditches and banks of civil society within which autonomous forms of life once flourished have been razed. All that exists is absolute power faced with the ultimately atomistic sources of resistance, monadic individuals who, however, have been stripped of all weapons and fortifications except guile, ruse and deception. (Bennett 1998: 177)

Against this background understanding, de Certeau wishes to preserve an idea of 'ruses' and 'tactics' through which power is subverted or evaded. But as Bennett points out, it is difficult to see how such countervailing forces are possible:

> Where do the ruses and tactics come from? What accounts for their guile and deception? No-one can say, and certainly not de Certeau, whose only account of these is to recast them as a series of images which convert any particular resistances on the part of particular actors into the mere contingent stand-ins for, variously, the opacity of popular culture, 'a dark rock that resists all assimilation', 'the enigma of the consumer-sphinx', or for an operational logic which stems from outside culture and history entirely and 'whose models may go back as far as the age-old ruses of fishes and insects that disguise and transform themselves in order to survive'. (Bennett 1998: 178–9)

As Bennett points out, de Certeau in fact *prohibits* himself from anything more than poetic allusions. He is obliged 'to forgo the possibility of describing practices in terms of an external analytic vocabulary since this would, *eo ipso*, place him on the side of knowledge and power' (1998: 180). The logic of his position requires an appeal to the 'domain of the ineffable' (1998: 179).

A similar form of argument can be found at a more concrete level in an intervention by Hunter into debates about the future of the humanities and social sciences in the early 1990s. The major catalyst for these debates in Australia was a Federal Government White Paper (Dawkins 1988) on the future of higher education, which outlined sweeping reforms aimed at harnessing the sector more fully to 'national priorities' such as productivity and debt reduction. This move was widely perceived by critics in somewhat similar terms to de Certeau's extended concept of power. An important text of the time was Michael Pusey's (1991) *Economic Rationalism in Canberra*, which presented a picture of a relentless advance by abstract technical reason, subsuming everything – like panoptic power – within a single comprehensive 'system'. Pusey's object of analysis was wider than the university system, but the concept of 'economic rationalism' provided – and indeed continues to provide – a major framework for understanding shifts in higher education. Against this background, the academic humanities and social sciences have often regarded themselves as a last bastion of 'resistance'.

The problem with this, for Hunter, is that the critical analysis of governmental control provides such a total explanation that it is unable to account for the position of the critics themselves:

> On the one hand, the governmental discourse seeks to constitute universities as legitimate objects of governmental intervention. It does so by conceiving of their educational activities in terms of the formation of skills and knowledges with calculable, hence plannable, economic outcomes. On the other hand ... the defence of the humanities seeks to establish their institutional autonomy by rendering their ends opaque to all purposive rationality... Pushed to its extreme, which is not in fact very far from its centre, this defence ends by identifying the autonomy of the humanities with their ineffability. (Hunter 1991: 11–12)

The sting in the argument comes in Hunter's diagnosis of the consequences of this for any considered assessment of the position and possibilities of humanities education and research: 'Needless to say significant intellectual and political penalties are incurred in trying to calculate one's situation and prospects by proclaiming their incalculability' (1991: 12).

Both Bennett and Hunter tend to generalize their objects of criticism, seeing individual cases as merely contemporary examples of tendencies stretching back to classical European romanticism and the formation of the modern university. But it is worth considering whether the problems they identify may have had a more immediate context. In his critique of de Certeau, Bennett describes his view of power as an extreme case of a bipolar model of domination and resistance: 'one in which it is carried to excess in the magnification of one pole of power to the point where it becomes all-encompassing and the diminution of the other to the point where it disappears entirely, becomes a zero power' (Bennett 1998: 177). The description resonates strongly with actual conditions as they were widely perceived at the end of the Cold war: an uncontested American military dominance and the evaporation of any alternative to Western market liberalism. If read in this context, the policy analysis could be seen as offering an acute diagnosis of the problems of maintaining oppositional discourses at the end of the Cold War. So long, at least, as the temptation remains to totalize power, any claim to resist it is left unable either to account for itself or to offer any framework in which it might be held to account. It runs a risk, in short, of intellectual and ethical bankruptcy.

The Exorcism of 'Principle'

The policy response to this problem was in many ways surprising. Rather than pulling back from totalizing visions of power, Bennett and Hunter suggest pushing them *further*. The strategy draws inspiration from Foucault's late work on governmentality (Foucault 1978) and a body of British and Australian writing which has sought to develop and extend it (Rose 1990; Miller and Rose 1992; Meredyth and Tyler 1993; Minson 1993). The distinctive feature of this work, in relation to questions of power, has been in stretching the concept of 'government' to apply well beyond the institutions and agencies of the state. In Foucault's original account, the instruments and techniques of governing were formed initially *outside* the state, in local and autonomous projects of managing and ordering, only subsequently being taken up and developed by the state (Foucault 1978: 103). The important corollary of this is that speaking or acting against the state – or indeed any centralized power – can be represented as itself an expression of governmental power.

The perspective is applied by Bennett in his critique of de Certeau. There is an irony in this: having sharply characterized totalizing tendencies in de Certeau's view of power, Bennett leapfrogs him with his own proposals. If, for de Certeau, there are still gaps and interstices – albeit mysterious – in the grid of power, the gaps, for Bennett, are closed and the interstices filled in. Admittedly, power has the capacity in Bennett's account to divide against itself so that it appears as having fluid characteristics. Citing Foucault, he argues that

> the mechanisms of modern forms of government ... are themselves partly responsible for generating counter-demands on government owing to their inability to entirely satisfy the demands they generate. It is, as Graham Burchell contends in summarizing this line of argument, 'in the name of forms of existence which have been shaped by political technologies of *government* that we, as individuals and groups, make claims on or against the *state*'. (Bennett 1998: 178)

The position allows for relations which are 'active and disputatious' (1998: 178). Nevertheless, everything is orchestrated by a single principle: the all-pervasive 'political technologies of government'. Even where conflicts arise which these technologies are unable to resolve, they are conflicts that the technologies have generated in the first place. There is – which is precisely the point – no 'outside'.

A similar position informs Hunter's writing on education. In *Rethinking the School*, he takes aim at the idea that intellectuals have any role to play in offering an external critique of the governmental management of modern schooling. When subjected to scrutiny, he warns, 'the idea that "transformative intellectuals" can exercise "emancipatory authority", based on their pure insight into the future form of human development, begins to look dangerously self-deluding. Under this degree of moral inflation the teacher's role threatens to break free of its professional and civic moorings, drifting into moral grandiloquence and political fantasy' (Hunter 1994: 30). The most immediate target of criticism here is the 'critical pedagogy' of Henry Giroux and his collaborators (see particularly, Giroux and McLaren 1989) – the term 'emancipatory authority' is Giroux's – but the arguments press towards more generalized conclusions. Any claim to speak from a position of exteriority to power needs, for Hunter, to be stripped of pretension. As he puts it earlier in the book:

> [W]e must learn to see abstraction as first and foremost a social gesture. The claim to 'pure' theory, made in the name of withdrawing from the power-tainted perceptions of the governmental sphere, is in fact a means of exercising power on and within this sphere, as the claimant reappears wielding the moral authority and social prestige of the untainted theoretical persona. (Hunter 1994: 14)

It is not just the understanding of the school which is at stake here; a larger claim is being made about any position which disavows an involvement in the exercise of power. As with Bennett's analysis of resistance, Hunter recognizes the position from which such disavowals are made but reduces them to an epiphenomenon of governmental power itself.

The governmental absolutism of the policy initiative served its function, in Bennett's words, as a means to 'undercut and disable those ways of thinking about intellectual work which situate the intellectual in some self-subsistent and transcendent site of critique' (Bennett 1998: 6). But it also involved its own costs. The most widely remarked of these was an intolerance of anything other than a declared alignment with governmental objectives – what Meaghan Morris described, in reference to Stuart Cunningham, as a 'desperately gung-ho corporatism' (1992: 546). This tendency was more than a matter of personalities; it was a requirement of the position: to allow any suggestion of a position independent from government was immediately to raise the spectre of the moral grandstanding of 'principled criticism' and had therefore to be denied. Hunter writes tellingly, at one point, of a need for a kind of 'exorcism' (1994: 2). The metaphor is appropriate: there was often a grim determination in the way the policy proponents sought to nail down their claims and an intolerance in the way they addressed alternative positions.

A second problem of the position was in accounting for how the *ends* of government are arrived at. As Tom O'Regan (1992: 416) pointed out, the policy arguments did little to revise critical caricatures of government as entirely given over to instrumental rationality. In 'Putting Policy into Cultural Studies', Bennett presents the policy initiative as matter of 'talking to the Ideological State Apparatuses'. What is clearly intended here is a rejection of a hostile Althusserian view of governing agencies as instruments of ruling class domination. But the assumption that these agencies are indeed 'apparatuses' – that they are reducible to an instrumental function of some kind – is carried over largely intact. This raises a question of the *objectives* for which they are deployed. One would normally look here, as Althusser did, to specifically political processes: the uses of the instruments of government are the outcome of contest and debate between different interests and groups. But if nothing is allowed outside of 'governmental rationalities', any space for politics is effectively eliminated. There was nowhere in the policy vision where ends might be decided.

There was, finally, a central contradiction in the policy arguments. It was assumed, on the one hand, that the arguments themselves might make a difference. There are frequent warnings in the policy writings of the need to respect the 'fragility' of government. In *Rethinking the School*, Hunter (1994: 157) refers darkly to sectarian violence in Northern Ireland and the disintegration of Yugoslavia as lessons of the costs of failing to do so. On the other hand, however, the arguments sought to explain away differences as merely illusory. If they were followed consistently, 'putting policy into cultural studies' would have to be seen as having precisely no effect: the field has *always been* completely enmeshed in government, hence *always already* involved in policy considerations. The most abstract dialectician, the most romantic aesthete, the most revolutionary ideologue are all, for Hunter and Bennett, agents of government, exercising power 'on and within the governmental sphere'. To enjoin them to adopt governmental functions can only be redundant.

Governmentality as Ethics

One might conclude from this that the policy initiative was a blind alley for attempts within cultural studies to reform concepts of power. While further contributing to an understanding of the problems, it was unable to offer satisfactory solutions. Such an analysis could be seen as confirmed by the fact that the policy 'moment' has clearly passed. In fact, a fatigue with policy began to be felt almost as soon as the case had been put. In a 1992 essay, McKenzie Wark expressed a feeling of many at the repetitive gambits of the policy proponents: 'Honestly, if I hear the words "cultural policy" one more time I'm going to grab the remote control and change channels' (Wark 1992a: 677). In their 1993 introduction to *Australian Cultural Studies*, John Frow and Meaghan Morris (1993: xxix) sum up the debate around policy, with a retrospective closure, as generating 'much heat and less light'. It should be said that the policy proponents have continued, individually, to be productive, but the energy generated by their arguments about power appears to have largely dissipated.

Something important would be lost, though, if the policy initiative were left to moulder as yet another ruin in the history of the concept of power. For it had another dimension than governmental absolutism. This was a rediscovery of a certain British style of political thought. It is easy here to be misled. The cover of *Culture – A Reformer's Science* carries an image of a pensive Foucault, the Gallic intensity of his gaze symbolically fused with Bennett's name overlaid as if as an autograph. But in the pages inside his real enthusiasm is for a rather different set of figures: Sir Henry Cole, William Stanley Jevons, James Kay-Shuttleworth, Thomas Greenwood, John Ruskin, James Fergusson and Edward Edwards. What unites this group is a very British tradition of practically minded public service idealism, a tradition whose legacy was institutionalized in free public libraries and museums, literary and debating societies, mechanics institutes and schools of art.

The function of Foucault in the policy arguments is, in fact, largely negative. It is, as Bennett puts it, 'to provide an *antidote* to the headier forms of thought and action that now too often go under the label of cultural studies' (Bennett 1998: 84, emphasis added). Similarly, in Hunter's work, Foucault is most often invoked as the most effective agent for driving out the moral claims of transcendent critique. The exorcism is only performed so that our attention can begin to be engaged by an unlikely group of unspectacular heroes: the nineteenth-century Scottish and English philanthropists and social reformers David Stow, Samuel Wilderspin, Henry Dunn and, again, James Kay-Shuttleworth. It is not to the prophets of moral and political philosophy but to figures such as these, for Hunter, that we owe the minor miracle of modern education. It is not to abstract 'principle', but 'to the inglorious micro-technics of conscience, patiently adapted from Christian spiritual discipline by the journeymen intellectuals of the state' (Hunter 1994: 142).

The significance for concepts of power of reconnecting with this British tradition are all but spelt out by Bennett in an analysis of Henry Cole's nineteenth-century conception of the South Kensington Museum in London. He compares the latter with the *envoi* system developed in Napoleonic France, which was organized around the theme of sovereignty: 'the system's primary purpose was to embody and circulate an image of state power throughout the nation... [L]ess importance was attached to the pictures selected ... than the labels accompanying them, which indicated that they were the gift of the Emperor or of the state' (Bennett 1998: 116). Cole and his associates were concerned, by contrast, with quite different questions. Schooled in utilitarianism, 'they constantly stressed art's divisibility, its capacity to be broken down into different quantities from which different degrees and kinds of benefits might be derived' (1998: 117). One indicator of the difference is that it was not essential in the British model that objects or works of art be originals; what was important were the educational effects their circulation could achieve.

As Bennett goes on to summarize:

> art was not, in this school of thought, envisaged as a means of representing or staging power... Instead, its circulation was conceived in accordance with a governmental logic in which art, rather than representing power, *is* a power – a power susceptible to multiple

subdivisions in a programme which has as its end not the exertion of specular dominance over the populace but the development of its capacities. (Bennett 1998: 118)

The shift here from the general 'power' to the singular and specific '*a* power' is barely remarked and is elsewhere obscured by a Foucauldian contrast between different *forms* of power ('juridico-discursive' and 'governmental'). But otherwise, all the elements are there for a regeneration of the pluralist vision, the vision of a 'multiplicity of semi-independencies', which I traced in Chapter 3 as emerging particularly from English patterns of state formation.

My analysis here resonates with some recent work of Thomas Osborne. Osborne has been loosely associated with the British work on governmentality. In *Aspects of Enlightenment – Social theory and the ethics of truth*, he acknowledges Hunter as one of those, along with Graham Burchell, Colin Gordon, Ian Hacking and Nikolas Rose, who have 'motivated this book in ways they do not know, and would probably not much like' (Osborne 1998: xv). He also works significantly from Foucault. But the Foucault that interests him is rather different from the one most often invoked in cultural studies and governmentality theory. He is not 'the subversive continental philosopher, the arcane prophet of transgression, the iconoclastic poststructuralist, the metatheorist of power, the functionalist theory of social control, or the gloomy prophet of the totally administered society', but 'a much more buttoned-up animal':

> An ethical thinker with a Kantian heritage, a good modernist rather than a faddish postmodernist, a rigorous and not so unconventional historical epistemologist concerned with the 'immature' human sciences and, most unlikely of all, something of an Anglo-Saxon empiricist *manqué*. (Osborne 1998: x)

This last suggestion marks a significant shift. The 'Anglo' themes that can be found in Bennett and Hunter are no longer authorized by Foucault but come to stand in their own right and even to restructure our understanding of Foucault himself. An 'English' intellectual style comes out from the shelter of its continental patron, projecting itself more clearly in its own terms.

This development is conditioned by the evaporation of a generalized concept of power. At a certain level, Osborne's arguments are consistent with Hunter's and Bennett's. But there is also a significant difference. It is a difference that is most evident in his understanding of governmentality, which is conceptualized in terms not of power but of *ethics*: 'To talk of modern arts of government is not the same as talking, in epochal terms, about the characteristics of whole societies. The *mentality* in 'governmentality' is important. What is at stake are quite restricted rationalities or mentalities for the governing of conduct, not the structural principles of whole societies…' (Osborne 1998: 30). Governmentality, for Osborne, is not a positive phenomenon; it is an ethical disposition which has been adopted unevenly in the practice of government – a disposition to govern in the name of truth:

Put schematically: to govern in a 'liberal' way – and in the highly restricted sense we need to give to the notion of liberalism here, which is not the sense that is usual in political philosophy – one had to subject the terrain over which one governed to apparatuses of truth, and the knowledge that this supplied would likewise supply the ends of government – the security, welfare and tranquillity of the population. (Osborne 1998: 30)

While the reference here to 'apparatuses' continues the use of mechanical metaphors, there can be no doubt about the implications of the position. To recognize the historical emergence of governmentality is not to apprehend a structural principle of social organization or a new modality of power. It is only to recognize a new ethic informing the conduct of those involved in the specific and limited sphere of government. It provides no grounds for general claims about 'relations between culture and power'.

Media Republicanism and the 'Knowledge Class'

'Media republicanism' – as I am calling it here – has not had quite the profile of the policy position and has not occasioned such a focused 'debate'. But it is sufficiently distinctive to be recognized as a contrasting intervention into the use of the concept of power, different in character but similarly ambitious in its claims. I will discuss the work here of John Hartley, McKenzie Wark and Catharine Lumby. This work does not have quite as clear a 'line' as the policy initiative or a rallying point in a figure such as Foucault, but there are clear similarities in the negotiation of questions of power. In this respect, it can also be seen as representative of wider tendencies. Hartley's arguments share themes, for example, with the work, among others, of Henry Jenkins, Mark Poster and Alan McKee. Wark's have connections with debates around new technologies and libertarian possibilities in cultural theory. Lumby's are broadly aligned with a range of attempts within feminism to avoid automatic condemnations of sexualized representations and popular media.

   Like the policy initiative, media republicanism has explicitly set out to address problems in the use of the concept of power. I have already quoted Hartley's warning, in the early 1990s, that the 'radical' claims of cultural studies 'may not be so bold and radical and new after all, but merely the beginning of a spoilt, arrogant, *pouting* phase' (Hartley 1992: 16). The analysis is quite similar to those of the policy advocates and is useful in more explicitly invoking a 'post Cold War' context. The challenge posed by this context – or, more specifically, the idea that there is a single, global 'field' of power – is, again, that claims to speak 'against' power come to seem merely gestural. Unable, any longer, to identify a concrete 'other' to what they oppose, a base from which to work, they assume the status of a pose or style rather than a part of a credible political programme.

But Hartley's scepticism has increasingly extended to the concept of power as such – and here there is a marked divergence from the policy advocates. In *The Politics of Pictures*, from which the above quote is also taken, he suggests that the focus on power may *always* have been unfortunate:

> In fact it might be argued that the oppositional intellectuals whose early efforts established the theoretical and analytical agenda for cultural studies as an academic subject were interested in television's potential to manipulate the masses because some time in the future they hoped they'd be able to have a go at doing that too. What's the point of Gramsci if not to show how the hegemonic can be countered, and, once the strategy is determined, who's going to direct it if not the strategists? (Hartley 1992: 25)

This line of argument comes closer to the reservations of James Carey, discussed in Chapter 9, about cultural studies' turn to questions of power in the 1970s. It points, like Carey, to the political and ethical costs of an instrumental view of social relations. Even where such a view takes the form of a critical analysis, it can easily become a self-fulfilling prophecy, leaving no conceptual space in which to project a democratic vision.

In his later *Popular Reality*, Hartley goes somewhat further, representing intellectual struggles over questions of power as an internecine struggle between different elements of what John Frow (1995) has dubbed the 'knowledge class' – those whose position depends not so much on a stake in material processes as on symbolic representations. Writing of Stuart Hall and his co-authors in *Policing the Crisis*, he suggests that the idea of a universal field of power has been merely as a pretext for exercising power over and against other knowledge-class factions:

> they [Hall et al.] need to theorize a *hegemonic* ideology which has the population at its mercy because they want to ride into town as organic intellectuals and impose a *counter-hegemonic* consciousness on those same people, in order to mobilize resistance to the 'ruling-class alliance'. They don't *really* give two hoots for what 'the people' might be thinking, saying, knowing and imagining for themselves. (Hartley 1996: 239–40)

The critical analysis of power relations comes to look here not just as holding certain dangers. It stands accused of knowledge-class practices 'every bit as anti-democratic as anything the media moguls have invented' (1996: 26).

Similar arguments have been developed by Lumby specifically in relation to feminism. In her 1997 book *Bad Girls*, she sets out to question common feminist conceptions of power:

> Feminism has historically been concerned with the dominant nature of one point of view in the production and consumption of images: a male, patriarchal perspective. Yet, the popular feminist critique of the media has *itself* become a dominant point of view. It has become self-satisfied and lazy. It has failed to take account of changes in popular culture

and the media more generally. It is out of touch with the way people consume images. (Lumby 1997: xxv)

In the same characteristic move as Hartley, Lumby turns the analysis of power back on the analysts. While patriarchy continues to hover ambiguously in the background, the 'dominant point of view' of most immediate concern has become feminism itself.

As noted in Chapter 2, there is a question whether this kind of turning of the tables does not simply exacerbate the problem it seeks to address. There is clearly some irony in launching an oppositional critique of those who engage in oppositional critiques. Lumby shows some awareness of this paradox, taking care to temper her differences with the older feminist 'establishment', but it is perhaps Wark who has addressed it in the most sustained way. In *The Virtual Republic*, he treads a delicate path between rejecting the idea of a 'dominant ideology' and elevating this idea as itself a 'dominant ideology' that needs to be opposed. As Wark notes, the latter tendency becomes identical at a certain point with the position of the conservative culture warriors and the campaign against a left-liberal 'politically correct' conspiracy. In a deft move, he parcels both left and right positions in the 'culture war' as paranoid fantasies, structurally dependent on the image of a 'bad other' to sustain themselves ('the white patriarch' or 'the phantom army of PC zealots' respectively). There remains little doubt, however, that the concept of power is as much a problem, for Wark, as it is positively enabling.

The Politics of Kissing

The media republican solution to this problem has been, in a sense, the opposite of the policy initiative. Rather than seizing further on the concept of power, in order to subject it to the rigours of Foucauldian reform, it has been simply to let it slip. The sharpest statements of the position are probably to be found, again, in Hartley. In *Popular Reality*, he suggests that the contemporary public sphere be approached not from a 'they' perspective – concerned with how 'other people' are manipulated or controlled – but a 'we' perspective – the perspective of those who participate themselves (either as 'writers' or 'readers') in the circulation and exchange of meanings. If we do so, he argues, we begin to recognize that '"mass" audiences may be seen to be discursively "decolonized" (ie. more free) to a much greater extent than is commonly admitted by critical coteries' (Hartley 1996: 57). This general proposition could be seen as framing the media republican project: to describe and analyse communication in the public sphere *without* reaching immediately for the concept of power.

As a provocative opening to this project in *Popular Reality*, Hartley suggests that we view public exchanges through the metaphor of the 'kiss':

Kissing is ... a remarkably apposite metaphor for thinking about the relationships between producers, texts and readers. For instance, a kiss is a communicative encounter between two parties and is obviously meaningful, though differently for each partner; it's a form of dialogue... Kisses are ... very like meanings, being soft, fleeting, immensely important, sometimes telling the truth, sometimes not, sometimes holding the universe still for a moment, sometimes betokening very little; always highly coded... (Hartley 1996: 4–5)

In a nice contrast to the high seriousness of Bennett's Foucault, Hartley adorns his cover with a *Vogue-a-Vision* image of Nicole Kidman dressed in MGM musical costume, blowing a heavily lipsticked kiss to the reader. If the policy initiative made a virtue of sobriety, prescribing a dour focus on the 'mundane technologies of government', media republicanism has identified unabashedly with the colour and passion of popular pleasures and desires.

The obvious question mark over this is whether it is not simply an extension of the familiar popul*ism* identified by Morris in 'Banality in Cultural Studies'. Hartley has fallen under particular suspicion here as a one time collaborator and continuing defender of the figure widely regarded as the field's arch-populist, John Fiske. I have already argued that there is greater complexity to Fiske himself than has generally been recognized, but there is a further significant difference between media republicanism and the characteristic positions of 'British cultural studies' in the 1980s. In the earlier work, 'the popular' was still framed in opposition to dominant regimes of power. This accounts for the tendency, noted by Morris, to repetition and reduction. Popular cultural practices tended to be emptied of any specific characteristics to figure simply as instances of a generic 'resistance'. In Hartley's work by contrast – and in media republicanism generally – the abstract postulate of dominant regimes of power has been avoided from the start. This removes the pressure for an obsessive overcoding of popular cultural forms, allowing them to be considered more in their specificity and diversity.

The avoidance of the concept of power does not mean, as might perhaps be assumed, an abandonment of 'the political'. Hartley asks us rather to question assumptions about what politics involves. A good example is an analysis of an issue of Paris *Vogue* published in collaboration with Nelson Mandela on the eve of the historic 1994 elections in South Africa in which he was elected as the country's first black president. The issue, which bears a cover-image of a beaming Mandela surrounded by doves of peace, is an illustration, for Hartley, of a 'new configuration of forces in the mediasphere':

a mediasphere that takes as its opening theme not the *logic* of critique but the *beauty* of Nelson Mandela. It is as much about style (as befits *Vogue*), as about politics. But still it is about politics, since the issue is given over to a man who was seeking election to lead a government; a man who, like the rest of his people, had never been allowed to vote in an election himself, and who had only recently been set free from 27 years in gaol for treason. (Hartley 1996: 128)

Although he never represents it in this way himself, Hartley could be seen as developing the possibility, recognized by Hall in the Gramsci's concept of hegemony, of a 'radical displacement' of Marxist inheritances in cultural studies. As I pointed out in Chapter 6, there is an implication in the concept of hegemony that the most central political processes cannot be understood in terms of power. If, as Gramsci suggested, the formation of hegemonic blocks is a *precondition* for domination, the process of formation itself cannot be understood in *terms* of domination. It can only be explained by something like 'beauty'.

The spectre of populism is probably banished most convincingly by Wark, whose writing tends, if anything, towards a forbidding *avant-gardism*. There are clear similarities to Hartley in a vision of the media as a space in which the salience of the concept of power is at least in question. In *Virtual Geography*, Wark extends the concept of media beyond television, print and radio to include the wider 'vector field' of electronic communication and information. Through a study of four 'weird global media events' – the 1991 Gulf War, the Tiananmen Square Massacre, the fall of the Berlin Wall and the 1987 stock market crash – he argues that this field has escaped the control even of those whose needs it has been designed to serve: 'While the ruling powers, be they military, political, or industrial, try to bend the vector to the will to power, the vector is not a tractable instrument. Every vector field is an opening, a clearing of densely defended military, social or cultural spaces. The vector presupposes a plane of action that is also a plane of freedom' (Wark 1994: 80). But the subject of this freedom, for Wark, is not 'the people'; it is a more fluid, shifting and indeterminate 'desire'. A significant inspiration in this is the work of Gilles Deleuze and Félix Guattari (1983; 1987), with its vision of the capacity of desire to escape attempts to contain it – to find 'rhizomatic', 'deterritorialized' networks which cannot be channelled or controlled.

Wark is also useful in explicating the sense in which the initiative can be described as 'republican'. In *The Virtual Republic*, he invokes a venerable tradition, which has generally gone by that name, of attempts to define the political forms appropriate to the 'self-governance of a free people' (Wark 1997a: xiii):

In the English language, the word republic has been with us for four hundred years. It means a state where power derives from the people. Whenever English-speaking peoples took the governing of their collective lives into their own hands, the word republic occupied some space in their minds and hearts, even though its meaning changes from place and time to place and time. (Wark 1997a: xi)

The definition of republicanism as an organization of power might suggest that the concept has not, in fact, been suspended. But the important point, for Wark, in the idea that power 'derives from the people' is that the people are *free*, that they are not subject to the instrumental designs of others and are therefore capable of assuming responsibility for their common collective life. The significance of the proposition that the media offer a space of relative freedom is in fostering a hope that such a political vision is still possible today.

Loving to Influence People

The central weakness of media republicanism has been that it has not resolved or addressed problems around the concept of power so much as simply *avoided* them. It might be fair, as Hartley (1999: 32) puts it, to toggle off the critical 'default setting' which insists that everything be interpreted in terms of power. But the question inevitably arises of how to address cases where – as it is never really denied – the concept *does* still apply. There is often a suggestion in the media republican writing that these cases are merely residual, being eclipsed by the expansion of a mediasphere which is increasingly feminized, 'youthful', driven by popular pleasures or deterritorializing desires. Even if we accept this, however, the kinds of phenomena which have been addressed under the rubric of power are not entirely excluded. An evasiveness in relation to these phenomena – and a prickliness, at times, towards those who continue to point to them – has tended to weaken the media republican case.

Where questions of power *have* been negotiated, the attempt has often been marked by awkwardness and contradiction. An example is a discussion by Wark of the feminism he encountered as an undergraduate student in the early 1980s. Looking back in the late 1990s, he dismisses its view of gendered power relations as merely a projection of an internal psychological need:

> I can vividly remember the arguments that went back and forth between the bean bags in the sociology seminar room... There *has* to be a patriarchy, otherwise there can be no feminism. So everything was organized around the fantasy of the patriarchal other and his all embracing power. This particular feminism was organised negatively around what it didn't have. Not the 'penis envy' of Freud's odd theories, but *power*. (Wark 1997a: 170)

Yet Wark clearly does not wish to be associated with a simple anti-feminist line. Finding a position of greater sympathy, he suggests that the fantasy of patriarchal power was 'a *useful* fantasy. It motivated a lot of women to go and do something about structural inequalities, in domestic life and in the workplace' (1997a: 171). The obvious question that arises here is why, if it is admitted that there are such things as 'structural inequalities', the patriarchy has not been something rather more than a fantasy. The admission disrupts Wark's whole analysis, but is casually passed over as if it were merely incidental.

Similar problems can be found in Hartley and Lumby. The examples they discuss often seem quite selectively chosen to suit their case. Hartley does not mention, for example, that Nelson Mandela had a life before *Vogue* as a militant anti-Apartheid activist or that majority rule in South Africa was achieved as much through blood on the streets as through efforts at 'cordialization'. Lumby's *Bad Girls* has an index entry for 'violence against women', but all the references are, in fact, to a violence *imputed* by feminists to media representations. The argument of the book – that such imputations are often questionable – is brilliantly developed. It is striking, however, that Lumby avoids any direct recognition of the fact that *real* violence does occur. The suppression of references to conflict and violence in media republicanism is similar, in many ways, to that noted by E. P. Thompson in the early work of Raymond Williams – and, it appears, for similar reasons. To admit such references is seen to invoke a generalized concept of power, reintroducing the instrumentalist perspective that the initiative has attempted to avoid.

But as in the case of the policy initiative, to reject media republicanism for these failings would be to miss its significance in opening new possibilities. With a slight twist, its weakness on questions of power can be seen, instead, as a strength. While Hartley, Wark and Lumby are still, in many ways, haunted by the concept, their efforts to limit and contain it also create the conditions for a transformation. This transformation is, again, a turn to a kind of pluralism. If, as the media republican arguments suggest, power is not continuously distributed; if it comes into view only sometimes, perhaps even as an exception; then we are subtly led to think not of a general phenomenon but of specific and discrete *phenomena*. We are led to think, in short, not of 'power', but of '*powers*'. Once this shift is made, invoking the repressive agencies of the Apartheid state in South Africa or the violence of some men against women is no longer to raise the spectre of a totalizing political vision. The way is opened to a grittier recognition of violence and conflict where they occur, but a recognition that does not extend to a prejudicial view of all social relations as conforming to some universal pattern.

The potential which arises here is best indicated in Hartley's case in an explicit reconnection with the 'Hoggartian' legacy in cultural studies. In his 1999 book, *Uses of Television*, Hartley reaches back before the turn to Marxism at Birmingham in the 1970s, before the emergence of anxieties about populism and banality, and before Foucault, to Hoggart's deceptively simple vision of the field in *The Uses of Literacy*. The move coincides with a noticeable reintroduction of references to concrete bearings, references that are sometimes missing in earlier efforts to screen out implications of power. One of the qualities Hartley values in Hoggart is an earthy sense of culture as a practical agent – as 'useful'. He picks up, for example, on a description by Hoggart of the 'kneading effect' of television, its 'detailed and intelligent presentation of the day-to-day texture of other people's lives, assumptions, hopes' (Hoggart quoted in Hartley 1999: 140). The medium appears, from this perspective, not as a space apart from power, but rather as *a power*, an almost corporeal force in the world.

There is a surprising convergence at this point between media republicanism and the policy initiative. Despite the strength of their differences, Hartley's attention to the 'kneading' effects of television comes very close to Bennett and Hunter's call for greater attention to 'useful culture'. The convergence is particularly marked around questions of pedagogy. Drawing again on Hoggart, Hartley suggests that the best teachers are those who 'love to influence others' (Hartley 1999: 29). The significance of the idea of 'influence' is that it indicates material effects without coding them immediately in terms of a generalized framework of power. For Hartley, as for Hoggart, 'loving to influence' has an uncomplicated directness; it is quite distinct from a love of power in the abstract, but nor is it associated with 'resistance' or 'subversion'. It is to be understood in similar terms to those urged by the policy advocates in their attempts to revive an appreciation for the 'useful' endeavours of public educators such as Henry Cole and James Kay-Shuttleworth – not through abstract oppositions between 'power' and its others, but in relation to more immediate and practical contexts and aims.

A similar reconnection with the early British matrix of cultural studies can be found in Wark. In *The Virtual Republic* he draws particularly on Williams's concept of 'structures of feeling', working very deliberately to restore the *integration* of 'structure' and 'feeling' which, as I argued in Chapter 6, was increasingly lost from the 1970s. A condition of a republican politics, for Wark, is that we regard social institutions not as repressive, as things which 'limit individual desires', but rather as enabling, 'as a positive means of artificially extending and integrating the kinds of creative and productive ingenuity of our particular little sympathetic worlds – to enable us to fly' (Wark 1997a: 13). Like Williams himself, Wark looks further back to David Hume and the Scottish Enlightenment for a deeper sense of this integration. The key to this tradition is a resistance, often in the face of good reason for doing so, to seeing political structures as external, impersonal, as simply imposed. This clearly translates also to a resistance to the tendency, widespread in modernity, to inflate the concept of power.

–12–

Orientalism and Occidentalism
'Power' in International Cultural Studies

If, as I suggested in the last chapter, there are recent strands of cultural studies which have reactivated some 'Anglo' perspectives on questions of power, there would be an obvious problem in closing with these. Since at least the 1990s, the field has increasingly come to be defined as international one. In important cases, this development has not even been initiated from Britain, the United States or Australia. The bi-annual 'Crossroads in Cultural Studies' conferences, for example, which have given birth to the International Association for Cultural Studies, were first organized by Pertti Alasuutari and colleagues at Tampere in Finland. Similarly, the Inter-Asia Cultural Studies network – which has produced a number of conferences, a journal and society – has been genuinely regional, being variously coordinated from Korea, Taiwan, Hong Kong, India, Singapore and Japan. A plausible case might be made, as I have tried to do in previous chapters, that certain parallels can be drawn between Britain, the United States and Australia. There are some clear similarities not just in histories of state formation, but in characteristic ways in which questions of power have tended to be addressed. But the same is not true of other significant sites where cultural studies has emerged around the world.

There is an urgency and interest in the internationalization of cultural studies and there are obvious reasons why this should be so. They are similar to the reasons that have made 'globalization' a major rubric for new work in the social sciences over the last twenty years. The increasing volume of international trade and financial transactions coupled with new communication technologies such as satellites and the internet have brought an increasing intensity of exposure to other parts of the world. When television audiences in Boston or Dallas can have a real-time missile-cam view of bombs hitting targets in Baghdad or when telephone call centres in India can market products in London or Sydney, there is clearly a need for frames of analysis which transcend the nation state. Such frames are also required in addressing what are shaping as the major political issues of the twenty-first century – terrorism and counter-terrorism, the environment, fair trade and the shape of the new international order following the rise of China and India.

These contexts are registered in the more recent work of a number of figures whose work I have discussed in previous chapters: Stuart Hall's interests, for example, have turned to globalization and diasporic cultural formations; Meaghan

Morris has worked on the development of Asian and international cultural studies from a position at Lingnan University in Hong Kong; John Hartley has launched an *International Journal of Cultural Studies* and developed projects in China. This work sits beside major contributions from others: Andrew Ross (2004), for example, on the global push for fair labour conditions; Stephanie Donald (2000) and Wanning Sun (2002) on Chinese audiovisual cultures; Arvind Rajagopal (2001) on television and Hindu nationalism in India.

Against this background, an emphasis on 'Anglo' themes and concerns might appear backward looking, perhaps suspiciously nostalgic for a time when their importance could simply be assumed. As Ackbar Abbas and John Nguyet Erni write in their edited collection *Internationalizing Cultural Studies*, 'A certain parochialism continues to operate in Cultural Studies as a whole, whose objects of analysis have had the effect of closing off real contact with scholarship conducted outside its (western) radar screen'. It is time, they suggest, 'to clear a space for an introduction to, a pluralization of, Cultural Studies work from diverse local and intellectual traditions' (Abbas and Erni 2005: 2). Such arguments have been widely accepted, bringing an important shift in cultural studies conference themes, publications and teaching programmes. It would be easy to make a case, in this context, that it is precisely *not* the time to allow British, American and Australian histories to assume a centrality. These histories are relatively well known. Is it not more important now that others should be told?

Differences here should not be overplayed. New international perspectives in cultural studies generally appear, as in Abbas and Erni's argument, in contrast to older ones (the 'parochial' past, 'the western radar screen'). Continuing to think carefully about the latter is therefore important to the way the former are framed and received. It may be flattering to new initiatives simply to set them off in positive terms against established work in cultural studies, but it is questionable whether it serves them more substantially. Moving on to new fields out of tiredness with where one has been is not a strong basis on which to proceed. It produces a tendency to exoticize – the reduction of 'other places' to colour and vibrancy in such a way that their actual complexity and interest disappears from view. It also denies the value that could be gained from *exchange* between 'old' and 'new', between established positions in British, American or Australian cultural studies and work that has developed elsewhere. There is no doubt that Asian, African and Latin American scholars and cultural workers have much to teach Anglo-American cultural studies, but a dialogue needs something be offered in return. The health of international encounters requires that all parties have a positive sense of what they have to contribute.

My argument in previous chapters might be seen, in this context, as *comple-mentary* to attempts to internationalize cultural studies. The intention in historicizing the concept of power has been to normalize the field, to counter a tendency, most marked in the so-called 'culture wars', to represent it in simple black-and-white terms. I have given strongest emphasis to the importance of this for the relation between cultural studies and its own past, its ability to draw realistically and constructively on the experience of the last fifty years. But attention could equally be drawn to the importance for the relation between Anglo-American cultural studies – still, for better or worse, by far the dominant strand – and work which is taking place elsewhere. To put it simply, a field that knows itself only through celebration or denunciation is not likely to be a careful listener or subtle interlocutor. It will be inclined, on the contrary, to remain self-obsessed, even in reaching out to engage with others. In scaling back the logic that has produced polarization over the status and achievement of Anglo-American cultural studies, we might also hope to put the internationalization of the field on a more constructive footing.

Even so, it is important to demonstrate that the new approach I have suggested to questions of power is not simply locked within an Anglo-American orbit, that it is capable of connecting in positive ways with wider contexts. This then is the aim of this final chapter. I want, in particular, to suggest that some of the qualities which I have been denominating as 'Anglo' might be seen, more abstractly, as attaching generally to approaches and traditions which are sensitive to the *formation*, rather than simply the conduct or behaviour, of agents which are considered as 'powerful'. I argued in Chapters 3 and 4 that such sensitivity can be found in English political thinking in relation to the power of the state. I will argue below that a similar sensitivity can be found in some recent writing by Latin American scholars on power in the international sphere. I make particular use of the work of the Argentinian-American Walter Mignolo, whose concept of 'occidentalism' suggests an interesting shift of perspective on the power of 'the West'.

Orientalism and Postcolonial Theory

But it is important first to set some context. The internationalization of cultural studies has been significantly formed by an earlier body of writing, known broadly as 'postcolonial theory', on global dimensions of power associated with European and American colonialism. Mignolo's 'occidentalism' is developed in critical counterpoint to what is probably still the most influential text here – Edward Said's *Orientalism*. The latter has been widely problematized since its publication in 1978 and is often seen as superseded by more recent work on the complexities and 'ambivalences' of colonial and neo-colonial relations. Indeed, the central argument was tempered and qualified in various ways by Said himself. Yet *Orientalism* has continued to set much of the tone for the discussion of international relations in cultural studies. Most centrally, it established a principle that the metropolitan intellectual culture of the West should be seen as thoroughly implicated in global relations of power – power being understood in its most generalized sense. This principle has proven remarkably influential, often becoming only further embedded as problems or shortcomings have been recognized in the way it has actually been applied.

There are obvious reasons why Said should have been more interested in the conduct of powerful agents than with the thematics of power as such. He was a Palestinian intellectual living in the United States and was passionately concerned about the nature of American involvement in the Middle East. *Orientalism* was written in the immediate aftermath of the 1973 Arab–Israeli war and the OPEC oil crisis, events which set the West on collision course with governments and movements in the region. The book is largely historical, focusing most closely on the nineteenth century, but the past is very directly articulated to the present. History provides purchase, for Said, in explaining and bringing to account ingrained assumptions of Western superiority, assumptions which 'flood the press and the popular mind':

> Arabs, for example, are thought of as camel-riding, terroristic, hook-nosed, venal lechers whose undeserved wealth is an affront to real civilization. Always there lurks the assumption that although the Western consumer belongs to a numerical minority, he is entitled either to own or to expend (or both) the majority of the world resources. Why? Because he, unlike the Oriental, is a true human being. (Said 1978: 108)

Studying the discourses of nineteenth-century colonialism allows Said to develop a case that current attitudes and actions reflect a deep-seated Western syndrome. This strategic logic is confirmed by the fact that *Orientalism* was only the first book in a trilogy, the second and third parts of which – *The Question of Palestine* (1980) and *Covering Islam* (1981) – were immediately engaged with contemporary concerns.

But the concept of power is given a status in *Orientalism* that cannot be explained simply as a natural expression of Said's political concerns. The book was by no means the first to engage critically with Western representations of non-Western people or to find structural tendencies to insensitivity, prejudice or complicity with colonial rule. As Said himself puts it in later reflections:

> What I said in *Orientalism* has been said before me by A. L. Tibawi, by Abdullah Laraoui, by Anwar Abdel Malek, by Talal Asad, by S. H. Alatas, by Fanon and Cesaire, by Pannikar, and Romila Thapar, all of whom had suffered the ravages of imperialism and colonialism, and who in challenging the authority, provenance, and institutions of the science that represented them to Europe, were also understanding themselves as more than what this science said they were. (Said 1984: 17)

Why then did the book gain the attention that it did? Why did it cause such a stir? Said's modesty may be admirable, but it obscures the respect in which he was *not* simply restating what had been said before. Something of the difference can be seen even in his synoptic vision of the figures to which he pays tribute. Most of these figures, with the exception perhaps of Franz Fanon, were involved in particular struggles over representation. Tibawi, for example, was concerned specifically with English language scholarship on Islam (see Tibawi 2000). Said's object is much wider than this. Despite his primary interest in Palestine, his argument extends not only to this or that struggle, but to a general regime of power which comprehends them all.

The most obvious influence in this is Foucault. As Aijaz Ahmad has put it, '[t]he striking novelty of *Orientalism* resided ... crucially in its explicit invocation of Foucault, its declaration that his object of study, namely Orientalism, was a *discourse* and his insistence that this was the constitutive discourse of Western civilisation as such' (Ahmad 2000: 286). The function of the concept of a discourse is first to draw attention away from claims to veridical reference in the texts being studied to patterns and forms of organization that can be identified independently of these. As Said puts it: 'The phenomenon of Orientalism I study here deals principally, not with a correspondence between Orientalism and the Orient, but with the internal consistency of Orientalism and its ideas about the Orient ... despite or beyond any correspondence, or lack thereof to a "real" Orient' (Said 1978: 5). This opens the way to introduce a proposition of the centrality of power. If Western writing on the Orient has an 'internal consistency' independent of any reference to the real, what explains this consistency? The answer is, at first, hesitantly phrased but moves unmistakably towards a bracing simplicity and clarity:

> [I]deas, cultures, and histories cannot seriously be understood or studied without their force, or more precisely their configuration of power, also being studied. To believe that the Orient was created – or, as I call it, 'Orientalized' – and to believe that things happen simply as a necessity of imagination, is to be disingenuous. The relationship between Occident and Orient is a relationship of power... (Said 1978: 5)

As might be recalled from Chapter 2, the general procedure here, a procedure of displacing other forms of explanation in order to explain in terms of power, is classically Foucauldian.

But Said's use of the concept of power might equally well be traced to the more immediate context in which he was writing. His politicization was closely related to the rise of the American New Left. He was not of the generation who participated in the movement as a student. Princeton in the 1950s, where he completed his first degree, was, as he later described it, 'unpolitical, self-satisfied, and oblivious... McCarthy was treated at Princeton as a bagatelle and no Princeton professor was known to us as having been persecuted for Communist views. In fact there was no left presence of any sort' (Said 1999: 278). He became active, however, while teaching at Columbia in the late 1960s: 'The big change came with the Arab-Israeli war of 1967, which coincided with a period of intense political activism on campus over civil rights and the Vietnam War. I found myself naturally involved on both fronts...' (Said 1998). There are obvious similarities between Said's biography and others who became intellectual leaders at the time. He always felt, by his own account, 'between worlds', 'out of place'. Despite having lived in the United States since the age of sixteen, he never felt he truly 'belonged'. This sense of alienation was greatly lessened, as it was for others, by involvement in the left. There were certainly tensions between Palestinian activism and other New Left causes; indeed the former was sometimes attacked as 'anti-Semitic and Nazi-like' (Said 1998). Yet Said clearly found a place of sorts in the fractious community on the left which formed in the late 1960s and 1970s around concepts of power.

Just as importantly, this is the context in which *Orientalism* has largely been received. Controversy over the book might be seen as one of the longest running battles in the 'culture wars'. It started in the early 1980s in an exchange between Said and the eminent Orientalist scholar Bernard Lewis in the *New York Review of Books*. The dispute was partly over the specifics of Said's case, but was more substantially over the emphasis given to questions of power. For Lewis, the elevation of these questions betrayed an ideological obsession that reduced historical understanding to a simplified caricature. For Said, it was Lewis's position that was ideological, insisting on a fantasy of pure, disinterested scholarship in the face of indisputable evidence of the implication of knowledge in political processes. The lines remained drawn even in obituaries for Said following his death in 2003, having become sharpened, if anything, by the politically charged climate following the terrorist attacks on New York and Washington on September 11 2001. Writing in the *National Review*, prominent neo-conservative David Frum described *Orientalism* as perhaps 'the most influential academic studies of the past quarter century', but also 'the most disastrous' (Frum 2003). By discrediting scholarship on the Middle East, Frum alleged, Said and his followers had eroded the kind of expertise on the region that might have warned of the rising tide of Islamist radicalism and the dangers of groups like Al Qaida.

Postcolonial theory cannot be reduced, by any means, to *Orientalism*. Even Said himself went on to modify his arguments and significant differences can be found in later work. In *Culture and Imperialism* he admits that more attention needed to be paid to *resistance* to colonial designs:

> What I left out of *Orientalism* was that response to Western dominance which culmin-
> ated in the great movement of decolonization all across the Third World. Along with
> armed resistance ... there was also considerable efforts in cultural resistance almost
> everywhere, the assertion of nationalist identities, and, in the political realm, the creation
> of associations and parties whose common goal was self-determination and national
> independence. (Said 1993: xii)

Other writers have gone further in complicating our understanding of colonial and neo-colonial relations of power. Homi Bhabha (1994), for example, has argued that these relations are shot through with ambivalence and ambiguity. The subject positions associated with power – whether of race, gender, generation, institutional locale, geopolitical location or sexual orientation – are, for Bhabha, more fluid and reversible than is suggested by simple binary oppositions of 'colonizer'/'colonized'. More troublingly, Gayatri Spivak (1988) has asked whether attempts to counter the dominance of Western systems of knowledge, particularly where they call forth an authentic 'subaltern' voice, may themselves reinscribe colonial relations.

But none of these extensions or modifications in any way displace the thematics of power as such. It is true that they have muted the simplifying *force* which has often been associated with the concept. As Peter Conrad (1979) put it in a contemporary review of Said's original contribution, much of the excitement of *Orientalism* was its 'salutary fury'. Some of this fury might be found in later work, but it is also more controlled and restrained. To identify resistance to Western dominance, after Said's later revisions, is to shift the emphasis from denunciation. To see fluidity and reversibility in colonial relations, after Bhabha, is to soften the distinction between colonizer and colonized. To find a complicity with neo-colonial practices of representation even in attempts to counter colonialism, after Spivak, is to deny any easy position of moral superiority. Through all these developments, however, there remains a clear thread of continuity: in its international dimension, cultural phenomena are read, with little reflection on the concept itself, as fundamentally imbricated in relations of power.

Internationalizing Cultural Studies

This principle has been central to the formation of international cultural studies. In some cases, the impulse to internationalize can be seen as a direct extension of postcolonial theory. Spivak's *Critique of Postcolonial Reason*, for example, traces 'a practitioner's progress from colonial discourse studies to transnational cultural studies' (Spivak 1999: ix–x). In the first chapter, 'Philosophy', she reads the work of Kant and Hegel in order to 'track a foreclosure: the native informant' (1999: 111). By the later chapters, 'History' and 'Culture', she is writing in a rather different register about the practice of *sati* or the self-immolation of widows in Bengal and child labour in Bangladesh. And yet this engagement with non-Western contexts unfolds very much within the critique of colonial discourse. Spivak is highly conscious of writing from a position within the American academy, maintaining a constant vigilance against staking knowledge claims over others. Despite her Indian background, she refuses to adopt the role of native informant herself, maintaining a rigorous attention to the *textuality* of any access to non-Western realities. As she puts it herself, 'I always attempt to look around the corner, to see ourselves as others would see us' (xii–xiii). The problematic remains very much, as in Said, colonial and neo-colonial relations of power.

This is also true of significant initiatives that have emerged outside North America, Europe and Australasia. One of the most interesting and productive of these has been the Inter-Asia Cultural Studies (or earlier 'Trajectories') project, already mentioned above. The project is impressive in the diversity of its geographic sites and has been constituted in such a way as to allow space for the assertion of local differences. An important indication of this is the commitment of the journal *Inter-Asia Cultural Studies* to receiving and translating work in languages other than English. It is difficult, given this diversity, to generalize, but like any network Inter-Asia Cultural Studies is bound by certain operating principles. Exchanges only occur because participants believe themselves to share some common understanding or commitment, and in the articulation of this the concept of power has played a major role. A useful text here is the introduction by Kuan-Hsing Chen to the edited collection *Trajectories: Inter-Asia Cultural Studies*, proceeding from two international conferences, in 1992 and 1995, at the National Tsinghua University in Taiwan. Chen, who is based at Tsinghua, has clearly been a central figure in the development of Inter-Asia Cultural Studies and in establishing some basic coordinates.

The starting point for an international or transnational cultural studies in Asia, for Chen, must be the 'decolonization question':

> [W]hy, thirty or forty years [after the post-war moment of decolonization], are we (who live in the (ex-)colonized globe) still deeply shaped by the questions posed by our forerunners in the critical tradition? Well, because of the neo-colonial structure. We have been 'made' to identify with intellectual formulations coming from the (ex-)imperial centers, and hence have completely forgotten the powerful interventions made by Fanon, Memmi or Nandy. (Chen 1998: 1)

Chen recognizes the 'seminal work' of Said and Spivak, also paying tribute to Stuart Hall and Paul Gilroy, as having 'projected a necessary desire against Euro/ America-Western-centrism' (1998: 5). But his concerns are also somewhat different. Less attention is given to the problem of Western dominance as such and more to the formations which have developed in reaction to it. These, for Chen, take three main forms: nativism, nationalism and 'civilizationalism'. Each has responded to colonialism by positing a pure position from which to oppose it, but each in their own way creates new forms of oppression. The one which was particularly ascendant at the time of the Tsinghua conferences and which occupied the first issue of *Inter-Asia Cultural Studies* was the civilizational discourse of 'Asian values'. Capitalizing on rapid economic growth in Asia through the 1990s, this discourse turned the tables on the West through the formula: 'Asia is becoming the center of the earth and we are at the center of Asia, so we are the world' (1998: 2). But it often constructed, in doing so, a narrow, conservative image of what it was to be 'Asian'.

As Chen points out, these problems are related to significant shifts in the global economy, shifts which require a vision beyond any one discipline or nation. The conjuncture is 'an intense moment of [the] so-called post-cold war era when all of us are forced to walk out of our own little disciplinary ghettoes and geographical sites in order to more adequately respond to the questions of globalization and subsequent regionalization posed by the imperatives of transnational and global capitals' (1998: 1–2). Cultural studies appears here as a space 'in which we might be able to get the necessary work done' (1998: 2). It has the virtue of insisting on 'historical contingencies and local specificities': 'it never pretends to a universality of cultural analysis and openly acknowledges the relative autonomy of cultures in different geopolitical locations' (1998: 4). Chen's formulations here draw particularly on Stuart Hall. As he puts it, with David Morley, in an earlier introduction to an edited collection on Hall, 'Hall's positions and concerns have always been conjunctural in nature, developing in response to emerging social and political questions' (Morley and Chen 1996: 4). This conjuncturalism has an obvious value in developing an open exchange between different regional positions and traditions. Cultural studies is invoked not so much for any definite theoretical propositions as for the sort of fluid intellectual space it is able to provide.

But there is also a definite point of closure in this constitution of international or transnational cultural studies. It is taken as a given, by Chen, that the field is fund-amentally organized around the concept of power:

> Having persistently questioned cultural relations of power in local social formations for the past forty years, cultural studies is now undergoing a critical phase of internationalization. Such a transformation is occurring very much in response to the changing dispositions and structure of global forces such as the transnationalization of capital, the realignment of the nation-states into regional super-states ... as well as the implementation of the interconnected high tech systems such as satellites and the Internet which makes talking across borders more possible. (Chen 1998: 3)

The emphasis on specificity and changeability of 'local social formations' stands in quite strong contrast here to the assumption that they are always appropriately framed in terms of 'cultural relations of power'. In fact, Chen goes further than this, suggesting that, beyond this, there are '"common" structures of domination'. The list of nominations for these structures is more or less identical with the analytic axes which have emerged from Anglo-American cultural studies: 'capitalism, patriarchy, heterosexism, ethnocentrism, neo-colonialism, etc.' (1998: 4) Whatever the 'specificities and intensities of oppression from place to place', gender, race, sexuality, ethnicity and class remain 'central co-ordinating categories across geographical, national, and regional boundaries' (1998: 4).

It would be possible, at this point, although it is not my intention to do so, to charge Chen himself with a kind of neo-colonialism – a problem which he appears uncomfortably aware of in hedging his reference to 'common structures' with scare quotes. His concepts of power are largely abstracted from work produced out of Britain, France and the United States – and even more specifically from 'New Left' contexts in those countries. While he lives and works in Taiwan, Chen undertook his graduate study at the University of Iowa and has continued to address much of his work to British and American readers and publication outlets. It would not be difficult to represent him as radicals in Asia are often seen by conservative governments in the region: as an agent for 'Western' ideas. Apart from any desire to side more with the 'radicals', however, there are two reasons to avoid this analysis. The first is that meanings are not simply determined by origins. Chen makes this point himself in relation to Marxism. While the latter is obviously, in its formation, a European intellectual formation, 'its critical elements have saturated into different geographical sites... [F]or at least a century now, Marxism has become part of the cultural subjectivity of intellectuals outside the imperial centers' (1998: 7). Traditions of use more specifically around the concept of power are probably shorter – as they have been in the West – but there have almost certainly been similar processes of indigenization. This is not to make the obvious and accepted point that the concept of power has been flexibly deployed to account for different contexts; it is to suggest that the *meaning* of the concept has been transformed in doing so.

The second reason for avoiding accusations of an imperialism of the concept of power is that to do so would be oddly circular and self-defeating. The accusation itself would seem to imply an analysis in *terms* of power while at the same time calling the concept into question. The logic that emerges here is the same vortex I observed in Chapters 1 and 2 in relation to the 'culture wars'. There has been a tendency in the latter, as I noted there, to use the concept of power against itself, representing those who *use* the concept as themselves making a bid for power. All that this achieves, however, is a tightening spiral of denunciation. My argument throughout the book has been that it is more productive, both intellectually and politically, to stand back a little and reflect on the concept itself. There is, again, some resonance between this argument and Chen's position on Marxism. The latter, he suggests, should be understood first not as an analytic but rather as an *imaginative* framework: 'the tradition of Marxism has established an imaginary discursive position "outside" capitalism from which to critique internal logics of the latter' (1998: 7). My suggestion has been that a similar understanding should be brought to the traditions that have developed in cultural studies around the concept of power.

Translating Theory

What might be gained by this? Or to turn the question around, what are the costs of a more 'literal' understanding of power? There is sometimes a suggestion that displacing cultural studies from its Anglo-American axis might offer an escape from the kinds of problems around the concept reviewed in previous chapters. Referring obliquely to these problems, Chen holds out the promise that engaging with transnational contexts 'might ... be able to change the terrain of dominant cultural studies practices (which have run into a moment of crisis – depoliticization, dehistoricization and lack of sense of vision)' (Chen 1998: 2). John Nguyet Erni has suggested, somewhat more bluntly, that the urgency of struggles outside the North Atlantic around democracy, political repression and the threat of historical amnesia 'should haunt North Atlantic Cultural Studies and suggest its continued banality' (Erni 2005: 297). There is probably a certain truth to these claims. As we have seen, 'culture war' debates around power have been quite particular to the United States, Britain and other Anglophone societies. To leave these debates aside and engage instead with queer cultural formations in Taiwan or with nationalism in China can certainly bring a breath of fresh air. It would be wishful thinking, however, to believe that it is possible to abstract concepts of power from Anglophone cultural studies while suffering none of the problems – and there is in fact evidence that a number of the latter have emerged.

Some these problems are recognized by Chen. He is particularly conscious of a danger, in fixing on global structures of power, of a politics of resentment. When concepts such as imperialism and colonialism are generalized away from specific historical formations, the phenomena come to appear as so massive and all-embracing that the only horizon becomes a negative and reactive strategy of opposing them. Such resentment is, for Chen, very active in Asia today: 'the inside/outside, self/other logic of colonialism lingers on ... and a constant resentment against the (past and present) colonial outsider and/or imaginary other is still at work' (Chen 1998: 20). To recognize the problem is, of course, already to have moved towards addressing it and Chen develops a number of responses. One of these, similar to the approach I have suggested in this book, is to rearticulate theoretical positions to the historical contexts in which they took form. This leads Chen to some important excavations of lesser known figures in the history of anti-colonial struggles: Albert Memmi, Octave Mannoni and Ashis Nandy. In respect of the concept of power, he tends rather to deploy a Foucauldian rhetoric of 'multiple resisting subjects of a micropolitics, gradually emerging on the historical platform' (1998: 7); he seeks to counter a 'territorialization of subjectivities and subject positions' through a pan-leftist attention to 'gay and lesbian, bi- and trans-sexual, feminist, labor, farmer, environmental, aboriginal, anti-racist, and anti-war groups' (1998: 28). The general point, however, is that the problems he address and the resources he calls on in doing so are remarkably similar to those of Anglo-American cultural studies. A non-Western location is not a golden alibi against the pitfalls of the latter.

Indeed in some respects, the internationalization of cultural studies could be seen as *exacerbating* problems around the concept of power. It has often tended, in particular, to focus attention on questions of identity and representation. A broad context for this has been a loss of a sense of the specificity of cultural studies itself as an intellectual formation. When the term was first coined in the 1950s, it functioned almost as a proper name, identifying a distinctive style of work emerging out of British adult education and with a niche in at the University of Birmingham. Through the 1970s and 1980s, it was broadened to include other Anglophone New Left formations. But in international contexts today, it has acquired a much more abstract meaning, suggesting a global forum for any discussion of cultural politics or of 'relations between culture and power'. The disjuncture between the older and newer sense of the term has been a source of ongoing tensions. In reality, the majority of work that calls itself cultural studies is still overwhelmingly from Britain, the United States, Canada, Australia and New Zealand, where the term has an established currency. The contradiction between this and claims to internationalism have been widely noted, resulting in charges against the field of 'exclusions' and 'marginalizations' of positions and traditions from elsewhere.

The disabling aspect of this development should not be surprising to anyone familiar with debates around 'identity politics' in the United States. It was sharply identified by Benjamin Bertram, a participant at a 1994 conference organized by Fredric Jameson and Masao Miyoshi on the 'cultures of globalization'. While the conference was valuable in developing international dialogue, it was also blighted, for Bertram, by a 'conspiracy effect': 'Somehow, somewhere, it was often suggested, someone was trying to keep some of us silent. Whereas critical reflection on procedures, arrangements, and so on often strengthened the conference, it often revealed an odd pathology, a desire for alienation, rather than a resistance to alienation' (quoted in Jameson and Miyoshi 1998: 372). The logic operating here is similar to the one I discussed in Chapter 8 associated with abstract models of representation which developed in the British and American new left in the 1970s. Within these models, power is understood as a generalized resistance to inclusion in a putatively universal forum. But as Tony Bennett has pointed out, no forum can ever meet the demand for universal inclusion. The result can often be a chronic worrying away at the failure to satisfy expectations that can never be satisfied. The loss of ability to articulate real prospects for change means that the resulting form of politics has a tendency to shrink to the space of the seminar room.

Some of the more interesting and productive initiatives in international cultural studies have avoided some of these problems by working with a problematic not of representation but of *translation*. The most ambitious project in this area has probably been *Traces – A Multilingual Series of Theory and Translation*, under the general editorship of Meaghan Morris in association with Gao Jianping, Yukiko Hanawa, Kang Nae-hui, Kojima Kiyoshi, J. Victor Koschmann, Thomas Lamarre and Naoki Sakai. The significance for the project of the theme of translation extends beyond the fact that *Traces* is published in four languages – Chinese, English, Korean and Japanese. It also frames the conception of the series of the sort of 'space', as the editorial statement of purpose puts it, in which international cultural studies may take form: 'Constituted in processes of translation, among multiple languages and registers, this social space is actualized in our exchanges and debates, and in debates among authors, commentators, translators, and readers' (*Traces* 2003). There is no claim in this to provide a universal forum and no expectation created of absolute inclusiveness. International or transnational cultural studies is seen not as an abstract stage to which one might lay claim or be excluded from laying claim, but as 'constituted', 'actualized' in concrete exchanges.

An important background text to the *Traces* project is Naoki Sakai's (1997) *Translation and Subjectivity*, described by Morris in a foreword to the book as offering a 'working model for transnational studies in culture' (1997: xiii). Sakai has been one of the most active figures in the project and a number of themes in the editorial prospectus for *Traces* are prefigured in his work. Abstracting from his own experience of working between English and Japanese, Sakai distinguishes between 'homolingual' and 'heterolingual' forms of address. 'Homolingual' address is not, as one might at first expect, an address to a single language community (say to speakers of English or Japanese); it is an address that assumes a homogeneity *within* such communities. 'Heterolingual' address assumes, by contrast, that 'every utterance can fail to communicate because heterogeneity is inherent in any medium, linguistic or otherwise' (Sakai 1997: 8). Heterolingual address, clearly valued by Sakai, corresponds to the idea of a 'nonaggregate community', one in which 'we are together and can address ourselves as "we" because we are distant from one another and because our togetherness is not grounded in a common homogeneity' (1997: 7). These concepts clearly provide a productive framework for thinking about exchanges within transnational cultural studies and for heading off the more paralysing effects of generalized concepts of power.

It is notable, however, that the framework is not brought to bear on concepts of power themselves. These concepts are drawn upon to *theorize* translation, not considered as possibly in *need* of translation. Homolingual address, for Sakai, is a 'regime' and clearly linked with relations of power, but the meaning of 'regime' is assumed as relatively transparent. The point is even clearer in the prospectus for *Traces*, which assumes the universality of a broadly 'Foucauldian' discourse on power, even as it seeks to relativize and particularize our understanding of 'theory':

> Global modernization has accelerated cultural, economic and political interchange between different regions and brought different forms of power-knowledge into more intense interaction. The globality of theoretical production in these various sites cannot be understood uniformly in terms of the Western Enlightenment or post-Enlightenment forms of power-knowledge. These forms of "theory" which are no longer merely "indigenous" make up the power-knowledge in everyday life not only in the Euro-American world but also in many parts of the world including East and South East Asia. (*Traces* 2003)

Everything is in question here – what counts as 'theory', the sites at which new theoretical insights may emerge, the forms of power-knowledge operating in those sites – everything that is, *except* the appropriateness of extending the concept of power-knowledge to any and every context. At this level, if only at this level, the heterolingual address of the project appears to evaporate; the 'community' of transnational cultural studies is not, in Sakai's terms, a non-aggregate community, but is 'grounded in a common homogeneity' – a shared assumption of the transparency of the concept of power.

The reason I have given such weight in previous chapters to the development of British and American cultural studies is that they provide a resource for questioning this transparency. There are some striking similarities between Sakai's idea of heterolingual address and central themes emerging from the experience of adult education in Britain in the 1950s and 1960s. It could be seen as corresponding closely, for example, to Raymond Williams's emphasis on the 'pause and effort' required for communication between classes or Richard Hoggart's view that middle-class intellectuals and artists were to the working class as 'snail eating Frenchmen'. Indeed, it would be fair to say that early British cultural studies emerged precisely out of the recognition of 'non-aggregate' communities. The difference from both *Inter-Asia Cultural Studies* and the *Traces* project, however, is that concepts of power were not exempted from scepticism over suggestions of transparency. As we saw in Chapter 4, the use of terms such as 'domination' and 'subordination' was always for Williams, even in his conversion to Marxism, a use of a particular *language*. The meaning of the terms was not assumed as universal, but understood in relation to specific historical *experiences*. As indicated above, however, I want to broaden the argument, finally, by suggesting another significant base in transnational cultural studies for sceptical approaches to concepts of power: some recent work from Latin America.

Latin American Scepticism

There are a number of reasons why the concept of power figures differently in Latin America than in Asia. The first and most obvious is a difference of position in the global system. In international comparative terms, the Latin American nations are poor and peripheral to the metropolitan centres of capital and technological development. Because of this, they have often been classified with Asia in conceptual groupings such as the 'Third world' or 'the South'. But they are, at the same time, European settler states, with historical similarities – in the displacement of indigenous people and the transfer of European languages, religions and economies – to the United States, Canada, Australia and New Zealand. This complicates any attempt to frame their position in terms of colonialism and neo-colonialism. While there have been some efforts to transpose Said's *Orientalism* to Latin America (Moreiras 2001), there has never been quite the 'Saidian moment' in cultural studies' orientation to Latin America as developed in the 1980s in its orientation to Asia. The dominant critical paradigm has tended to be located in political economy – in dependency and world-systems theory – rather than in more specifically cultural analysis. These approaches have not given the same theoretical centrality to the concept of power.

A second important context is a certain caution in Latin America about a straightforward alignment with political radicalism. It is a caution born of bitter experience: after half a century or more on the continent of revolutionary and counter-revolutionary violence, the major political theme since the 1980s has been *democratization*. The priority in this context, including often on the left, has been not to sharpen but to *moderate* political conflict. As the Chilean-American sociologist J. Samuel Valenzuela puts it: 'Nothing is more destructive of democracy than frequent confrontation in the streets, the legislature, the state administration, and elsewhere between groups who view themselves as engaged in a zero-sum conflict' (1992: 82). Similar themes can be found, closer to cultural studies, in Sonia Alvarez's (1990) important work on women's movements in Brazil. Alvarez is far from unsympathetic to the more radical elements in these movements; they have often articulated deeply felt responses to authoritarianism, machismo, violence and economic desperation. But she is also concerned to question assumptions of necessary political oppositions – particularly between women's interests and the state – and to recognize the importance of mobilization around 'feminine' issues that are not fully 'feminist'. Her interest generally is not so much in the oppositional rhetoric of the movements as such, as their positive or constructive dimension.

In a 1990s' essay, 'Reweaving the Fabric of Collective Action', Alvarez distances herself from a tendency to see social movements as 'heroic forms of resistance to dictatorship', urging attention to 'the less visible, less heroic, but perhaps equally valiant, efforts of what I shall call an emergent social movement sector' (Alvarez 1997: 87). The significance of this sector, she suggests, has been in building 'social movement webs', providing a social and cultural density to the democratization process. As she puts it in a particularly striking statement:

> Democratization is more than just a technocratic/institution-building process; it is also an "art", a profoundly cultural process. Perhaps institutional engineering must be balanced by ... a choreography – one that enables the fluid and creative articulation *in society* of needs, interests, and identities historically excluded from the dominant democratic publics – if the foundations of Brazilian democracy are to be inclusive, solid and enduring. (Alvarez 1997: 110)

It is important to recognize that this suggestion is not calculated to *displace* reference to power. Alvarez's emphasis on culture might raise the ghost of E. P. Thompson's charge against the early Raymond Williams: that he screened out conflict. But the point is only that moments of conflict not be given a theoretical *priority*. This has the effect not of eliminating the concept of power, but of normalizing it, placing it on a level with other concepts as similarly conditioned by context and conjuncture.

A similar transformation of the concept can be found in the work of the Mexican anthropologist/sociologist Néstor García Canclini. On first impression, García Canclini's *Hybrid Cultures* might appear thoroughly consistent with Anglo-American postcolonial theory. Although written in Spanish, it references familiar theoretical figures such as Bourdieu, Gramsci and Foucault and addresses themes of post-modernity and cultural hybridity. But it also shows a consistent scepticism towards the reduction of social relations to relations of power:

> Hegemonic, subaltern: heavy words that helped us to name the divisions between people but not to include movements of affection and participation in solidary or complicit activities... The ideological dramatization of social relations tends to exalt so much the oppositions that it ends by not seeing the rites that unite and connect them; it is a sociology of gratings, not of what is said through them or when they are not there. (García Canclini 1995: 259–60)

Again, García Canclini does not dismiss concepts of power, even 'Manichean and conspiratorial representations of power'. The latter, he suggests, 'find partial justification in some contemporary processes' (1995: 258). The point is rather that these concepts are not assumed to have an obvious veridical reference, a transparency that gives them a theoretical priority over other kinds of explanation. García Canclini goes somewhat further here than Alvarez, suggesting explicitly that we recognize their figurative dimension: 'When we do not succeed in changing whoever governs, we satirize him in Carnival dances, journalistic humour, and graffiti. Against the impossibility of constructing a different order, we establish masked challenges in myths, literature, and comic strips. The struggle between classes or ethnic groups is, most of the time a metaphorical struggle' (1995: 261). There is an interesting resonance here with Dick Hebdige's analysis of punk and Rastafarianism in *Subculture* which, as I argued in Chapter 7, also drew attention to the figurative dimension of power. There is a further connection between García Canclini and the Birmingham CCCS in a shared enthusiasm for Gramsci. While there is no evidence of any direct influence, García Canclini often uses Gramsci, as Stuart Hall put it, to 'displace some of the inheritances of Marxism' – or, as I have suggested, to allow a bracketing or backgrounding of the concept of power.

But perhaps the most interesting reason for a different vision of transnational cultural studies in Latin America is a sensitization to an earlier moment in the formation of supranational or global entities than is generally considered in debates around colonialism in Asia. It is here that I want to suggest the significance of the work of Walter Mignolo. In *Local Histories/Global Designs*, Mignolo distinguishes between two phases in the development of the contemporary global system: 'first' and 'second' modernity. The first was a product of the Spanish and Portuguese empires, which saw the creation, in the sixteenth century, of the geosocial entity 'the Americas' (Mignolo 2000: 52–3). The second, closely associated with the emergence of industrial capitalism, followed the expansion of England and France towards Asia and Africa in the eighteenth and nineteenth centuries. There are obvious reasons why the legacy of first modernity, despite its relatively antique status, should be of ongoing interest in Latin America. But the significance of starting with this legacy goes beyond the particularities of language, religion or colonial experience; it also affects our general understanding of modernity, colonialism and power.

The implications of thinking from 'first modernity' are most sharply articulated by Mignolo in his differences with Said's *Orientalism*. It should be said that these differences are more positional than absolute or theoretical. Mignolo does not wish to minimize 'the tremendous impact and the scholarly transformation Said's book has made possible', or dismiss it because it 'doesn't do exactly what I want it to' (Mignolo 2000: 57). He wishes rather to place it as belonging to a particular perspective – the perspective of 'second modernity'. The most significant consequence of this is that, even in drawing attention to the constructed character of 'the Orient', Said tends to assume 'the West' as a given. It is this assumption which is brought into question by the perspective of 'first modernity'. Orientalism, for Mignolo, presumes an 'Occidentalism':

> Without Occidentalism there is no Orientalism, and Europe's "greatest and richest and oldest colonies" are not [as Said suggests] the "Oriental", but the "Occidental": the Indias Occidentales and then the Americas. "Orientalism" is the hegemonic cultural imaginary of the modern world system in second modernity when the image of the "heart of Europe" (England, France, Germany) replaces the "Christian Europe" of the fifteenth to mid-seventeenth century (Italy, Spain, Portugal). (Mignolo 2000: 57)

If we wish to understand the contemporary meaning of the 'the West', for Mignolo, we need to recognize the quite different character of colonial expansion in the Americas as against Asia and Africa:

> The Occident ... was never Europe's Other but the difference within sameness: Indias Occidentales (as you can see in the very name) and later America (in Buffon, Hegel, etc.) was the extreme West, not its alterity... Occidentalism was a transatlantic construction precisely in the sense that the Americas became conceptualized as the expansion of Europe, the land occupied by Japheth whose name inscribed his own destiny: "breath", "enlargement," and, as such, will rule over Shem (located in Asia) and Ham ("hot not in wisdom but in willfulness," located in Africa). (Mignolo 2000: 58)

The relevance of this for concepts of power is not directly articulated by Mignolo, but is nevertheless unmistakable. Occidentalism is quite different from Orientalism because it cannot be referred back to a powerful agent preceding it. It is the complex through which the powerful agent is *formed*. Attention is directed not to the uses of power as an already accomplished force in the world, but to how it is that we are able to *talk* of power in the first place.

The strength of Mignolo's analysis is that it allows us to situate concepts of power in historical processes rather than assuming power as a universal and being faced with a choice of asserting or denying its 'reality'. He is not exceptional in bringing into question the substantial unity of 'the West'. Similar questions have been asked in cultural studies in Asia. The first issue of *Traces*, for example, was titled 'Specters of the West' and was concerned with just this issue. But there is often a tendency in such questioning to oscillate between assertions of the unreality of 'the West' – precisely its 'spectrality' – and continuing Saidian assumptions of the West as an accomplished hegemonic presence or real agent of power. Mignolo's 'Latin' perspective permits a third alternative – a kind of 'both/and' or 'neither/ nor'. As suggested by the reference to biblical figures in the emergence of the West, the latter has always had an imaginative dimension. But it has also been constructed through practices of maritime exploration, bloody conquest, settlement and economic exploitation. If the early modern sense of 'the West' had roots in almost mythological ideas of 'breath' and 'expansion', it was also realized through an economy of precious metals: 'between 1531 and 1660 a minimum of 155,000 kilograms of gold and 16,985,000 of silver entered Spain legally... These amounts transformed the economic relations between Spain and the rest of Europe and also the commerce with the "extreme" Orient.' (Mignolo 2000: 57)

Productive comparisons might be drawn between the emergence of the West as a global agent and the emergence within Europe of the modern state. As I argued in Chapter 2, the latter was associated with an abstraction from particular *powers* – in Hobbes's terms the 'Strength, Eloquence, Riches or Reputation' of individual men – to a concept of power *in general*, to be put theoretically at the disposal of the sovereign. A similar process of abstraction can be found in the international domain. The power of the West is conceptually distinct from the particular powers of Spain, Portugal, Britain, France or the United States. It has tended to be thought of not as *a* power but, like the sovereign, as simply embodying 'power' as such. In this respect it is, like the state, a fiction, going beyond anything that could ever be demonstrated and closely bound up with utopian imaginings. It is, like the state, a *material* fiction, only too real in its effects. But it is nevertheless open to a properly cultural analysis, an analysis that locates its particular meanings in the contexts in which it has taken form. If, as I have argued, British cultural studies provides openings for such a history within national frameworks, Latin American scepticism offers similar openings in the global domain.

Conclusion
Reconfiguring Cultural Studies

When culture met power in the 1980s and 1990s, culture was the first to blink. But in the long run it may be culture that has the last laugh.

Stanley R. Barrett (2002), *Culture Meets Power*, 113

How should we address questions of power today? Cultural studies has a long history of offering urgent answers to this question. The field has had a propensity for staging revolutions, a propensity that is particularly marked when it comes to questions of power. From the break into Marxist theory and the emergence of feminism in the 1970s, through postmodernism, postcolonialism and theories of popular agency in the 1980s, to queer theory, governmentality and media republicanism in the 1990s, there have been countless calls for 'new directions' in how the concept is used. In each case, these calls have been driven by a conviction in having identified flaws in approaches that have gone before: they have 'neglected' power, they have failed to recognize that there are multiple 'axes' of power (gender, race, sexual preference, etc.), they have overlooked (or overstated) popular resistance to power, they have assumed a critical position external to power, they have imputed power relations where in fact there are none... And in each case, passionate positions have been taken on how the field should respond.

My aim in this book has been somewhat different. It has been to suggest that we suspend the search for 'correct positions' on power in order to consider more openly what has been invested historically in the *concept* of power. The approach is similar to one Thomas Osborne has described, in relation to his own work on the social sciences, as a 'deliberately parasitic' approach to questions of theory. A basic contention of this approach is that 'we already have plenty of good practices in the social and human sciences, and things are not quite as bad in theory ... as many seem to think; indeed, that we do not have to fear that the sky is about to fall on our heads at any or every moment' (Osborne 1998: xiii). Osborne's aim is not 'to reinvent social theory from scratch, to provide a swingeing critique of everything that has gone before', but 'to contribute to a reconfiguration of a discipline that is in effect already there'. This involves 'a kind of fieldwork into existing practices', or as he also puts it, a 'diagnostics': 'Doctors diagnose by decomposing the elements of a condition, thus producing a profile of the disease – its characteristics, the possible forms of

203

treatment, the prognosis' (1998: 9). The previous chapters might be described, in this sense, as a diagnostics of the concept of power.

Another way of describing it might be to say that I have attempted to 'culturalize' the concept of power. Without wishing to claim an equal stature, I drew a comparison in Chapter 1 between the project of the book and Raymond Williams's attempt in the 1950s to 'culturalize' the concept of culture itself, to embed it in the evolving historical and material conditions – the 'tradition' – in which it has taken form. One of the most stable qualities of the concept of culture, a quality which Williams clearly valued, is that it does not admit simple judgements of 'right' or 'wrong'. Cultures may enable or disable certain actions and possibilities – they are certainly open to *criticism* – but they cannot, in any meaningful sense, be *disproved*. The concept of power has always been somewhat in tension with this. From E. P. Thompson's insistence on a distinction between 'good' and 'bad' men to the spectre of political 'correctness', it has consistently been associated with more absolute forms of judgement. But as I hope to have demonstrated, there is at least a case that this tendency can be reversed, that the principles of 'cultural' evaluation can be brought to precisely the concept which has most threatened to displace them.

It is probably inevitable that some will find this argument unsettling. It clearly runs counter to attempts to ground the concept of power in veridical reference – to defend it by pointing to simple 'facts' about the organization of the world. As I noted in Chapter 1, there are understandable sensitivities in this area. There have been continual campaigns over the last twenty years – most notably, but by no means exclusively, in the 'culture war' debates of the 1990s – to trivialize and discredit critical discourses on power. In this context, any attempt to bring the concept into question can easily be read as just another extension of these campaigns. Indeed it may fair to conclude, in some cases, that the first priority must be for the authority of the concept to be simply defended.

For the sake of clarity, however, it is important to insist that to 'culturalize' is not to dismiss as insubstantial or unreal. The argument of the book has emphatically *not* been that the generalized concept of power – power in the singular – is somehow 'false' and should not be used. It has been only – as is widely accepted for many other concepts – that its meanings are not universal. They inhere rather in particular contexts of use: the psychological dynamics of cat and mouse games, the pitting of 'good' against 'evil' in children's fiction, the formation of the modern state, slavery, colonialism, the Cold War, the domestic division of labour, the post-war expansion of higher education, the global projection of American military forces, the Bomb... Where there are still phenomena such as these, it is unlikely that the concept of power will lose much of its currency. If it does not name a single or simple 'truth', it organizes experience in ways that are not arbitrary or fanciful but a part of a substantial and ongoing collective practice.

A more troubling objection to the argument might be that it suggests a rather dispassionate perspective on cultural studies. One of the reasons for the tradition of 'urgent answers' to questions of power is, undoubtedly, that those who have proposed them have *cared* – and cared not only for themselves but also for the collective project of the field. To resist the temptation to suggest such answers requires a certain moderation of the passions. Osborne (1998: xii) describes his approach as frankly *deflationary*, as one 'that seeks to take the heat out of some of the extremes of controversy that beset social theory and social sciences, an approach that bids that we adjust our ideas to at least some of our existing practices'. Recognizing that he could have opted instead for a more 'dyonysiac' sense of laughter, he notes wryly that his book 'is unfortunately not the barrel of laughs that it might have been' (1998: 5). In taking a similar approach, my own book might perhaps be seen as relentlessly measured in tone, without the colour or interest which is able to convey strongly enough a sense of why cultural studies *matters*.

The problem is not a new one. It is the central point on which the radical generation of the 1970s took their leave from what Terry Eagleton described as the 'Olympian impersonality' of Raymond Williams. My best response in relation to the present is that while the concept of power may still excite passions, it is not clear that this translates any longer to care for any *collective* form. Even at the point of its introduction to cultural studies, there were problems here. In its generalized form, the concept has always been, to some degree, a separating agent. In the first phase, class, race, gender and other identity-based perspectives came to be seen as competing with each other. The 'dawn-raid' by feminism and the disintegration of the study groups at Birmingham in the late 1970s were an early indication of more general tendencies. In a second phase, a proliferation of more theoretical differences emerged – between 'structuralists' and 'culturalists', 'radical' and 'liberal' feminists, Marxists and Foucauldians, political economists and textualists – over the ways in which power should be addressed. Many of these divisions have become so familiar and entrenched that they are now most often greeted not by passion but a sophisticated yawn.

The difficulty of maintaining a more vital conversation about power should be taken seriously, for if there is any way in which cultural studies *has* mattered it has been in its capacities for inclusion of diverse experiences and points of view which nevertheless find ways to speak to each other. In Stuart Hall's much-quoted phrase, there has been a sense that there is 'something is at *stake* in cultural studies' (1992: 278). But this something has been more than simply a sum of the individual enthusiasms of those involved. The reason the field has been important is that its participants have cared about the form of their common encounter. They cared in the 1950s and 1960s that the rising number of working-class entrants to higher education and public life be able to join in debates without being made to feel secondary or inferior. They cared in the 1970s and 1980s that the contributions of women, sexual minorities and people of colour be shown a similar respect. And in many ways they continue to care. But if power is taken to be a central concept, and the only options for discussing it are a shouting match or a retreat to private worlds of passionate intensity, then something has clearly been lost.

I would like to think that moderating cultural studies' attachment to the concept of power may allow conversations around it to be rejoined. There is plenty to be discussed. There are major questions, for example, of how 'totalist' concepts of power derived from the Cold War should be adapted or modified in response to the rather different circumstances that confront us as we dip our feet further into the twenty-first century. For a time, at the end of the Cold War, it seemed that no modification was necessary; indeed, the elimination of one pole in the global system appeared only to confirm the 'undifferentiated inclusiveness' of power. But in recent years, this assumption has come to look increasingly shaky. As ex US Secretary of State, Madeleine Albright, put it in a 2003 speech:

> Today America is at the height of our power. We have a president [George W. Bush] who is determined to assert and use that power. And yet if you look around the world, you have to wonder just how much control over events we actually have. In Iraq, we are dependent on the UN, our allies and various internal factions. In fighting terror, we rely heavily on the help of two individuals, the presidents of Afghanistan and Pakistan, both of whom have recently been the target of assassination attempts. In Asia, we are counting on, of all nations, China to put pressure on North Korea not to build nuclear weapons. Economically, we depend increasingly on the willingness of Tokyo and Beijing to purchase our skyrocketing debt. (Albright 2003)

One response to this would be to say that even the United States is, in the end, only *a* power. And yet it is likely that more generalized concepts of power will continue to circulate – not just in the rarefied spaces of global strategy, but in workplace politics, arguments around gender relations, science fiction and action movies, concerns about the environment and the management of cultural difference and diversity. The way they do so should be a matter of common concern.

References

Abbas, Ackbar and John Nguyet Erni (eds) (2005), *Internationalizing Cultural Studies – An Anthology*, Malden, MA: Blackwell.

Agger, Ben (1992), *Cultural Studies as Critical Theory*, London and Washington DC: Falmer Press.

Ahmad, Aijaz (2000), 'Between Orientalism and Historicism', in A. L. Macfie (ed.) *Orientalism: A Reader*, Edinburgh: Edinburgh University Press: 285–97.

Albright, Madeleine (2003), 'A Conversation with Madeleine Albright', The Commonwealth Institute, 23 September, http://www.commonwealthclub.org/archive/04/04-02albright-speech.html (accessed 11 August 2006).

Althusser, Louis (1971), *For Marx*, trans. B. Brewster, London: New Left Books.

Alvarez, Sonia (1990), *Engendering Democracy in Brazil – Women's Movements in Transition Politics*, Princeton, NJ: Princeton University Press.

Alvarez, Sonia (1997), 'Reweaving the Fabric of Collective Action – Social Movements and Challenges to "Actually Existing Democracy" in Brazil', in Richard G. Fox and Orin Starn (eds) *Between Resistance and Revolution – Cultural Politics and Social Protest*, New Brunswick, NJ: Rutgers University Press: 83–117.

Anderson, Perry (1964), 'Origins of the Present Crisis', *New Left Review* 23: 27–53.

Anderson, Perry (1968), 'Components of the National Culture', *New Left Review* 50: 3–57.

Anderson, Perry (1980), *Arguments Within English Marxism*, London: New Left Books.

Anderson, Perry (1983), *In the Tracks of Historical Materialism*, London: Verso.

Anderson, Perry (1992a), *English Questions*, London: Verso.

Anderson, Perry (1992b), 'Origins of the Present Crisis', in *English Questions*, London: Verso: 15–47.

Appignanesi, Lisa (1994), 'Liberté, Égalité and Fraternité: PC and the French', in S. Dunant (ed.) *The War of the Words – The Political Correctness Debate*, London: Virago Press: 145–63.

Barker, Martin and Anne Beezer (eds) (1992), *Reading into Cultural Studies*, London and New York: Routledge.

Barrett, Stanley R. (2002), *Culture Meets Power*, Westport, CT and London: Praeger.

Baudrillard, Jean (1987), *Forget Foucault*, New York: Semiotext(e).

Bennett, Tony (1992a), 'Putting Policy into Cultural Studies', in L. Grossberg, C. Nelson and P. Treichler (eds), *Cultural Studies*, New York and London: Routledge: 23–33.

Bennett, Tony (1992b), 'Useful Culture', *Cultural Studies* 6(3): 395–408.

Bennett, Tony (1995), *The Birth of the Museum: History, theory, politics*, London and New York: Routledge.

Bennett, Tony (1998), *Culture – A Reformer's Science*, St Leonards: Allen & Unwin.

Benton, Ted (1984), *The Rise and Fall of Structuralist Marxism – Althusser and his Influence*, London: Macmillan.

Berlin, Isaiah (1976), *Vico and Herder: Two studies in the history of ideas*, New York: Vintage Books.

Bhabha, Homi K. (1994), *The Location of Culture*, London and New York: Routledge.

Bourdieu, Pierre and Jean-Claude Passeron (1979), *The Inheritors: French Students and Their Relation to Culture*, trans. R. Nice, Chicago: Chicago University Press.

Bourdieu, Pierre and Jean-Claude Passeron (1990), *Reproduction in Education, Society and Culture*, trans. R. Nice, London: Sage.

Bourdieu, Pierre, Jean-Claude Chamboredon and Jean-Claude Passeron (1991), *The Craft of Sociology: Epistemological Preliminaries*, trans. R. Nice, New York: Walter de Gruyter.

Bourdieu, Pierre, Jean-Claude Passeron and Monique de Saint Martin (1994), *Academic Discourse: Linguistic Misunderstanding and Professorial Power*, trans. R. Teese, Cambridge: Polity Press.

Brabazon, Tara (2000), *Tracking the Jack*, Kensington, NSW: University of NSW Press.

Bratich, Jack Z., Jeremy Packer and Cameron McCarthy (eds) (2003), *Foucault, Cultural Studies and Governmentality*, New York: SUNY Press.

Brunsdon, Charlotte (1996), 'A thief in the night: Stories of feminism in the 1970s at CCCS', in D. Morley and K.-H. Chen (eds), *Stuart Hall: Critical Dialogues in Cultural Studies*, London and New York: Routledge: 276–86.

Buck-Morss, Susan (2000), 'Hegel and Haiti', *Critical Inquiry* 26: 821–64.

Canetti, Elias (1992), *Crowds and Power*, trans. C. Stewart, London: Penguin (orig. pub. *Masse und Macht*, 1960).

Carby, Hazel (1982), 'White women listen! Black feminism and the boundaries of sisterhood', in CCCS (ed.) *The Empire Strikes Back – Race and racism in 70s Britain*, London: Hutchinson: 212–35.

Carey, James W. (1989a), *Communication as Culture – Essays on Media and Society*, Boston: Unwin Hyman.

Carey, James W. (1989b), 'Overcoming Resistance to Cultural Studies', in *Communication as Culture – Essays on Media and Society*, Boston: Unwin Hyman: 89–110.

Carey, James W. (1991), "'A Republic, If You Can Keep It": Liberty and Public Life in the Age of Glasnost', in Raymond Arsenault (ed.) *Crucible of Liberty – 200 Years of the Bill of Rights*, New York: The Free Press, 108–28.

Carey, James W. (1997a), 'Reflections on the Project of (American) Cultural Studies', in M. Ferguson and P. Golding (eds), *Cultural Studies in Question*, London, Thousand Oaks and Delhi: Sage: 1–24.

Carey, James W. (1997b), 'Political Correctness and Cultural Studies', in E. S. Munson and C. A. Warren (eds), *James Carey – A Critical Reader*, Minneapolis: University of Minnesota Press: 270–91.

CCCS (1978), *Women Take Issue – Aspects of Women's Subordination*, London: Hutchinson.

CCCS (1982), *The Empire Strikes Back – Race and racism in 70s Britain*, London: Hutchinson.

Chen, Kuan-Hsing (1992), 'Voices from the Outside: Towards a New Internationalist Localism', *Cultural Studies* 6(3): 476–84.

Chen, Kuan-Hsing (1996a), 'Post-marxism: Between/beyond critical postmodernism and cultural studies', in D. Morley and K.-H. Chen (eds), *Stuart Hall: Critical Dialogues in Cultural Studies*, London and New York: Routledge: 309–25.

Chen, Kuan-Hsing (1996b), 'The formation of a diasporic intellectual – An interview with Stuart Hall', in D. Morley and K.-H. Chen (eds), *Stuart Hall – Critical Dialogues in Cultural Studies*, London and New York: Routledge: 484–503.

Chen, Kuan-Hsing (ed.) (1998), *Trajectories – Inter-Asia Cultural Studies*, London: Routledge.

Conrad, Peter (1979), Review of Edward Said's *Orientalism*, *New Statesman*, 26 January, 117–18.

Critcher, Charles (1974), 'Women in Sport [1]', *Working Papers in Cultural Studies* 5: 3–20.

Cunningham, Stuart (1992), *Framing Culture: Criticism and Policy in Australia*, Sydney: Allen & Unwin.

D'Souza, Dinesh (1991), *Illiberal Education: The Politics of Race and Sex on Campus*, New York: Free Press.

D'Souza, Dinesh (1992), 'The Visigoths in Tweed', in P. Aufderheide (ed.) *Beyond PC – Towards a Politics of Understanding*, St Paul, Minnesota: Graywolf Press: 11–23.

Davies, Ioan (1995), *Cultural Studies and Beyond: Fragments of Empire*, London: Routledge.

Dawkins, John (1988), *Higher Education: A Policy Statement*, Canberra: Australian Government Printing Service.

Deleuze, Gilles and Félix Guattari (1983), *Anti-Oedipus – Capitalism and Schizophrenia*, trans. R. Hurley, M. Seem and H. R. Lane, Minneapolis: University of Minnesota Press.

Deleuze, Gilles and Félix Guattari (1987), *A Thousand Plateaus – Capitalism and Schizophrenia*, trans. B. Massumi, Minneapolis: University of Minnesota Press.

Denfeld, Rene (1995), *The New Victorians: A Young Woman's Challenge to the Old Feminist Order*, New York: Warner Books.

Diamond, Sara (1995), 'Managing the Anti-PC Industry', in C. Newfield and R. Strickland (eds), *After Political Correctness – The Humanities and Society in the 1990s*, Boulder: Westview Press: 23–37.

Donald, Stephanie (2000), *Public Secrets, Public Spaces – Cinema and Civility in China*, Oxford: Rowman and Littlefield

Dunant, Sarah (1994), 'Introduction: What's in a Word', in S. Dunant (ed.) *The War of the Words – The Political Correctness Debate*, London: Virago Press: vii–xv.

Eagleton, Terry (1976), 'Criticism and Politics: The Work of Raymond Williams', *New Left Review* 95 (Jan–Feb): 2–23.

Elias, Norbert (1994), *The Civilizing Process*, trans. E. Jephcott, Oxford and Malden, MA: Blackwell (orig. pub. *Über den Prozess der Zivilisation*, 1939).

Epstein, Barbara (1995), '"Political Correctness" and Collective Powerlessness', in M. Darnovsky, B. Epstein and R. Flacks (eds), *Cultural Politics and Social Movements*, Philadelphia: Temple University Press: 3–19.

Eribon, Didier (1992), *Michel Foucault*, trans. B. Wing, London: Faber and Faber.

Erni, John Nguyet (2005), 'Section introduction to Popular Practices', in Ackbar Abbas and John Nguyet Erni (eds) (2005) *Internationalizing Cultural Studies – An Anthology*, Malden, MA: Blackwell: 297–9.

Farshtey, Greg (2003), *Bionicle Collector's Sticker Book*, New York: Scholastic Inc.

Fiske, John (1993), *Power Plays, Power Works*, London and New York: Verso.

Fiske, John (1996), 'Opening the Hallway: some remarks on the fertility of Stuart Hall's contribution to critical theory', in D. Morley and K.-H. Chen (eds), *Stuart Hall: Critical Dialogues in Cultural Studies*, London and New York: Routledge: 212–22.

Foucault, Michel (1978), 'Governmentality', in G. Burchell, C. Gordon and P. Miller (eds), *The Foucault Effect: Studies in Governmentality*, London: Harvester/ Wheatsheaf.

Foucault, Michel (1979), *Discipline and Punish – The Birth of the Prison*, trans. A. Sheridan, Harmondsworth, Middlesex: Penguin.

Foucault, Michel (1980), *Power/Knowledge – Interviews and Other Writings*, Brighton, Sussex: Harvester.

Foucault, Michel (1981), *The History of Sexuality – Volume 1*, trans. R. Hurley, Harmondsworth, Middlesex: Penguin.

Foucault, Michel (1983), 'Preface', in Gilles Deleuze and Félix Guattari, *Anti-Oedipus – Capitalism and Schizophrenia*, Minneapolis: University of Minnesota Press: xi–xiv.

Foucault, Michel (1988), *Technologies of the Self: A Seminar with Michel Foucault*, L. H. Martin, H. Gutman and P. H. Hutton (eds), Amherst: University of Massachussets Press.

Foucault, Michel (1994) *Dits et Écrits – 1954–1988*, Volume II 1970–175, Ed. Daniel Defort and François Ewald, Paris: Gallimard

Foucault, Michel (2000a), 'Questions of Method', in J. D. Faubion (ed.) *Power: Essential Works of Foucault 1954–1984, Volume Three*, New York: The New Press: 223–38 (orig. pub. 'Round Table of 20 May 1978', 1980).

Foucault, Michel (2000b), 'Interview with Michel Foucault', in J. D. Faubion (ed.) *Power: Essential Works of Foucault 1954–1984, Volume Three*, New York: The New Press: 239–97 (orig. pub. Interview by D. Trombadori *Il Contributo*, 1980).

Foucault, Michel (2000c), 'Truth and Juridical Forms', in J. D. Faubion (ed.) *Power: Essential Works of Foucault 1954–1984, Volume Three*, New York: The New Press: 1–89.

Foucault, Michel (2000d), 'The Subject and Power', in J. D. Faubion (ed.) *Power: Essential Works of Foucault 1954–1984, Volume Three*, New York: The New Press: 326–48.

Frank, Thomas (2002), *One Market Under God – extreme capitalism, market populism and the end of economic democracy*, London: Vintage.

Franklin, James (2000), 'The Sokal Hoax and Postmodernist Embarrassment', *Continuum* 14(3): 359–62.

Frow, John (1995), *Cultural Studies and Cultural Value*, Oxford: Oxford University Press.

Frow, John and Meaghan Morris (1993), 'Introduction', in *Australian Cultural Studies: A Reader*, Sydney: Allen & Unwin: vii–xxxii.

Frum, David (2003), 'Edward Said', *National Review*, 29 September (accessed online at http://frum.nationalreview.com/archives/?q=MjAwMzA5).

Garber, Marjorie, Beatrice Hanssen and Rebecca Walkowitz (eds) (2000), *The Turn to Ethics*, London and New York: Routledge.

García Canclini, Néstor (1995), *Hybrid Cultures – Strategies for Entering and Leaving Modernity*, trans. Christopher L. Chiappari and Silvia L. López, Minneapolis: University of Minnesota Press.

Gibson, Mark (1998), 'Richard Hoggart's Grandmother's Ironing: Some questions about 'power' in international cultural studies', *International Journal of Cultural Studies* 1(1): 25–44.

Gibson, Mark (2001), 'Myths of Oz Cultural Studies: The Australian Beach and "English" Ordinariness', *Continuum: Journal of Media and Cultural Studies* 15(3): 275–88.

Gibson, Mark and John Hartley (1998), 'Forty Years of Cultural Studies – An Interview with Richard Hoggart', *International Journal of Cultural Studies* 1(1): 11–23.

Gikandi, Simon (1996), *Maps of Englishness – Writing Identity in the Culture of Colonialism*, New York: Columbia University Press.

Gilroy, Paul (1987), *There Ain't No Black in the Union Jack – The cultural politics of race and nation*, London: Hutchinson.

Gilroy, Paul (1992), 'Cultural studies and ethnic absolutism', in L. Grossberg, C. Nelson and P. Treichler (eds), *Cultural Studies*, London and New York: Routledge: 187–98.

Gilroy, Paul (1993), *The Black Atlantic: Modernity and Double Consciousness*, London: Verso.

Giroux, Henry A. and Peter L. McLaren (eds) (1989), *Critical Pedagogy, the State, and Cultural Struggle*, New York: University of New York Press.

Gitlin, Todd (1987), *The Sixties: Years of Hope, Days of Rage*, New York: Bantam Books.

Gordon, Colin (2000), 'Introduction', in J. D. Faubion (ed.) *Power: Essential Works of Foucault 1954–1984, Volume Three*, New York: The New Press: xi–xli.

Goux, Jean-Joseph (1990), *Symbolic Economies – After Marx and Freud*, trans. J. C. Gage, Ithaca, NY: Cornell University Press (orig. pub. *Freud, Marx: Economie Symbolique* and *Les iconoclastes*, 1973, 1978).

Grossberg, Lawrence (1997), *Bringing It All Back Home – Essays on Cultural Studies*, Durham, NC and London: Duke University Press.

Hall, Stuart (1958), 'A sense of classlessness', *Universities and Left Review* 1(5 (Autumn)): 26–32.

Hall, Stuart (1972), 'The Social Eye of *Picture Post*', *Working Papers in Cultural Studies* 2: 70–120.

Hall, Stuart (1977a), 'Culture, the Media and the "Ideological Effect"', in J. Curran, M. Gurevitch and J. Woollacott (eds), *Mass Communication and Society*, London: Edward Arnold: 315–48.

Hall, Stuart (1977b), 'On Ideology', *Working Papers in Cultural Studies* 2(Spring): 9–32.

Hall, Stuart (1980), 'Cultural Studies and the Centre: some problematics and problems', in S. Hall, D. Hobson, A. Lowe and P. Willis (eds), *Culture, Media, Language: Working Papers in Cultural Studies, 1972–79*, London: Unwin Hyman: 15–47.

Hall, Stuart (1982), 'The rediscovery of "ideology": return of the repressed in media studies', in M. Gurevitch, T. Bennett, J. Curran and J. Woollacott (eds), *Culture, Society and the Media*, London: Methuen: 56–90.

Hall, Stuart (1992), 'Cultural Studies and its Theoretical Legacies', in L. Grossberg, C. Nelson and P. Treichler (eds), *Cultural Studies*, New York and London: Routledge: 277–86.

Hall, Stuart (1994), 'Some "Politically Incorrect" Pathways Through PC', in S. Dunant (ed.) *The War of the Words – The Political Correctness Debate*, London: Virago Press: 164–83.

Hall, Stuart (1996a), 'Cultural Studies: two paradigms', in J. Storey (ed.) *What is Cultural Studies?*, London: Arnold: 31–48.

Hall, Stuart (1996b), 'The Problem of Ideology: Marxism without guarantees', in D. Morley and K.-H. Chen (eds), *Stuart Hall: Critical Dialogues in Cultural Studies*, London and New York: Routledge: 25–46.

Hall, Stuart (1996c), 'Cultural studies and the politics of internationalization: An interview with Stuart Hall by Kuan-Hsing Chen', in D. Morley and K.-H. Chen (eds), *Stuart Hall: Critical Dialogues in Cultural Studies*, London and New York: Routledge: 392–408.

Hall, Stuart (1996d), 'The formation of a diasporic intellectual: An interview with Stuart Hall by Kuan-Hsing Chen', in D. Morley and K.-H. Chen (eds), *Stuart Hall: Critical Dialogues in Cultural Studies*, London and New York: Routledge: 484–503.

Hall, Stuart and Paddy Whannel (1964), *The Popular Arts*, London: Hutchinson Educational.

Hall, Stuart and Tony Jefferson (eds) (1976), *Resistance through rituals: Youth subcultures in post-war Britain*, London: Hutchinson.

Hall, Stuart, Chas Critcher, Tony Jefferson, John Clarke and Brian Roberts (1978), *Policing the Crisis*, London: Macmillan.

Hartley, John (1992), *The Politics of Pictures*, London and New York: Routledge.

Hartley, John (1996), *Popular Reality – Journalism, Modernity, Popular Culture*, London and New York: Arnold.

Hartley, John (1999), *Uses of Television*, London and New York: Routledge.

Hartley, John (ed.) (2005), *Creative Industries*, Malden, MA, Oxford and Carlton, Vic: Blackwell.

Hebdige, Dick (1979), *Subculture: The Meaning of Style*, London and New York: Methuen.

Hebdige, Dick (1988), *Hiding in the Light – On Images and Things*, London and New York: Routledge.

Herman, Peter C. (ed.) (2004), *Historicizing Theory*, Albany, NY: State University of New York Press.

Hindess, Barry (1996), *Discourses of Power: from Hobbes to Foucault*, Oxford: Blackwell.

Hindess, Barry and Paul Hirst (1975), *Pre-Capitalist Modes of Production*, London: Routledge & Kegan Paul.

Hindess, Barry and Paul Hirst (1977), *Mode of Production and Social Formation*, London: Macmillan.

Hobbes, Thomas (1914), *Leviathan*, London: J. M. Dent & Sons Ltd. (orig. pub. 1651).

Hodge, Bob (1999), 'The Sokal "Hoax" – Some Implications for Science and Postmodernism', *Continuum* 13(2): 255–69.

Hoggart, Richard (1957), *The Uses of Literacy*, London: Chatto & Windus.

Hoggart, Richard (1970), *Speaking To Each Other Volume 1: About Society*, London: Chatto & Windus.

Hoggart, Richard (1982), *An English Temper: Essays on Education, Culture and Communications*, London: Chatto & Windus.

Hoggart, Richard (1988), *A Local Habitation: Life and Times Volume 1: 1918–1940*, London: Chatto & Windus.

Hume, David (1978), *A Treatise of Human Nature*, Oxford: Clarendon Press.

Hunter, Ian (1991), 'Personality as a vocation', in I. Hunter, D. Meredyth, B. Smith and G. Stokes (eds), *Accounting for the Humanities: The Language of Culture and the Logic of Government*, Brisbane: Institute for Cultural Policy Studies, Griffith University: 7–66.

Hunter, Ian (1992), 'Aesthetics and Cultural Studies', in L. Grossberg, C. Nelson and P. Treichler (eds), *Cultural Studies*, New York and London: Routledge: 347–67.

Hunter, Ian (1994), *Rethinking the School – Subjectivity, bureaucracy, criticism*, Sydney: Allen & Unwin.

Jameson, Fredric and Masao Miyoshi (eds) (1998), *The Cultures of Globalization*, Durham, NC and London: Duke University Press.

Jensen, Joli and John J. Pauly (1997), 'Imagining the Audience: Losses and Gains in Cultural Studies', in M. Ferguson and P. Golding (eds), *Cultural Studies in Question*, London, Thousand Oaks and New Delhi: Sage: 155–69.

Kagan, Robert (2003), *Of Paradise and Power: America vs Europe in the New World Order*, New York: Knopf.

Kimball, Roger (1990), *Tenured Radicals - How Politics has Corrupted our Higher Education*, New York: Harper and Row.

Kinder, Marsha (1991), *Playing with Power in Movies, Television, and Video Games – From Muppet Babies to Teenage Mutant Ninja Turtles*, Berkeley, Los Angeles and Oxford: University of California Press.

Knight, P. G. (1997), 'Naming the Problem: Feminism and the Figuration of Conspiracy', *Cultural Studies* 11(1): 40–63.

Kuhn, Thomas (1970), *The Structure of Scientific Revolutions*, Chicago: University of Chicago Press.

Laclau, Ernesto and Chantal Mouffe (1985), *Hegemony and Socialist Strategy – Towards a Radical Democratic Politics*, London and New York: Verso.

Lumby, Catharine (1997), *Bad Girls: The Media, Sex and Feminism in the 90s*, Sydney: Allen & Unwin.

McGuigan, Jim (1992), *Cultural Populism*, London and New York: Routledge.

McRobbie, Angela (1980), 'Settling Accounts with Subcultures: A Feminist Critique', *Screen Education* 34, Spring: 37–49.

McRobbie, Angela (1992), 'Post-Marxism and Cultural Studies: A Post-script', in L. Grossberg, C. Nelson and P. Treichler (eds), *Cultural Studies*, New York and London: Routledge: 719–30.

Mercer, Kobena (1992), '1968: Periodizing Politics and Identity', in L. Grossberg, C. Nelson and P. Treichler (eds), *Cultural Studies*, New York and London: Routledge: 424–8.

Meredyth, Denise and Deborah Tyler (eds) (1993), *Child and Citizen: Genealogies of Schooling and Subjectivity*, Brisbane: Institute for Cultural Policy Studies.

Meyrowitz, Joshua (1985), *No Sense of Place: The Impact of Electronic Media on Social Behavior*, New York and Oxford: Oxford University Press.

Mignolo, Walter (2000), *Local Histories/Global Designs – Coloniality, Subaltern Knowledges, and Border Thinking*, Princeton, NJ: Princeton University Press.

Miller, Peter and Nikolas Rose (1992), 'Political power beyond the State: Problematics of Government', *British Journal of Sociology* 43(2): 173–205.

Millett, Kate (1970), *Sexual Politics*, Garden City, NY: Doubleday.

Mills, C. Wright (1956), *The Power Elite*, New York: Oxford University Press.

Milner, Andrew (1997), 'Cultural Studies and Cultural Hegemony: Comparing Britain and Australia', *Arena journal* 9: 133–56.

Minson, Jeffrey (1993), *Questions of Conduct: Sexual Harassment, Citizenship and Government*, London: Macmillan.

Mitchell, Juliet (1971), *Women's Estate*, Harmondsworth, Middlesex: Penguin.

Mitchell, Juliet (1974), *Psychoanalysis and Feminism*, London: Allen Lane.

Mitchell, Juliet (1995), 'Twenty Years On – Revisiting *Psychoanalysis and Feminism*', *New Formations* 26(Autumn): 123–8.

Moreiras, Alberto (2001), *The Exhaustion of Difference: The Politics of Latin American Cultural Studies*, Durham, NC and London: Duke University Press.

Morley, David and Kuan-Hsing Chen (1996), 'Introduction', in David Morley and Kuan-Hsing Chen (eds) *Stuart Hall – Critical Dialogues in Cultural Studies*, London and New York: Routledge, 1–24.

Morris, Meaghan (1984), 'Room 101 Or a Few Worst Things in the World', in A. Frankovits (ed.) *Seduced and Abandoned – The Baudrillard Scene*, Sydney/ New York: Stonemoss/Semiotext(e): 91–117.

Morris, Meaghan (1988), *The Pirate's Fiancée: Feminism, reading, postmodernism*, London and New York: Verso.

Morris, Meaghan (1990), 'Banality in Cultural Studies', in P. Mellencamp (ed.) *Logics of Television*, Bloomington: Indiana University Press: 14–43.

Morris, Meaghan (1992), 'A Gadfly Bites Back', *Meanjin* 51(3): 545–51.

Morris, Meaghan (1996), 'Banality in Cultural Studies', in J. Storey (ed.) *What is Cultural Studies? A Reader*, London: Arnold: 147–67.

Morris, Meaghan (1997a), 'A question of cultural studies', in A. McRobbie (ed.) *Back to reality? Social experience and cultural studies*, Manchester and New York: Manchester University Press: 36–57.

Morris, Meaghan (1997b), 'Ticket to Bundeena – An Interview with Meaghan Morris', in J. Mead (ed.) *Bodyjamming – Sexual Harassment, Feminism and Public Life*, Sydney: Vintage: 243–66.

Morris, Meaghan (1998), *Too Soon Too Late: History in Popular Culture*, Bloomington and Indianapolis: Indiana University Press.

Morris, Meaghan and Paul Patton (eds) (1979), *Michel Foucault: Power, Truth, Strategy*, Sydney: Feral Publications.

Muecke, Stephen (1997), *No Road (bitumen all the way)*, Fremantle: Fremantle Arts Press.

Nelson, Cary and Lawrence Grossberg (eds) (1988), *Marxism and the Interpretation of Culture*, Basingstoke: Macmillan Education.

Oakeshott, Michael (1996), *The Politics of Faith and the Politics of Scepticism*, New Haven and London: Yale University Press.

O'Regan, Tom (1992), '(Mis)taking Policy: Notes on the Cultural Policy Debate', *Cultural Studies* 6(3): 409–23.

Osborne, Thomas (1998), *Aspects of enlightenment – Social theory and the ethics of truth*, London: UCL Press/Taylor & Francis.

Parsons, Talcott (1994), 'On the Concept of Political Power', in John Scott (ed.), *Power – Critical Concepts*, vol. 1, London and New York: Routledge: 16–61.

Passeron, Jean-Claude (1971), 'Introduction to the French Edition of Uses of Literacy', *Working Papers in Cultural Studies* Spring: 120–31.

Pusey, Michael (1991), *Economic Rationalism in Canberra: A Nation-Building State Changes its Mind*, Melbourne: Cambridge University Press.

Rajagopal, Arvind (2001), *Politics after Television – Hindu Nationalism and the Reshaping of the Public in India*, Cambridge: Cambridge University Press.

Robbins, Bruce (1993), *Secular Vocations – Intellectuals, Professionalism, Culture*, London and New York: Verso.

Roiphe, Katie (1993), *The Morning After: Sex, Fear and Feminism*, New York: Penguin Books.

Rojek, Chris (1998), 'Stuart Hall and the antinomian tradition', *International Journal of Cultural Studies* 1(1): 45–65.

Rose, Nikolas (1990), *Governing the Soul: The Shaping of the Private Self*, London: Routledge.

Ross, Andrew (2004), *Low Pay, High Profile – The Global Push for Fair Labor*, New York and London: The New Press.

Rowbotham, Sheila (1973), *Woman's Consciousness, Man's World*, London: Penguin.

Sahlins, Marshall (1995), *How "Natives" Think: about Captain Cook for example*, Chicago: University of Chicago Press.

Said, Edward W. (1978), *Orientalism*, New York: Routledge and Kegan Paul.

Said, Edward W. (1980), *The Question of Palestine*, London: Routledge and Kegan Paul.

Said, Edward W. (1981), *Covering Islam – How the media and the experts determine how we see the rest of the world*, London: Routledge and Kegan Paul.

Said, Edward W. (1984), 'Orientalism Reconsidered,' in F. Barker, P Hulme, M. Iverson and D. Loxley (eds), *Europe and Its Others*, vol. 1, Essex Sociology of Literature Conference, Colchester: University of Essex: 14–27.

Said, Edward W. (1993), *Culture and Imperialism*, New York: Alfred A. Knopf.

Said, Edward W. (1998), 'Between Worlds', *London Review of Books*, 20.9, 7 May (accessed online at http://www.lrb.co.uk/v20/n09/said01_.html).

Said, Edward W. (1999), *Out of Place – A Memoir*, New York: Alfred A. Knopf.

Sakai, Naoki (1997), *Translation and Subjectivity – On 'Japan' and Cultural Nationalism*, Minneapolis: University of Minnesota Press.

Sassoon, Donald (1981), 'The Silences of *New Left Review*', *Politics and Power* 3.

Shumway, David R. (2004), 'The Sixties, the New Left, and the Emergence of Cultural Studies in the United States', in P. C. Herman (ed.) *Historicizing Theory*, Albany, NY: State University of New York Press: 235–54.

Simpson, David (1993), *Romanticism, Nationalism and the Revolt against Theory*, Chicago: Chicago University Press.

Sokal, Alan (1996), 'A Physicist Experiments with Cultural Studies', *Lingua Franca*, May/June, 62–4 (Accessed Online at http://linguafranca.mirror.theinfo.org/9605/sokal.html, May 2006).

Sparks, Colin (1974), 'The Abuses of Literacy', *Working Papers in Cultural Studies* 6(Autumn): 7–23.

Sparks, Colin (1996), 'Stuart Hall, cultural studies and marxism', in D. Morley and K.-H. Chen (eds), *Stuart Hall: Critical Dialogues in Cultural Studies*, London and New York: Routledge: 71–101.

Spivak, Gayatri Chakravorty (1988), 'Can the Subaltern Speak?', in Cary Nelson and Lawrence Grossberg (eds) *Marxism and the Interpretation of Culture*, Urbana: University of Illinois Press, 271–316.

Spivak, Gayatri Chakravorty (1999), *A Critique of Postcolonial Reason – Toward a History of the Vanishing Present*, Cambridge, MA: Harvard University Press.

Steele, Tom (1997), *The Emergence of Cultural Studies, 1945–65: Cultural Politics, Adult Education and the English Question*, London: Lawrence & Wishart.

Stratton, Jon (1998), *race daze – Australian identity crisis*, Annandale, NSW: Pluto Press.

Stratton, Jon and Ien Ang (1996), 'On the impossibility of a global cultural studies: "British" cultural studies in an "international" frame', in D. Morley and K.-H. Chen (eds), *Stuart Hall: Critical Dialogues in Cultural Studies*, London and New York: Routledge: 361–91.

Sun, Wanning (2002), *Leaving China – Media, Migration, and Transnational Imagination*, Oxford: Rowman and Littlefield.

Thompson, E. P. (1961), 'The Long Revolution', *New Left Review* 9: 24–33 and 10: 34–9.

Thompson, E. P. (1963), *The Making of the English Working Class*, London: Gollancz.

Thompson, E. P. (1965), 'The Peculiarities of the English', *The Socialist Register* 2: 311–62.

Thompson, E. P. (1978), *The Poverty of Theory and Other Essays*, London: Merlin Press.

Tibawi, A. L. (2000), 'English-Speaking Orientalists,' in A. L. Macfie (ed.) *Orientalism: A Reader*, Edinburgh: Edinburgh University Press, 57–76 (originally published 1964).

Traces (2003), 'Purpose' and 'Prospectus', *Traces – Multilingual Series in Cultural Theory and Translation*, http://www.arts.cornell.edu/traces/index.htm (Accessed 26 May 2006).

Turner, Graeme (1992), '"It Works for Me": British Cultural Studies, Australian Cultural Studies, Australian Film', in L. Grossberg, C. Nelson and P. Treichler (eds), *Cultural Studies*, New York and London: Routledge: 640–53.

Turner, Graeme (1996), *British Cultural Studies – An Introduction*, New York and London: Routledge.

Valenzuela, J. Samuel (1992), 'Democratic Consolidation in Post-Transitional Settings: Notion, Process, and Facilitating Conditions', in Scott Mainwaring, Guillermo O'Donnell and J. Samuel Valenzuela (eds) *Issues in Democratic Consolidation – The New South American Democracies in Comparative Perspective*, Notre Dame, Indiana: University of Notre Dame Press: 57–104.

Volosinov, V.N. (1986), *Marxism and the Philosophy of Language*, Cambridge, MA: Harvard University Press.

Wark, McKenzie (1992a), 'After Literature: Culture, policy, theory and beyond', *Meanjin* 51(4): 677–90.

Wark, McKenzie (1992b), 'Speaking Trajectories: Meaghan Morris, Antipodean Theory and Australian Cultural Studies', *Cultural Studies* 6(3): 433–48.

Wark, McKenzie (1994), *Virtual Geography: Living with Global Media Events*, Indianapolis: Indiana University Press.

Wark, McKenzie (1997a), *The Virtual Republic*, St Leonards, NSW: Allen & Unwin.

Wark, McKenzie (1997b), 'Free speech, cheap talk and the Virtual Republic', in P. Adams (ed.) *The Retreat from Tolerance – A Snapshot of Australian Society*, Sydney: ABC Books: 162–87.

West, Cornell (1992), 'The Postmodern Crisis of Black Intellectuals', in L. Grossberg, C. Nelson and P. Treichler (eds), *Cultural Studies*, London and New York: Routledge: 689–705.

West, Cornell (2001), *Race Matters*, Second Edition, New York: Vintage Books.

Williams, Raymond (1958), *Culture and Society 1780–1950*, London: Chatto & Windus.

Williams, Raymond (1965), *The Long Revolution*, Harmondsworth, Middlesex: Penguin.

Williams, Raymond (1977), *Marxism and Literature*, Oxford and New York: Oxford University Press.

Williams, Raymond (1979), *Politics and Letters – Interviews with New Left Review*, London: New Left Books.

Williams, Raymond (1983), 'David Hume: Reasoning and Experience', in *Writing in Society*, London and New York: Verso: 121–41.

Williams, Raymond (1989a), *The Politics of Modernism*, London and New York: Verso.

Williams, Raymond (1989b), 'Culture is Ordinary', in *Resources of Hope*, New York: Verso: 3–18.

Willis, Paul (1980), *Learning to Labour: How working class kids get working class jobs*, Westmead, Farnborough and Hampshire: Gower.

Index